GARDENS of the WORLD

THE ART AND PRACTICE OF GARDENING

Consulting Editors
Penelope Hobhouse and Elvin McDonald

Written by
Elvin McDonald, Penelope Hobhouse, Allen Paterson,
Teiji Itoh, Ann Lovejoy, Katherine Whiteside,
John Brookes, and Madison Cox

Foreword by
Audrey Hepburn

Photography by
Mick Hales
and Erica Lennard,
Elvin McDonald, Allen Paterson, Art Schronce

Garden plans by
Perry Guillot

Conceived by
Janis Blackschleger

Macmillan Publishing Company • New York

Collier Macmillan Canada • Toronto

Maxwell Macmillan International
New York • Oxford • Singapore • Sydney

Macmillan Publishing Company
866 Third Avenue, New York, NY 10022

Collier Macmillan Canada, Inc.
1200 Eglinton Avenue East, Suite 200
Don Mills, Ontario M3C 3N1

Library of Congress Cataloging-in-Publication Data
Gardens of the world: the art and practice of gardening/Penelope
Hobhouse and Elvin McDonald, consulting editors.
p.   cm.
Includes bibliographical references and index.
ISBN 0-02-583127-5
1. Gardens—Design.   2. Gardens.   3. Landscape gardening.
4. Flower gardening.   I. Hobhouse, Penelope.   II. McDonald, Elvin.
SB472.G35   1991
635.9—dc20   90-48433   CIP

Macmillan books are available at special discounts for bulk purchases for sales promotions,
premiums, fund-raising, or educational use. For details, contact:

Special Sales Director
Macmillan Publishing Company
866 Third Avenue
New York, NY 10022

10   9   8   7   6   5   4   3   2   1

Printed in the United States of America

ACKNOWLEDGMENTS

The evolution of the idea to the reality of *Gardens of the World* would have been impossible without the excellent support and contribution of many, each bringing an important discipline, perspective, expertise, or enthusiasm to bear.

We are grateful to our eight authors, whose individual diversity and talent we have had the privilege of sharing with you. Penelope Hobhouse made us reconsider the definition of the word brilliant with her brightness of spirit and mind. Elvin McDonald was instrumental in helping to keep it all together and championed our efforts tirelessly. Mick Hales took a simple request for "beauty and substance" into a whole new dimension with his photography; no detail or nuance escaped his attention. Erica Lennard captured the gardens of Italy and Japan with distinct clarity and sympathy. Pam Hoenig courageously took charge to bring this highly collaborative endeavor to fruition. Felicity Bryan, Carla Glasser, and Helen Pratt helped keep everything and everyone on track all along the way. The Brooklyn Botanic Garden; Huntington Botanical Gardens in San Marino, California; Royal Botanical Gardens in Hamilton, Ontario; the International Bulb Center of Holland; and the National Trust of England are just a few of the many gardens and horticultural organizations we wish to thank for their cooperation and assistance.

The relationship between the television series and the book has been an exciting one, each fueling the other. Without the contributions and support of Polaroid Corporation and Jackson & Perkins, neither would have been possible. We are grateful to Polaroid for providing major underwriting for the television series; Polaroid Pro-Chrome D was used for much of the photography in the book. Jackson & Perkins also supplied major underwriting and promotional support for the series and we are very proud that they have selected a 'Gardens of the World' rose in our honor. Finally, a special thanks to A&I Color Lab and Wallen Green Design in Los Angeles.

While those who were instrumental in creating the television series will be credited appropriately in that context, the "cross-pollenization" of creative effort and spirit cannot go unacknowledged. We wish to recognize and thank, in alphabetical order, Julian Bercovici, Glen Berenbeim, Stuart Crowner, Frank DeMarco, Bruce Franchini, Michael Gendler, Peter Hawkins, Tony Iler, Ralph Lauren, Donald Lehr, Julie Leifermann, Walt Louie, Jeff Mackler, Bonnie Martin, Vicki Merrick, Doris Milsen, Bill Mulligan, Felix Racelis, Lois Scali, Justin Schwartz, Ken Short, Diana Skene, Jeri Sopanen, Blair Spangler, Gustavo Tavares, Caroline Taylor, Wayne Warga, and Robert Wolders.

To Audrey Hepburn we are most especially grateful. Her ability both to find and appreciate beauty in the world around us speaks to the very heart of the aspirations of *Gardens of the World*. The most simple definition we've heard for a garden—that it is a place for humans and plants—is one we like, yet the vast range of interpretation of this simple reality, both past and present, is nothing short of wondrous.

FOREWORD

We all have within us a need to create beauty. And we all can in a garden, however small. It is this need which has written the history of gardens. By looking at our world through its gardens today, we reaffirm the simple human capacity to create beauty on this earth.

The vocabulary of gardens is remarkably both an individual and collective one. Art, science, history, culture, and all the wonders of nature combine to create a universal, everchanging language that can enrich each of us through a lifetime.

We are most fortunate to have a truly fine group of writers and photographers dedicate their talents and expertise to *Gardens of the World*. Through their words and eyes we cross the boundaries of time and distance, culture and climate.

Each garden included has been carefully selected to illustrate a particular aesthetic, practice, or concept. Over sixty gardens are featured. I had the pleasure of filming in fifteen of them in the spring and summer of 1990.

After years of challenge and reward in my own garden, I greatly looked forward to spending time in some of the world's most beautiful gardens. I never imagined they would reveal the diverse range of expression they did.

The garden of old roses at Mottisfont Abbey contrasts delightfully with the orderly abundance of layout of the French rose gardens, yet each garden helps us know a new dimension of this most revered of flowers. The Japanese stroll garden at Shinshin-an in Kyoto challenges our sense of detail and nuance in the natural world. The Italian Renaissance gardens appeal to our sense of order and proportion, even hundreds of years after they were conceived and created. George Washington's gardens at Mount Vernon are a lovely statement of simplicity and lack of pretense. Tulips in spring eternally bring a sense of renewal and hope; in the soft, blue light of Holland one can glimpse the elements that inspired great Dutch and Flemish flower painters over two hundred years ago. And mysterious, romantic Ninfa, south of Rome, a country garden so artfully and carefully realized, that one would think nature alone had created it.

In the early planning meetings, when gardens were being selected with Penelope Hobhouse and Elvin McDonald, we realized that it would be simply impossible to include all of the world's most beautiful gardens in one book or television series. We were, at first, disappointed. But then we were heartened—even in these threatened environmental times, there are more beautiful places on this earth than any one of us may hope to see.

Perhaps if we now take a closer look at our gardens we will better understand how to find a way to save our lovely earth. Have we not lost sight of our only source of life? Or have we at last awakened to the fragility of our beautiful planet?

Audrey Hepburn

CONTENTS

CHAPTER ONE

ROSES AND ROSE GARDENS

Whatever its emotional impact on the individual person, "rose" is a word that almost always conjures an image of a perfectly formed flower bud that will slowly unfurl to become one of nature's most beguiling creations. "The image," says Stephen Hutton, a third-generation American rose grower whose family was instrumental in introducing the 'Peace' rose, "is one of grace, of beauty and perfection, and centers almost entirely around the flower produced . . . and not the plant itself. It is the perfection of the flower that has won the rose its exalted place in our very human appreciation of the plant kingdom." The precise moment in the life of a rose when the beholder sees that it is "perfect" depends both on personal taste and cultural conditioning. Americans tend to prefer a half-open blossom, whereas the English worship the full-blown, and the French can see beauty even as the petals are starting to fall.

In a most simplistic way, there are two kinds of roses: the species and varieties that occur in nature, without human interference; and the hybrids or cultivars that have been developed in cultivation. Altogether botanists have recognized well over a hundred species of *Rosa*, almost all occurring naturally in the temperate climates of the Northern Hemisphere, and these, together with the varieties and cultivars, are at present placed in fifty-six horticultural classifications. Although all of this can be made to seem quite tidy on paper, in practice the complexities are such that rosarians themselves have come to cultivate only two kinds—the bottom line, so to speak, being the "old" roses and the "modern" roses.

For most of us, our first encounter with this elusive flower will be with one or more of the modern roses, for they are the most widely distributed, as the florist's cut flowers, and the most widely cultivated in gardens.

Beyond their obvious beauty and pleasures lies the larger if more subtle world of the "old" roses, which, according to noted English journalist John Fisher, "Many writers treat as . . . those that were most written about and painted before the early part of the nineteenth century, when the arrival of the China Roses and other newly imported species led to extensive hybridization and a flood of new varieties." In 1966 the American Rose Society gave this definition sharper focus and pinpointed the cutoff date when it resolved henceforth to define an "old rose" as one belonging to a group that existed before 1867, the year in which 'La France', the first hybrid tea, was introduced. Also accepted as old roses are the newer hybrids that by origin and appearance are directly linked with indisputably old classes of roses, such as bourbons, centifolias, hybrid perpetuals, and tea roses. Excepting these new cultivars that are inherently "old," all others developed since 1867 are considered "modern."

Before venturing further into a consideration of the perfection of the rose and its role in garden design, it would be well to see how the genus *Rosa* fits into the larger context of its botanical family. Other members of the botanically allied though diverse clan of the rose family, or Rosaceae, include such favored ornamentals and edibles as *Alchemilla* (the herb known as lady's-mantle), *Chaenomeles* (flowering quince), *Cotoneaster*, *Crataegus* (hawthorn), *Cydonia* (quince), *Fragaria* (strawberry), *Malus* (apple), *Potentilla*, *Prunus* (apricot, cherry, peach, and plum), *Pyrus* (pear), *Rubus* (raspberry, blackberry, dewberry), *Spiraea*, and over two thousand widely distributed species of herbs, shrubs, and trees. Of particular note within the context of the family is that the genus *Rosa* is not known to have been successfully crossed with any other member of the family, yet the smell of the rose is often unmistakably "fruity" and, one senses, related to what we taste when savoring the likes of strawberries, apricots, pears, apples, and raspberries.

Graham Stuart Thomas, the grand old man of old roses in the twentieth century, has concluded, "There is no doubt that the Rose

Previous page: *At La Roseraie de l'Hay les Roses on the outskirts of Paris, the temple of love is covered by rambling roses, most noticeably pink-clustered 'Dorothy Perkins', introduced by the American firm Jackson & Perkins in 1901. The dark red in the back is 'Excelsa' and 'American Pillar' is seen in the front.*
Above: *A crested moss rose in the gardens of Josephine at Malmaison. 'Chapeau de Napoleon' (its name refers to the mossy, elongated, feathery sepals that enclose the bud, which suggest the feathered headpieces of Napoleon's men) has large pink flowers composed of nearly a hundred petals, and is possessed of a heavy perfume.*

was first treasured for its fragrance, long before plants were fully assessed and regardless of beauty." Considering that the rose entered written history through the invention of rosewater around 3000 B.C., Thomas is probably correct. So strong is our expectation of fragrance in the rose that mischievous persons have been known to proffer as fragrant a blossom they have found scentless, only to have the innocent companion press nose to the same bloom and exclaim, "Oh, yes, like an old rose!" There is certain black humor here, for henceforth the jokester will be troubled by a ray of doubt as to who has the more sensitive olfactories. Nurseryman Thomas Rivers, whose *Rose Amateur's Guide* was published in 1837, dismissed the prairie roses *(Rosa setigera)* as not worth cultivating, whereas the noted plantswoman Ellen Wilmott (1858–1934) disagreed, even though she admitted they were "deficient in scent." Graham Thomas's last word on the subject is that the broad-petaled, mallow-pink flowers ". . . are very fragrant in spite of numerous statements to the contrary."

Although Thomas describes as "unique" the lasting scent of the dried petals of roses, he says "the distillation of rosewater from the flowers was a great discovery: this was a commodity which, in its day, was the supposed antidote for innumerable ills. The much more precious Attar, an oil floating on the surface of rosewater, was worth more than its weight in gold." Henceforth, the rose came to be cultivated in herb gardens as a medicinal plant, the elusive benefits of fragrance ultimately overshadowed in a purely practical sense by the value of the vitamin C contained within the rose hips, appreciated for its efficacy in the treatment of scurvy some centuries before the vitamin itself was isolated and named in 1932. Nevertheless, fields of damask roses continue to be cultivated today in Bulgaria for the precious attar and Louise Beebe Wilder (1878–1938), an American garden writer, observed in her article "Pleasures of the Nose": "We all know persons who are affected for better or for worse by certain odours. . . . Over and over again I have experienced the quieting influence of Rose scent upon a dis-

The famed La Roseraie de Bagatelle, also on the outskirts of Paris, is a garden created at the turn of the twentieth century as an exhibition of modern roses. The garden was designed by Monsieur Forrestier, who was inspired by his friend Monet. Its development was made possible through the help of Monsieur Gravereaux, the founder and creator of La Roseraie de l'Hay. The garden is a series of carefully laid out symmetrical beds, edged with clipped boxwood, surrounded by gravel paths. The viewing pavilion is situated above the garden on a low rise, the better to see the examples of bush, standard, and climbing roses in all styles and varieties.

This view from the pavilion at the Bagatelle looking down from the main section of the rose garden shows the contestants for the coming year's rose competitions and many of the spectacular tripods that support the climbers. 'New Dawn', pale pink, is prominent in the foreground. Another interesting feature of this garden is the yew clipped in symmetrical shapes, such as the cone (foreground left).

A DOORYARD ROSE GARDEN

The garden sketched here stood directly outside The Hut, the house where Gertrude Jekyll lived until she moved to Munstead Wood in 1897. Published originally in 1908 in her book *Colour in the Flower Garden*, it was designed to be at its best in June, and featured two tree-form standard roses, as well as 'The Garland' ("a very old summer-flowering climber of distinct habit and foliage"), cabbage or Provence roses ("No rose surpasses it in excellence of scent"), damask ("charming with its . . . wide-open crimson flowers") and other varieties of *Rosa damascena* (especially 'York and Lancaster'), and rose hoops, most likely hybrid perpetuals ("in the spring only a few of the longest and best shoots . . . should be retained. After cutting off just the ends of these . . . they should be carefully bent and pegged down to within a few inches of the soil"). Framing the roses were boxwood and a single red cedar for accent. Planted among the roses were herbaceous plants, including peony, lily, fern, foxglove, snapdragon, columbine, myrrhis, Solomon's seal, penstemon, and bergenia. While she did not include any in this particular plan, Jekyll was also fond of planting alchemilla (or lady's-mantle), lavender, and rosemary in the company of roses. It is somehow reassuring that Jekyll chose to bring roses and flowers compatible with them right up to her windows and doors instead of setting them alone in some isolated part of the landscape.

turbed state of mind, feeling the troubled condition smoothing out before I realized that Roses were in the room, or near at hand."

LANDSCAPING WITH ROSES

Historically roses have been mostly treated as prima donnas, ill suited to sharing beds with any other plants save themselves and possibly the framing device of low, clipped hedges of boxwood or yew. As recently as the early twentieth century, gardeners were advised to position the rose garden far from the sight of the house, since the bushes were considered wretched looking in the winter. Although this view may not be shared today, in times past roses were often relegated to the serviceability of the vegetable or kitchen garden, or isolated in the landscape so that the rose garden had a mysterious hideaway quality, a place one deliberately visited, and came upon as something of a surprise. The arrival of the relatively well-behaved modern roses, which coincided with the Victorian rage for bedding out, may have done little to improve the overall image of the rosebush, yet since that time the rose has become increasingly the flower of the masses, a universal symbol of love, as welcome and as likely to be found in cottage and dooryard gardens as in the extensive landscapes of the ruling classes.

Not until the end of the nineteenth century did anyone see that the rose might play an important role in the larger landscape, one that was to be espoused in the writings of William Robinson and in the designs planted and documented by his disciple, Gertrude Jekyll. Today, near the turn of another century, this view is once again in vogue as holistic thinkers have come to see the rose plant itself as both ornamental and serviceable in the landscape. Implicit is that the plant will be tough enough to prosper without undue pampering, that it will be disease resistant, that there will be season-long flowering, and that the petals from spent blooms will wither, drop, and disappear into the environment, essentially self-cleaning. The rosarian intent on growing an exhibition-quality large-flowered hybrid may find such goals of little interest, but out in the big world, people want roses that are self-reliant and neither chemically dependent nor labor-intensive.

Stephen Hutton, in a brief talk delivered in New York City on the occasion of the introduction of the 1991 All-American Rose Selections, challenged members of the gardening press to reinterpret the rose as a plant that can serve many roles in both private and public landscapes. He noted that ". . . for a number of decades Europeans have been using other established classes [besides the hybrid tea] in landscape designs. In fact, in many years the top-selling varieties in Europe are not hybrid teas but floribundas and other lower growing, heavier flowering types. It is the appreciation of an orderly, well-balanced plant producing a mass of flowers throughout the season that has won the floribunda its place and continued popularity. Cultivars like 'Iceberg' and 'Europeana' have become immensely popular in Europe as well as North America because of their profusion of bloom and tidy plant habits which allow them to be put both in a formal rose bed as well as the informal, open landscape. More recently in America, the AARS floribundas 'Sun Flare' and 'Show Biz' have given us the chance to plant repeat-blooming, even everblooming, hardy ornamental plants which can stand on their own as such."

The person whose mind-set of the rose is of a labor-intensive plant that cannot be brought to perfection unless it is sprayed weekly with a potent combination insecticide, miticide, and fungicide can perhaps be no more quickly broken of this idea than by introduction to the rugosa roses and their hybrids. These are rugged shrubs, extremely hardy, disease resistant, and essentially care-free, that produce flowers and handsome fruit, extending their interest over three and into four seasons. The old-fashioned rose fragrance that emanates from many rugosas, combined with the attractively coarse, quilted foliage and orderly plant habit, gives this class of rose an appeal few ornamental shrubs can match.

Another broad class of roses seen thriving in mixed borders and the big landscape picture are those viewed as "old." These are the centifolias, gallicas, damasks, and other hybrids that were created largely before 'La France'. Breeding of these old roses has continued since that time and has come to the forefront recently through the appearance of David Austin's English roses. Preeminent horticulturist John Elsley writes, "These new hybrids are the culmination of nearly forty years of work, the thought behind them being the same as that which brought about the Hybrid Musk roses—the creation of repeat-flowering . . . shrubs for the smaller gardens of today." Aus-

A large old shrub rose, Rosa gallica, 'Officinalis', the apothecary's rose, is seen spilling over a walkway at Tintinhull in England. The individual rose-pink blossoms are composed of eight to ten petals and display a prominence of yellow stamens in the center. The foliage is grayish green on long, arching canes that are covered with flowers at the once-yearly blooming in late spring, but that have relatively few prickles.

Below: 'Peace', one of the
most popular and enduring
of all hybrid tea roses, can
vary in color throughout
the growing season, but it
is always in some
combination of shades of
yellow, with tinges of pink
and orange. Large ovoid
buds rise on exceptionally
strong and straight stems
that are clothed with
noticeably dark, glossy,
leathery foliage. It was
developed in France at
Cap d'Antibes by the
House of Meilland and is
known variously over the
world, but the most
universally accepted name
is 'Peace', in recognition of
the peace talks held in San
Francisco at the end of
World War II.

tin has included in parentage the old shrub roses for their vigor, fragrance, and full doubling of the flowers, and floribunda or cluster roses to add modern colors, scents, glossy leafage, and the propensity to flower repeatedly through the season. Among his achievements so far is the re-creation of the tea fragrance and also the myrrh scent, captured in 'Constance Spry' (1961), one of Austin's original crosses, a climber of unbelievable richness of flower and perfume.

Beyond the Austin English roses is an increasingly accepted class of landscape roses, perhaps best defined by saying what it is not, namely not hybrid tea, floribunda, grandiflora, miniature, climber, or old-fashioned varieties of lax habit. Anything left over may be considered a landscape rose. Early prototypes in this class were 'The Fairy' (1932) and 'Sea Foam' (1964), both of which continue with notable success in today's market. More recently 'Simplicity' has become the standard for

this hedge-type landscape rose. The millions of plants of this cultivar sold in the last decade have made it the top-selling rose in the world of the 1980s, although it is worth noting that the best-selling roses in China in 1981 were 'Peace', 'Chicago Peace', and 'Super Star', all large-bloomed, long-flowering roses descended from the Chinese "studs" of two hundred gardening seasons past.

Also considered landscape roses are the newly created cultivars classified as "shrubs," 'Bonica' being the first such rose ever to win an AARS award (1985), followed in 1991 by 'Carefree Wonder', the second shrub rose to gain this coveted distinction. More contenders in this class are already showing their stuff in gardens around the world where new roses are tested and critically assessed. Since all roses can be characterized as having a permanent woody growth, botanically speaking they are all shrubs. However, "shrub" has particular meaning to rosarians and does not necessarily mean a rose that is too large for the average flower garden. Today the World Federation of Rose Societies classifies shrub roses under three main categories:
1. shrubs that can be identified with the old shrub roses of tradition;
2. modern shrub roses introduced more or less since the beginning of the twentieth century, subdivided according to whether they are remontant (repeat flowering) or not; and
3. wild shrub roses.

'Bonica' and 'Carefree Wonder' fit in the second class, both being decidedly remontant, and eminently suited in size, habit, and performance for planting in a wide variety of landscape situations. They can be used alone as care-free hedging, or mixed and matched with other roses, other shrubs, herbaceous flowers, and ornamental grasses.

MINIATURE ROSES

The last category of rose I would like to put forward as uniquely suited to our time is the miniature, which by today's standards denotes a plant usually less than eighteen inches (46 centimeters) tall that in all parts is diminutive. Microminiatures are even smaller, sometimes unfurling tiny perfect roses from buds hardly bigger than a grain of wheat. The class is thought to have originated from crosses of *Rosa chinensis* 'Minima', discovered early in

the nineteenth century, with hybrid teas and other roses, but naturally small growers have also appeared in general populations of seedlings not necessarily from miniature strains. Some have unusually long, flexible stems and are accepted as climbing miniatures; in time one of these can cover a wall or trellis to shoulder height or more, but the individual flowers will always be miniature. Other miniatures of lax habit have been adopted for growing in hanging baskets, to spill from window boxes and planters, or to cascade over rocks in naturalistic plantings. Excepting those that are grafted as small tree-form standards, all miniatures in North America grow on their own roots, and are often able to live through winters that decimate hybrid teas and other grafted roses that may be growing in the same beds.

The modern miniature rose began its rise to fame among gardeners and its acceptance as a distinct and separate class by the rose establishment in 1936 with the introduction of 'Tom Thumb' from Spanish breeder Pedro Dot. After the war Ralph Moore of California concentrated his early breeding efforts on the development of miniatures in a full range of colors and bicolors, some fragrant, some even showing mossiness on the buds like an old moss rose. As gardens have grown increasingly smaller, the appeal of the miniature rose has also increased. The little bushes and even the tree-form standards adapt readily to being grown in pots, and the microminiatures are surprisingly adaptable as all-year-blooming plants in sunny or fluorescent-lighted indoor gardens.

Although the human element has romanticized the rose perhaps more than any other flower, the logic and science of botany suggest that the rose, like other flowers, exists to perpetuate itself, shameless in its appeal to pollinators, successfully attracting both insects and humans for over a millennium of coexistence. Geologists have found impressions of a five-petaled rose, much like those that still grow with abandon in American hedgerows, that grew along the Crooked River in Oregon some thirty-five million years ago. Such records permit us to see that what makes a rose a rose does not change even as the complexity within the genus *Rosa* increases with each new generation of roses and rosarians.

One of the most fascinating aspects of the rose is that when pollen from the blossom of one species or variety is applied to the stigma contained by the blossom of another, each seed that forms in the resulting hip is genetically different from all the others. This behavior seems at odds with Mendel's laws of inheritance and adds an extraordinary element of chance to the palette of the rose breeder. One example of this factor can be seen in the work of American breeder Eugene S. Boerner, as recounted by biographer Robert W. Wells in *Papa Floribunda*:

> Of the million or more crosses Boerner made during his career, [the] 1943 marriage between 'Pinocchio' and 'Crimson Glory' was the luckiest. From just one of the rose hips that resulted, four seeds were obtained. He planted them and up came four tiny rose plants. Two were nothing special. But the remaining pair of siblings, born of the same seed pod, turn[ed] out to be AARS [All-America Rose Selections] winners.
>
> Even as seedlings, they showed promise. One produced small blooms of coral-peach, the other of cherry-coral. The shades were so new and striking that Gene could hardly wait to bud the twins onto greenhouse stock for a quick check on what the full-sized blossoms would look like. The two new roses, still unnamed, survived every test.

The coral-peach half of the pair was introduced as 'Fashion' in 1949, one of the first truly fragrant floribundas, and the cherry-coral other half was introduced as 'Vogue' in 1951.

MOTTISFONT ABBEY AND THE OLD ROSES

There could be no better place to begin an acquaintance with old roses than in the garden started by Graham Stuart Thomas in 1972 at Mottisfont Abbey, located in Hampshire in the south of England, four and a half miles (7¼ kilometers) northwest of Romsey. Built in the twelfth century as an Augustinian priory and eventually converted to a private house, this National Trust property is visited today mostly for its roses, since only the monks' cellarium and one large room of the house are open to the public. The placement of this garden seems entirely appropriate in historical context, for it is located next to the parking lot at some distance from the house in what was once the kitchen garden, a walled, nearly square space divided by gravel paths into four plots of approximately the same size, with a

'Madame Ernest Calvat', introduced in 1888, is a very fragrant pink bourbon, which can be grown with perennials such as columbines and campanulas. Like bourbons in general, this one has a large globular bud that develops into a voluptuous, multipetaled blossom.

rounded space at the center for a pool and fountain. Michael Gibson, in *The Rose Gardens of England*, notes, "There are no hidden corners or secret bowers so all that can be said is that here is a collection of old roses, second to none in the country," and, one might add, "in the world," owing in part to the widespread influence of Thomas's books and other writings.

Perhaps the most surprising thing about the garden of old roses at Mottisfont Abbey is the limited number of species and the abundance of trees and herbaceous plants that mix successfully. Lessons can be learned here about the art and discipline of garden making. A preponderance of species roses would emphasize their propensity to bloom mostly in late spring and early summer, whereas the exclu-

sion of other kinds of plants would weaken the architecture and render the garden comparatively colorless through much of the gardening season. All gardens have limitations and here, in relatively limited space but with great natural resources, Thomas has chosen to include only the old roses he likes best, or which hold for him some special significance, in particular the old French roses of the nineteenth century. (A triangular walled garden adjoining the first and entered through the wall of the old garden farthest from the entrance was opened in 1987 and features many rare old roses newly brought from Sangerhausen in Germany, where the vast collections are said to include upwards of six hundred varieties and six hundred species and variants.)

Boxwood hedges line the graveled path-

The bourbon rose 'Madame Isaac Pereire' can be treated as a climber, as seen here at Mottisfont. This old rose is extremely fragrant and is an example of the repeat-blooming bourbons that have arisen from the original crosses of the pink China rose with a damask. The large red-pink flowers have reflexed petals and quartered centers.

Rambling and climbing roses grow along the walls that enclose the mixed border at Mottisfont. Lower-growing old-fashioned shrub roses blend beautifully with such herbaceous flowers as dianthus, digitalis, campanula, and geum. Once-a-year-blooming bourbons, centifolias, and damasks, along with the repeating Chinas and teas, make excellent bedmates for perennials that extend and enhance the season of flowering.

ways at Mottisfont, with tall, sheared English yews serving as exclamation point accents among the otherwise bounteous, exuberant, and generally curvaceous growth of the old roses. The mixing in of herbaceous perennials enhances the garden as a whole, with white campanulas, white foxgloves, and the creamy white aruncus, or goatsbeard, lacing the old roses at peak bloom in early summer. By autumn the blues, lavenders, purples, and pinks of hardy asters and the indigo blue of monkshood predominate, at once also accentuating the ripening rose hips in their peppery shades of orange, scarlet, and red.

Besides the old roses that grow as bushes in beds at Mottisfont, more or less as one might expect, others are trained along the walls, over arches across the paths, and up

into the trees. In addition, those having long arching canes are pegged down in Victorian fashion. Gibson notes that this method of training suits ". . . even the immense thorny canes of the Rugosa hybrid 'Ferdinand Conrad Meyer', which makes it produce so many flowers that it is worth its place despite persistent rose rust every year."

Ultimately it can be said that the garden of old roses at Mottisfont is a living museum in which are housed numerous collections, individually distinct but also inextricably linked. There are ancient treasures from nature along with those developed by gardeners through the ages, especially the varieties featured at Malmaison in the years 1798 to 1814 and immortalized in the paintings of Pierre-Joseph Redouté.

Bourbon roses are seen growing in front of the circular water-lily pool in the center of the old garden at Mottisfont Abbey. Old-fashioned cluster-flowered roses look inexplicably beautiful and at home when planted in close juxtaposition to a garden water feature.

THE STUD ROSES AND MALMAISON

Christopher Columbus discovered the West Indian island of Martinique in 1502, on his fourth voyage to the New World. The French began colonization in 1635. It is perhaps not surprising that a baby girl born there in 1763 would be christened Rose, but what seems a remarkable coincidence is that this ". . . beautiful Creole from the West Indies" would one day marry Napoleon Bonaparte and become the Empress Josephine at the moment when the first of the "stud" roses from China arrived in the West.

The term "stud" bears explanation, for it does not have quite the same meaning in the plant kingdom as it does in the animal. "Stud" in the case of a rose may indeed imply prowess, but the blossom contains both male and female parts, and may be employed by the breeder as either parent in a cross designed to combine, it is hoped, the desired traits from both plants while dropping or minimizing others. "Stud" as applied to certain old Chinese roses em-

bodies the same meaning within a larger acknowledgment of what these roses brought to the rose world, most notably the trait of blooming more than once in a season—they were particularly remontant—and the "tea" scent.

Today all of the modern large-flowered hybrid roses can be traced directly to one or more of the "four studs," as they have come to be known, listed here in the order of their arrival in the West:
• *Rosa chinensis* 'Semperflorens' (1792; also known as Chinese Monthly Rose, the Crimson China Rose, and Slater's Crimson China, the last for Gilbert Slater, a director of the East India Company, who brought the cuttings to his home in Essex, England);
• Parsons' Pink China (also known as Old Blush, first flowered at Kew 1795; a hybrid between *Rosa chinensis* x *R. odorata* 'Gigantea', the tea rose);
• Humes' Blush Tea-scented Rose (1809; also a hybrid between *R. chinensis* x *R. odorata* 'Gigantea', but, because of its unique fragrance, known originally as *R. indica odorata)*; and

This view of the temple of love at l'Hay les Roses shows in the foreground early-twentieth-century rambling roses, which bloom early in the rose season. 'Excelsa', red, covers the pergola in the distance. Also to be seen are examples of ramblers trained as tree-form standards, 'Dorothy Perkins' and 'Excelsa', and in the right foreground is one of the 'Seven Sisters', a multiflora by origin that is controversial as to exactly which rose correctly bears the name. The white standards are 'White Dorothy', a sport of 'Dorothy Perkins'. This is the typical French-style formal rose garden, featuring gravel paths, clipped box, and minimal lawn areas.

• Parks' Yellow Tea-scented Rose (1824; brought home from China by John Damper Parks for the Royal Horticultural Society and named *R. odorata* 'Ochroleuca').

"Rose" of Martinique married Napoleon in 1796, acquired the estate Malmaison two years later, and set out with single-minded determination to create what may have been the greatest rose gardens the world has ever known, extending to forty-five hundred acres and including every rose known at the time, some twenty-five hundred varieties. Upon Josephine's death in 1814 the great rose gardens soon began their decline, leaving little record other than the rose portraits painted by Redouté. Many of the same roses that Josephine grew remain in cultivation, however, and the idea of Malmaison lives on in the inspiration it gives each succeeding generation of rosarians. In a larger sense it can be seen that the Empress Josephine was something of a trailblazer as an aristocrat for whom horticulture was a primary interest. At least in spirit she was perhaps not that different from the lover of roses described by the Reverend A. Foster-Melliar in *The Book of the Rose* (1894):

The man of business, who rises at daybreak to attend to his roses before his day's work

The only area exhibiting modern roses at La Roseraie in a massive display is in front of the pavilion, itself covered with 'Alexandre Girault'. The pink modern roses in the foreground are hybrid tea 'Princess Margaret'. Interspersed throughout the beds are standard forms of climbing and rambling roses, including 'Paul Noel', 'New Dawn', and 'Paul's Scarlet'.

The arches at l'Hay les Roses are constructed of metal. In the foreground is 'Mrs. F. W. Flight', a rambler, appearing along a walkway over which different ramblers are displayed. Most of the old wood is removed after the once-yearly flowering, and the new wood trained in its place. This keeps the walkways tidy so that visitors can walk through without becoming caught on wayward shoots.

in the town; who is quite prepared if necessary to go out with a good lantern on a November night to seize a favourable condition of soil for planting at once some newly arrived standards or dwarfs; and who later in the winter will turn out in the snow after dark to give some little extra protection that may be required for his beds; that is the sort of man for me, and for the rose as well.

Each of us who has ever nurtured a rosebush can identify with both Josephine and the man described by the Reverend Foster-Melliar. When I planted my first flower garden, at age five, there was a rose in it, no doubt

because I had been sniffing the 'Harison's Yellow', a shrub rose that grew in the farmyard garden of the neighbors, Mr. and Mrs. Manning, the latter being one of the first adults to encourage my flower-gardening efforts. (My own mother thought it would be a better idea for me to concentrate on helping her with the vegetable garden.) Together, Mrs. Manning and I dug up one of the extremely stickery shoots, and I skipped back to our farm and planted it behind the house. The profusion of sweet-smelling yellow flowers the following June thrilled me beyond all reason and probably confirmed yet another lifelong rosarian. Now, having passed the half-century mark, I have come to theorize that within all of us,

miraculously programmed into our DNA, is a familiarity with the rose and all it represents that always remains with us. Meanwhile, the shoot of 'Harison's Yellow' that I planted has gotten along nicely without me, spreading into an irregularly shaped thicket that covers roughly thirty square feet (9 square meters) in what has become my stepmother's garden on an impossibly windswept hill in western Oklahoma. There the constant buffeting of the wind keeps 'Harison's Yellow' quite low and compact, at most four feet (1¼ meters) high, whereas at the Brooklyn Botanic Garden, where I walk by it nearly every day, the bush grows to three times this height, fairly billowing over the tall trellis walls.

'American Pillar', right foreground, is one of the most popular rambling roses in European gardens. It was introduced in 1902 by America's foremost breeder at the time, Dr. Walter Van Fleet. As seen, it is trained on a metal archway at La Roseraie that serves as an entrance to the Theater of the Rose, an area where poetry and theatrical pieces that celebrate the rose are presented.

This view of La Roseraie is through the wood lattice structure that is covered with 'Blaze' climber. Again are seen beds of hybrid perpetual roses hedged with clipped boxwood. Gravereaux conceived this as a garden that would be a living museum of roses, with as many of those in existence as possible. Today, almost a century later, it remains one of the most complete collections of roses in the world.

Above: *Here is another view showing the formal arrangement of the beds at La Roseraie, with clipped boxwood hedging, gravel paths, and closely clipped lawns. Besides the roses, there are only two other plants in this garden, the boxwood and the lawn. Again, the French use many different types of roses in standard form, underplanted with the bush form of the same variety. An example would be 'Princess Margaret' bush with 'Princess Margaret' standard interspersed throughout the bed.*
Right: *The pink rambler 'Mrs. F. W. Flight' and an unidentified white rambler are trained as festoons, with uprights provided by wood posts that are in turn connected by metal chains. The complete covering and intertwining reveals the work of a talented horticulturist and patient rosarian.*

A FORMAL ROSE GARDEN

The varied growth habits, sizes, and flowering seasons of roses suit them to an endless variety of applications in the garden. They are especially adapted to formal plans like that shown here. For scale, estimate that the square within the water feature in the very center of the plan measures six feet (almost 2 meters) square. It could be hedged with dwarf boxwood *(Buxus sempervirens* varieties, or *B. microphylla* varieties, which are hardier in North American gardens), gray or green santolina, stephanandra, or germander *(Teucrium chamaedrys)*. The roses surrounding the fountain could be a white to pale yellow or light pink miniature, or one of the dwarf landscape types, such as 'White Meidiland'.

The four L-shaped beds surrounding the center square might be framed with any of the previously mentioned hedging plants. Clipped evergreen globes could be ground level or tree-form standards, or they could be standard roses. They could be underplanted with a flat-growing, tidy ground cover such as creeping thyme or bronze bugle *(Ajuga reptans* 'Giant Bronze'). The roses could be the delightful, low-maintenance 'Sea Foam', a lovely carefree shrub that is broad and low growing, covered all season with foamy masses of pure white, teardrop-shaped buds that open into two- to three-inch- (5- to 7½-centimeter-) wide creamy pink flowers. It grows to a maximum of three feet (about 1 meter) tall.

The four large square beds, two at either end of the garden, suggest plantings of hybrid teas and floribundas in ever-intensifying colors, moving out from the white roses at the very center of the garden. Here again the beds are hedged, a technique that works well with roses since the low hedge helps hide the part of the rosebush that is perhaps the least attractive.

The four long sidebeds in this plan are devoted to the old-fashioned species, shrub, and heritage roses, some of which bloom only once each year, at the very end of spring or in earliest summer, and others that bloom constantly from early summer to frost. One of the most outstanding recent introductions, 'Bonica', is a pink shrub rose that is unusually hardy and disease resistant, and produces a large number of blossoms over the longest season imaginable. In autumn 'Bonica' has clusters of bright orange fruit (hips), yet it will still be covered with pink flowers.

How closely to plant the roses will be partly a matter of personal preference and partly a matter of how much money you have available. Where lots of color is the goal, bushes may be planted on eighteen-inch (46-centimeter) centers, although slightly wider spacing, to two feet (⅔ of a meter) apart in all directions, permits better air circulation and facilitates access for grooming and cultivation.

The four pedestals placed in the sidebeds give structure and architectural interest in all seasons. The fences on either side give a place to train climbing and rambler roses, such as pale pink 'New Dawn', vibrant pink with white eye 'American Pillar', rose-red 'Excelsa', scarlet 'Blaze', double yellow 'Golden Showers', and primrose yellow 'Mermaid'. The main pergola and arbors on either side provide a place to grow these and other similar roses. The four rounded trees at either end could be Cornelian cherry *(Cornus mas)* or any of a variety of flowering crab apples. Note the combination of flagstone paving and clipped grass for the pathways.

THE CRANFORD ROSE GARDEN

To stroll along the paths of the Cranford Rose Garden, set like a one-acre jewel in the fifty-two-acre Brooklyn Botanic Garden in Brooklyn, one of the five boroughs of the city of New York, is to enter the reality of all rose gardens. When one first glimpses it from the vantage of an earth-bermed and relatively high overlook to the north of the rose garden, it is not unusual for the visitor to experience *déjà vu:* Is this not something of a dream come true, the perfect setting for roses?

The Cranford, designed by landscape architect Harold Caparn and first planted in 1927, is set on a rectangular flat parcel of land that receives nearly full sun. It is framed by eight-foot- (2½-meter-) tall panels of white-painted wood trellising that are secured between slender concrete pillars. Toward the south end on a slight mound of earth stands a white lattice viewing pavilion with classic round columns, also constructed of white-painted wood, with both oval and rectangular windows cut in the trellis walls. From here the viewer is empowered by a sense of dominion that comes from being somewhat higher than the surrounding garden, in this case about four feet (1¼ meters), with each opening in the structure, whether window or doorlike, affording a frame for endlessly varied pictures or vistas of the roses throughout the garden.

Although no garden could be more democratic in its purpose than the Cranford, the axial symmetry imposed by the viewing pavilion suggests the influence of French Baroque, in vogue at a time when clear axis was seen as the manifestation of the autocratic power of one man—the king—over nature and all other people. The floor plan of the Cranford is forthrightly formal, but it can just as well be interpreted as hardly more than a straightforward layout, designed to suit the growth habits of all the different types of roses and to accommodate the human element, in this case perhaps a half-million visitors annually, from late May until the last roses of summer, which may not be finally frostbitten until late November or early December. The species and old-fashioned shrub roses grow in wide beds that run the length of the garden's long sides, with climbers woven through the trellis walls. Next, on either side, are wide

pathways of old bricks with double arches occurring at intervals, on which grow both rambling and climbing roses. The middle of the garden is an emerald lawn into which are cut rectangular beds for modern roses variously classified as polyantha, hybrid tea, grandiflora, and floribunda. Shapely concrete pillars set into these beds are connected by small-gauge chains that facilitate training ramblers into festoons.

Today's experience of the Cranford is strongly enhanced by horticultural practices that are so old they have become "new," to wit: At the time the first roses were planted more than sixty years ago, the ground was broken by a team of horses pulling a moldboard plow. It is likely that the original beds were enriched with well-rotted horse and other animal manures, as well as composted vegetable matter. Until World War II there would have been limited use of petrochemically derived fertilizers and pesticides. Beginning in the late 1940s, however, and continuing for some forty years, the Cranford was tended according to what were considered at the time the best possible practices. Chemical fertilizers were used, along with the latest pesticides, including insecticides against insects, fungicides against diseases, and herbicides to keep down weeds. Further, the beds were mulched with buckwheat hulls so as to reduce labor-intensive upkeep. Each spring the old mulch was left in place, along with any diseased leaves that might have fallen there during the previous season, and simply top-dressed with fresh hulls.

By the spring of 1985 when Stephen Scanniello, a young graduate biologist, was put in charge of the Cranford, he recalls, ". . . the garden as a whole seemed to have lost its vigor. My first clue as to what might be wrong lay in the soil itself. On my knees, I began to go around the garden, pulling back the mulch and finding in all cases a bricklike soil surface beneath that sometimes required the use of a small pickax to break up." In short, hardpan had developed, a condition that portends slow death to the living earth and inevitable decline of the plants growing therein. According to Scanniello, "Hardpan renders the soil airless, unable to absorb water, and effectually dead to biological activity."

That spring Scanniello and his helpers, I among them, immediately set out to remove and carry to the compost heap all of the old mulch. Then we moved into the beds and

Seen through one of the double arches that bower the paths at Cranford Rose Garden, Brooklyn Botanic Garden, 'Harison's Yellow' is one of the first roses to bloom. It has grown to about eight feet (2½ meters) high and twelve feet (3½ meters) wide and suckers freely, to produce many, many clusters of fragrant yellow flowers on long arching canes. 'Harison's Yellow' is a cross between an unknown spinosissima *and possibly a* foetida *rose, which occurred on a farm on the island of Manhattan in the nineteenth century and was then transported west with the early settlers.*

broke up the hardpan, which in some cases extended to a depth of five or six inches (13 or 15 centimeters). That first season Scanniello practiced clean cultivation of the beds, meaning that they were cultivated regularly in order to break up any surface crusting that normally follows rainfall or irrigation, and any weeds that might have sprouted were manually evicted rather than herbicidally destroyed. Spent flowers were promptly deadheaded and any petals or leaves that fell to the ground raked up and removed, thereby reducing the incidence of disease and with it the need for fungicidal treatments.

The following late fall and early winter, leading into the 1986 season, Scanniello topdressed all the exposed soil of the Cranford with nearly thirty tons of well-rotted cow manure. By early spring, when seasonal pruning began, this topdressing had mostly broken down into the ambient soil. Beginning with

the first flush of bloom in June, and continuing all that season, it was astonishingly apparent that new life was surging in this old garden, and that some of the oldest roses, dating from the first plantings, were behaving like energetic youths. What might easily have been attributed to beginner's luck on the part of the new rosarian was accepted instead in an otherwise cautiously scientific setting as living proof that healthy soil produces healthy roses, inherently stronger and less likely to fall victim to predatory insects and diseases.

In the ensuing seasons Scanniello has been able to spend progressively less time and resources on spraying and fertilizing and more and more on growing and training the vigorous roses so that their natural beauty becomes all the more evident. At present he is top-dressing every other winter with well-rotted manure, a practice that admittedly "brings weeds into the garden, but they are easily re-

Landscape architect Harold Caparn, the Cranford's designer in 1927, believed that the rose garden must look attractive in all seasons and not just in the full tilt of bloom. He chose to enclose the garden with white-painted wood latticing, to add a lattice viewing pavilion, and to bower the old brick paths with double arches on which rambling and climbing roses are trained.

This view of the Cranford is from the pavilion, looking northward to the Overlook at the Brooklyn Botanic Garden. In the foreground are beds of floribunda roses in which are displayed (with labels) nearly two hundred different cultivars. These cluster-stemmed roses produce flowers all summer. In the immediate foreground is a popular floribunda called 'Summer Snow'. The pavilion is situated on a low rise, which permits visitors to view most of the garden's collection from this one vantage point.

moved and added to the compost pile so that by the very next season their remains can serve remains can serve as new energy for the roses."

What is noteworthy about Scanniello's management of the Cranford is that it is not all that different from the way roses were grown throughout the nineteenth century, beginning at Malmaison, extending across the Continent, into England, and thence to America. Gibson observes, "This was a time when labour was cheap and manure was free. It came direct from the stables of the stately homes that grew the roses to their flower beds, dug in by platoons of gardeners." Today, however humble our "stately homes," or no matter that we ourselves more likely than not serve as our own "platoons of gardeners," we are embracing in ever increasing numbers the belief that quick-fix chemicals are not the answer for long-range health, but rather that nature's way produces the rose in all its glory.

The white climber on the left is a climbing form of the floribunda 'Summer Snow', and on the right is 'City of York', also a climbing rose. Climbing 'Summer Snow' is not a rampant plant and does best on a pillar or a low fence where it will reach a maximum height or length of about eight feet (2½ meters). 'City of York' can grow twenty to twenty-five feet (6 to 7½ meters) a season and is an incredibly floriferous rose that will repeat sporadically in the cooler days of autumn.

'Blaze', one of the most popular climbing roses found in gardens around the world, is of American origin, introduced in 1932. This repeat-blooming red rose took over the popularity that had previously belonged to one of its parents, 'Paul's Scarlet', which was crossed with the red bourbon 'Gruss an Teplits'. 'Blaze' makes an attractive showing when trained around a window or on a low-lying fence or garden wall.

EVERY PERSON'S FLOWER

Up until the founding of The Royal National Rose Society in England in 1876, it was generally held that roses were the province of the wealthy. Dean Hole, the principal founder, and his associates changed all that, proving that the rosarian having the most modest of resources could win at the show table. The American Rose Society, founded in 1899, and countless others that have followed around the world have reinforced this belief that the noble rose is indeed everyone's flower.

Perhaps in the end, nothing is so endearing about the rose as the observation of Theophrastus early in the third century B.C. as to

". . . the miraculous way in which the torch of life passes from one plant to another through the medium of small cuttings." By this awareness we can know that an old rose we grow and cherish in our garden because it has been passed down to us by way of our known family tree may actually have come to life first in the presence of the Empress Josephine hundreds of years before. By the same token, all the unknown roses yet to be are already represented in the DNA amassed through millennia of evolution. Finally we may see that roses are as much a part of what the gardener carries to the compost pile as what we stoop to smell. Dust to dust, the rosarian is sustained and comforted, ever reminded that in the dead of winter is born the other side of life.

Right: *Lawn areas are important in a rose garden to set off the various beds or plantings. Viewing across the Cranford through floribunda and hybrid tea beds, one sees a pergola covered with white climbing roses, 'City of York' (left) and 'Paul's Lemon Pillar' (right), a relatively rare climber. The double arches are metal-and-wire structures that cross over the walkways, creating a wonderful place to seek refuge from the hot sun and take in the smells of the roses.*

Following pages: *White 'City of York' (left) and pale pink 'New Dawn' (right) are extremely bountiful white-blooming climbers that will cover arches or walls in record time. They are readily trained and highly resistant to disease, also very cold-hardy. Both also possess generous perfume. City of York occasionally gives a light repeat blooming in autumn and 'New Dawn' is a profuse repeat bloomer. Here they form an enticing canopy over a walkway in the Cranford.*

CHAPTER TWO

FORMAL GARDENS

Today we are more intimately concerned with our environment than ever before. At a time when nature's very survival seems threatened, gardening with a formal theme and an architectural emphasis derived from older cultures may appear at first a gross irrelevance. Today we want to save and savor plants, not regiment them. Gardeners, in a threatened world, put more and more emphasis on "wild" gardening, using native plants in natural ways to recreate the scenes and nuances of vanishing nature. But in whatever style a garden is laid out, the rules formulated by formal gardeners act as guidelines to the composition. Gardens are not just slices of nature modified to suit our needs; they are self-consciously designed works of art and their roots are deep in history.

Many of us have visited Versailles or at least know of its grandeur and scale; it seems the epitome of the great architectural conceits of a bygone age. To a modern gardener, Versailles, with its sweeping water vistas and avenues to the horizon, appears sterile; it is architecture, not gardening. There even the plants play a contrived role to match the fine sculpture. Tall, smoothly clipped hedges form allées and dwarf boxwood frame scrolled parterres where annuals are massed. Orange trees and palms in tubs are arranged like parade-ground soldiers in front of the *orangerie*.

Today gardeners can pick and choose exotic plants from all corners of the world; we have an embarrassment of riches. Yet at the end of the seventeenth century not only was the plant palette restricted by the existing limits of exploration, but the cultivated plants were strictly used to implement the language of formality. Is what we see at Versailles all there really is—is this the greatest formal garden in the world; the Sun King's masterpiece?

THE GRAMMAR OF FORMALITY

Versailles and the rules it formulated remain universal; it is both wonderful and awe-inspiring. At Versailles the formal style, the garden treated as architecture, can be studied and then interpreted anew for the twentieth century. Versailles was not invented overnight; it was the architect-gardener's ultimate expression of man's triumph over nature. From earliest times people laid out gardens in order to counteract the lack of order in their environment; gardens developed as enclosures from which nature and chaos were banned. Formality is order; it is the opposite of chaos. In gardening it implies control, and the formal garden, with its straight lines, right angles, and symmetry, developed as a logical progression from the first functional enclosures, recorded around 1400 B.C. in the Mediterranean basin, to the supreme works of art created by Renaissance man in the sixteenth and seventeenth centuries.

The formal garden is not always as cold and grand as seem the echoing spaces of Versailles. Nor are the design principles involved necessarily the complicated exercises in perspective, symmetry, and balance they were in seventeenth-century France. In a formal garden the layout is symmetrical; pattern repeats pattern and views into the distance, and more intimate focal points are framed by paired architectural details or sculptured plant forms. In grand gardens, steep slopes are leveled into terraces, where patterned parterres are mirrored right and left. In 1731 the English poet Alexander Pope described the fashionable formal garden typified by contemporary French layouts in his *Epistle to Lord Burlington:*

> . . . each Alley has a brother,
> And half the garden just reflects the other.

Elegant ramps and stairways link the separate levels and water is harnessed into quiet reflecting canals or fills the air with sparkling jets. In the formal garden, clipped yew, box, and bay rival the shining marble statues in their effects, and even tender myrtle bushes are cut into tight shapes to decorate the box parterres. In the *potager* citrus fruits, aligned in serried ranks for summer display, are also shaped, while apples, pears, peaches, and plums are developed into fancy espalier, palmettes, and cordons to be productive as well as architectural and symmetrical. Pope satirized this fashion for elaborate topiary, inventing a "Catalogue of Greens" available for the aspiring gardener:

Previous page: *At Hidcote in Gloucestershire double lines of pleached hornbeam accentuate the formal layout of this early-twentieth-century garden and frame the view into the Cotswold countryside. Hidcote, made by the American Lawrence Johnston and today maintained by the English National Trust, remains a supreme example of an Italian-style formal garden planted with a twentieth-century flair for romantic profusion and rich flower colors.*

Bottom left: *The gardens of the sixteenth-century Villa Gamberaia, situated on the outskirts of Florence, were restored in the early years of this century. A water parterre is framed by clipped box hedges. Arcades, cut into the cypress screen at the end of the garden, allow views to the hills of Vallombrosa beyond the valley of the Arno.*

At Gamberaia some of the original features dating to the Renaissance period are still intact. A giardino segreto to the side of the main garden has sixteenth-century tufa stonework and decoration.

A pair of Giants, stunted, to be sold cheap,
A Queen Elizabeth in Phyllyraea, a little
    inclined to the Green
Sickness, but of full growth . . .
An old Maid of Honour in Wormwood.

If one studies the "grammar" of formality, even the remote magnitude of features at Versailles becomes comprehensible. In formal gardening on the grander scale, avenues stretch into the countryside to frame a distant view or, in close-up, arch overhead to give cathedrallike effects. Allées of soaring cypresses or clipped French-style *charmille* provide living green walls to enclose walks, with pergolas to provide essential shade, especially important in Mediterranean countries with hot sun; head-high mazes, symbols of our struggle through life to eternity, deliberately amuse and confuse the unwary and stylized birds or other fanciful topiary shapes demonstrate the gardener's use of shears. At ground level, geometric areas of grass or water contribute to the overall plan, and beds of flowers or colored gravels are framed by low patterns of box.

Formality is organization; even flower borders in repetitive color schemes extend the formal theme. There is nothing informal about organized swaths of grasses, perennials, and annuals planted in "natural"-looking drifts; it is a subtle form of patternmaking disguised to imply a relaxed garden style. The garden can be subdivided into compartments by walls or hedges in which geometric enclosures provide further space for gardening with separate themes. And there are many small gardens, both old and new, where small details provide elements of formality that can turn disorder into a logical sequence. In a formal garden, architectural features (these include plants) are repeated to give symmetry; two terra-cotta pots or fine clipped yews flank a gateway, double hedges border and accentuate the lines of a path. Often the formal treatment of a garden consists of extending the architectural rules of the house into the grounds that surround it, so that house and garden seem linked.

The classical elements of formality which evolved when few plants were available still hold as viable principles today but can be enriched and softened by judicious planting to please the passionate plantsman. The straight lines, right angles, and geometry, executed in isolated stone and marble at Versailles, can also be used to make a background frame for maximum informality in planting. The underlying structure, made with masonry walls or walls of "living" plants, still holds the garden together in a "formal" mold, while rich and

Left: *At the Château de Courances south of Paris the garden was laid out in the formal style in the seventeenth century. Tall trees soar overhead to be reflected in the long canals that are arranged in a geometric pattern.*
Above: *A cross canal at the Château de Courances emphasizes the strong horizontal lines. Framed by grass panels it reflects the overhanging linden trees.*

luxuriant shrubs and flowers spill over hard edges to soften and disguise rather than emphasize architectural detail. Tall dividing hedges (or walls) in Renaissance style make geometric garden compartments where color or plant themes follow in sequence through the gardening season. Some of the best twentieth-century gardens, such as Hidcote and Sissinghurst in England and Filoli in California, are of this type. Their formality is implied rather than implicit. In fact, formal gardening, working to a set of rules, is much simpler to execute and maintain than a more naturalistic style. In "informal" gardening much depends not only on how an individual eye sees and evaluates shape and color, but also on an intimate understanding of *how* plants develop when allowed to grow as they would in nature.

HISTORICAL EVOLUTION OF THE FORMAL GARDEN

Three thousand years ago the enclosed "formal" pleasure gardens of the Egyptians developed out of irrigated small holdings in the desert. Nature in the raw was the enemy and man, with quite limited plant material, imposed order and beauty behind the safety of

Bottom: *At Courances still reflecting water is an essential feature in the composition, the trees arching overhead to give a cathedrallike effect.*
Right: *At Les Quatre Vents on the St. Lawrence River north of Quebec, the garden has traditional formal lines that give essential background structure to the flower planting. Tall poplars close in the view.*

barricades erected against the alien outer world. The most important requisites were water and shade; symbolic lotus and papyrus bloomed in rectangular central water tanks flanked by regularly spaced fruit trees and date palms. Water nymphs lurked in the clear waters and tree goddesses distributed bounty from the fruit trees.

From these gardens we can trace the line of succession of formal gardening to the twentieth century. But from the beginning of recorded garden history, gardening development is split into what appears to be two distinct traditions, that of the enclosed geometric gardens of the Mediterranean basin and the naturalistic hunting parks of contemporary Imperial China. In one style lines and angles are symmetric; manipulated plants are subservient to an overall conception. In the other flowing lines follow natural contours and free-growing plant shapes develop to create a landscape that, although closely resembling nature in aspect, is, in reality, almost as artificial and controlled as the architectural garden. In the West, nature was to be shunned; in Oriental gardens, with their strong religious and philosophical overtones, copying nature's art became the dominant theme and the first recorded hunting parks developed as a form of cooperation with life-giving nature. By simulating nature's gifts the Chinese expressed an ideal of the universe in harmony; instead of controlling nature, man felt part of it. It is the synthesis of the "formal" classical Western style with the "informal" Oriental which has produced some of the great modern gardens of the world.

In the flower-filled gardens of Islam and the almost legendary garden oases of the Mogul emperors in the East, the heavy hand of man and the light touch of nature effected a subtle compromise. Under the Muslims after 800 A.D., the Islamic gardens in Persia developed as a high form of art where religious meanings and poetic imagery combined with a love of flowers and beauty to produce some of the most beautiful gardens in the world.

Above all, the presence of life-giving water was essential. To a Muslim the earthly garden is much more than a terrestrial experience; it represents the anticipation of the Heavenly Paradise promised by Muhammad. The Koran abounds with accounts of paradise in the form of a garden, "with plenteous shade and water everywhere" and above all scented flowers—tulips, irises, jonquils, violets, and anemones growing in scented profusion. In Muslim gardens, two canals representing the Rivers of Life would converge at a central point and divide the garden into squares, representing the four corners of the universe, in which fruit trees and flowers grew in sunken beds. Woven garden carpets show us vivid representations of these cross-axial rivers and the delicate tapestry of a myriad of flowers growing in the flanking beds. In spite of the regularity of layout, there was nothing sterile about the imagery of Persian gardens; scents and beauty, fading blooms, and falling leaves provided poets with endless themes, ranging from the earthly and sensual to the abstract and mystical.

The Arabs, learned botanists as well as skillful gardeners, developed their own version of the Islamic Persian gardens in Spain from the tenth century onward. Although the Christians recaptured southern Spain at the end of the fifteenth century and parts of the gardens at the Alhambra and neighboring Generalife at Granada reflect much later trends, enough remains of the thirteenth- and fourteenth-century layouts, with the superb background of Nasrite architecture, constructed of latticed ivory-colored stone, marble fretwork, and glazed tiles, to convey some of the magic of these gardens where, behind high enclosing walls, bubbling and sparkling water jets cool the air and spreading fruit trees provide essential shade. These rectangular enclosures have central watercourses, flanked with paths, as their main axes; at right angles secondary axes lead to further garden "rooms" where more water rills spill from carved stone basins.

The Persian garden also traveled to the East; by the end of the fifteenth century the Mogul emperors spread their empire into Afghanistan and India, where they made some of the most sumptuous gardens ever conceived. These are revealed to us in Mogul miniatures of the period.

While the Arabs in Spain were developing their sophisticated flower gardens the rest of Europe was in cultural eclipse; the only gardens made were useful, not ornamental. But even in the enclosed monasteries the culinary herbs, simples for medicinal use, and fragrant flowers for altar decoration were laid out in beds edged with boards or woven willow in convenient straight rows in a simple grid system that pleased the ordered mind.

In the fifteenth century, as Europe

The Generalife gardens above the Alhambra at Granada, with narrow water channels and flower beds hemmed in by hedges and tall cypresses, convey the Islamic concept of the garden as a terrestrial paradise, a foretaste of heaven to come.

Left: *At Villa La Pietra summer colors contrast with the clipped formality of evergreen box, bay, yew, cypress, and oak. Rose and wisteria arch to make tunnel arbors among the deep green.*

Right: *Sir Harold Acton's terraced garden at Villa La Pietra outside Florence is a reconstruction of an early-sixteenth-century Renaissance garden with cool allées of clipped evergreens. Steps link the descending terraces, which broaden out to create geometric shapes for other garden features. In spring wisteria twines around the central pergola.*

Bottom right: *Elegant stonework, steps, ramps, and fountains at the sixteenth-century Villa Lante near Viterbo north of Rome. Sparkling water rills and jets, and cascades descending into a series of pools and stairways, provide the central focus to the garden, which is set deep in surrounding woods.*

Following pages: *At the Villa Lante, set on a steep hill, the central water features provide continual sound and movement. The water falls down terraces from a high grotto, broadening out into wide balustrated pools at the bottom of the valley.*

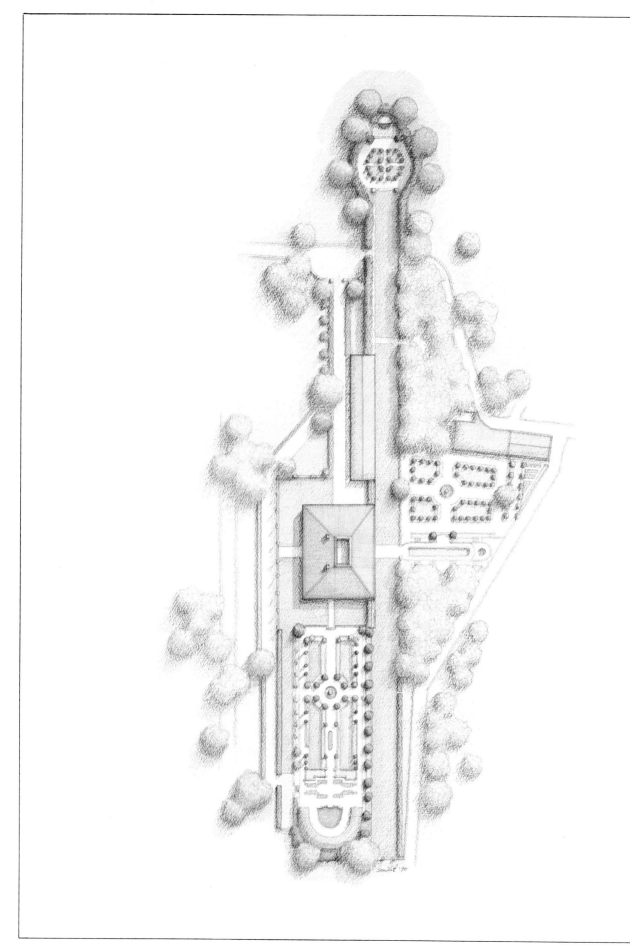

VILLA GAMBERAIA

As Europe emerged from the Dark Ages, the Italian Renaissance villa and its garden, with perfection of proportion and expert manipulation of space, developed gradually as a country retreat for humanist man. In these villas, often set on hillsides with views out into the surrounding landscape, the emphasis was on axial alignment and symmetry. A series of intimate garden rooms were linked together with the villa itself. Little remains of the early sixteenth-century villa and garden at Gamberaia, on the slopes outside Florence, but successive and brilliantly executed "restorations," after periods of neglect, have ensured that the whole layout expressively catches the true spirit of the original era, with a series of interrelated spaces linked with the dwelling. Today only the long bowling alley and grotto garden with eighteenth-century rocaille work are genuine features; the immaculately kept water parterres and arcaded semicircle of cypresses which reveal views to the hills around Vallombrosa were introduced by the Serbian Princess Ghyka and her American friend Miss Blood in the early 1900s. The water panels, edged with low box and pebbled paths, frame flower beds of roses, peonies, and annuals, which fill the garden with evocative scent. On the west, the balustrading, decorated with stone dogs, frames further views, this time of Florence in the valley below.

emerged from the Dark Ages, Renaissance gardening drew its inspiration from the precepts of Greece and Rome. Classical writings on architecture, gardens, farming, and plants by authors such as Theophrastus, Vitruvius and Pliny, Virgil and Varro were adapted and reinterpreted for humanist man, extending gardening design into a new realm of balanced proportion and manipulated space. Gardens became, as they had been for the peripatetic philosophers of Athens, walking under the shade of plane trees, the meeting places for poets and philosophers, providing a setting for discussions as well as a traditional refuge. In 1452 Leon Battista Alberti's influential *De Re Aedificatoria* was published. In it he recommended that villas should be sited in salubrious surroundings, on hillside sites with exposure to wind and sun with "the Delights of Gardens" in the foreground; gardens in which, adhering to architectural forms and strict geometry, plants such as box and sweetly scented herbs were clipped into topiary shapes. In 1499 another influential treatise, *Hypnerotomachia Poliphili* (translated into English in 1592 as *The Strife of Love in a Dream*), showed intimate garden areas illustrated by a series of woodcuts; a labyrinth, trelliswork arbors, topiary, hedges, colonnades, and knots (by the seventeenth century pattern books were publishing knot designs for the gardener to copy), and a "flowery mede" provided the classic ingredients of the Renaissance garden.

The Italian villa and garden became an integral unit, with a series of axial "rooms" on quite an intimate scale, aligned with the villa itself. These gardens were not displays of power but, as recommended by the classical writers, were for the individual's own enjoyment and health. It is not only the sense of order and proportion of the Italian garden which appeals to our senses today; it had many other ingredients. In some layouts sculptures excavated from Greek or Roman sites were displayed as in a gallery (by the seventeenth and eighteenth centuries statues from the *commedia dell'arte* peopled the stages of their fanciful "green theaters"), *giardini segreti* provided privacy and shade, and in their bosky woodlands we can catch a glimpse of sixteenth-century thought and attitudes that, emphasizing the beauty of nature, harked back to classical Greece and Rome. In the midst of all this seriousness the garden architects took time to devise fantastic water jokes and jets that even today can soak the unwary at a turn of a tap.

*The view from the
Château de Courances
carries the eye across the
parterre of box and gravel
down the long central
canal, into the distant
forest and onward to
infinity. The French
formal garden was an
expression of man's control
over nature and often a
demonstration of ownership
of the surrounding
countryside.*

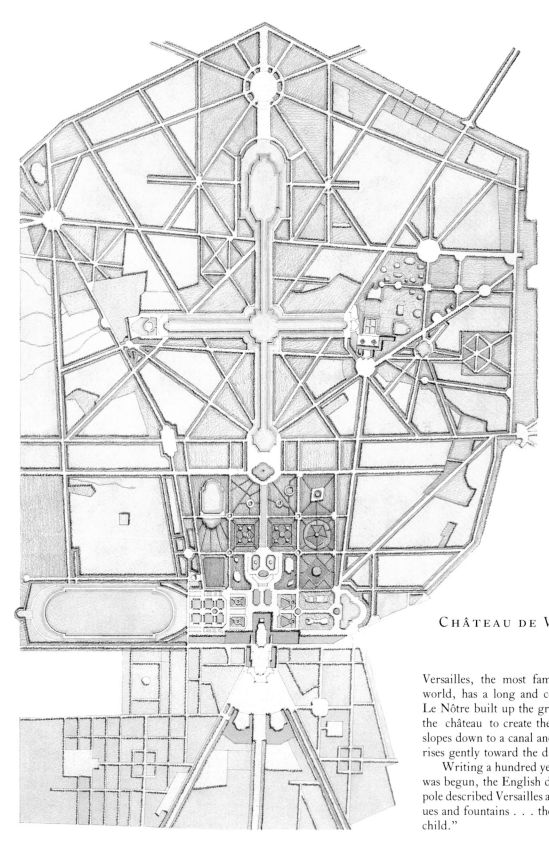

CHÂTEAU DE VERSAILLES

Versailles, the most famous garden in the world, has a long and complicated history. Le Nôtre built up the ground to the west of the château to create the main vista, which slopes down to a canal and fountain and then rises gently toward the distant horizon.

Writing a hundred years after the garden was begun, the English diarist Horace Walpole described Versailles as "littered with statues and fountains . . . the gardens of a great child."

The water theater, one of the bosquets *concealed in the woods at Versailles, became a setting for king and courtiers. When turned on for the king, seventy-five jets of water made spectacular patterns of spray. (A Bosquet at Versailles: The Water Theater by Jean Rigaud, The Metropolitan Museum of Art, Harris Brisbane Dick Fund, 1953— 53.600.1279)*

Nor were the gardens flowerless; in many sixteenth- and seventeenth-century gardens the latest exotic plants, including tulips from Constantinople, fritillaries, jasmine, roses, amaranth, carnations, and flowers from the New World, grew in the flower beds between the box hedging.

The Italian gardens captured the imagination of Europe. By the seventeenth century they developed, especially in France, a more dramatic Baroque aspect, visually extending the garden from the building on a vast scale, but always with a powerful axial emphasis, into the landscape. These gardens became symbols of man's power over and ultimate control of nature. Distorted perspective, theatrical water cascades and *bassins* were almost intimidating in their grandeur. Parterres in box were laid out under the château windows; the geometric dwarf hedges typical of the Renaissance were elaborated into much more complicated scroll- and featherwork *parterre-de-broderie* effects. The most influential designer was André Le Nôtre, whose masterpieces at Vaux-le-Vicomte and at Versailles (among many other still extant gardens) set the tone for European gardening for a century.

At Versailles, created for Louis XIV from 1661, the essence of Le Nôtre's scheme, with geometrically placed parterres, *pièces d'eau*, radiating avenues, and great works of sculpture, was to ensure the complete subjugation of nature. There was nothing spontaneous about the design; besides being an architectural tour de force it was a triumphant allegory of power—even Apollo's fountain extended

the theme of Louis as the Sun King, with the divine right to rule over the natural world as well as his kingdom. Nor, at the time, were idle visitors allowed to wander at will. (The history of gardening, told through its masterpieces, echoes the story and tastes of princes and courtiers who, like actors on a stage, peopled the theatrical garden layouts.) The king himself had written instructions for viewing the gardens *(Manière de Montrer les Jardins)*; the route, down steps, past fountains (ironically only turned on for the king's passing—in spite of the magnificence, water was scarce), and traversing the vast *parterres-de-broderie*, allowed diversions in the *bosquets* where tall trees filtering sunlight hid water theaters, other extravagances, and fine statuary, immortalized by the paintings of Jean Cotelle and recorded by Rigaud's engravings (1741). Versailles's grandeur was, and is, unassailable. In his old age Louis made the circuit in a three-wheeled *roulette* propelled by footmen.

In an age when the great princes of Europe associated power with wealth and display, Versailles spawned many almost equally imposing layouts, sometimes with their own distinctive national style. In 1685 a Dutch architect, Jacob Roman, rebuilt the Palace of Het Loo in the hunting forest near Apeldoorn for William of Orange (King William III of England). The interior decoration and the garden were completed by the French designer Daniel Marot (a Huguenot refugee after the Edict of Nantes in 1685). The layout depended again on unity of house and garden with a central axis, featuring mirror image parterres as com-

Left: *A garden was laid out for William and Mary in the 1680s at the Palace of Het Loo in Holland. Much of the decorative work, including the metalwork designs and the patterns for the Baroque parterres, was done by the French refugee Daniel Marot and shows French influence. The Dutch adapted Versailles styles to their flat, more treeless landscape and to the more confined garden spaces. The garden at Het Loo has recently been restored with authentic period planting.*
Right: *The Queen's, or Princess's, Garden at Het Loo, lying under the eastern walls of the palace, had parterres as well as trelliswork arbors. Exotic plants in pots were placed around the edge of the garden and sheltered in greenhouses during the winter.*

ponents on either side. Unlike Versailles, here water abounded in the low-lying terrain and cascades and fountains were vital ingredients of the integrated formal plan.

If Versailles and Het Loo expressed extreme developments in formalism, they provoked their own antithesis. In the eighteenth century man sought a new expression of freedom; instead of demonstrating his control over nature, man wished to express and experience his own reactions to beauty. In England, by the middle of the eighteenth century, within a few years of Pope's criticisms of the symmetric style in the 1720s, many of the great formal gardens were swept away in favor of "natural" landscaping; allées, hedges, knots, and parterres around the house disappeared to allow sweeping parkland to stretch to the windows of the house. Sheep and cattle grazed outside the drawing-room windows in place of elaborate topiary shapes; flowers were banished to the productive garden. Garden and park, separated only by a ha-ha, merged into one landscape.

With Pope, William Kent, Charles Bridgeman, and "Capability" Brown as its chief exponents, the landscape style developed its own English idiom, in which man's sublime reactions to a garden became of increasing importance, rather than the measure of man's control over it. Trees were felled to break up the line of avenues. Separate groves of trees and lakes were arranged naturalistically on newly contoured land with hills and valleys flowing with gentle swells into each other. This evolution did not take place overnight; the development was gradual, but after the middle of the eighteenth century the English landscape style was adopted in many new gardens throughout Europe. As in England, ear-

The eighteenth-century Baroque-style box-and-gravel parterre at Quinta da Bacalhoa, south of Lisbon, shows how French gardening styles were adopted all over Europe in the years after Versailles was laid out. It lies under the house walls; groves of fruit trees are located beyond. In another part of the garden the original sixteenth-century tiles line the walls of the pavilion above the water basin.

lier terraces and parterres in some of the great old formal gardens were obliterated to make way for the new romantic parks. As a style the landscape garden survives today, accommodating itself to plant collections, arboreta, and cemeteries, where rigid geometry would be less appropriate, and to small private gardens. Since the eighteenth century it has played as significant a role in the development of gardens as the more formal and traditional "rule book" gardening.

In Europe the "new" natural style took longer to establish; during the first three quarters of the eighteenth century gardens modeled on Versailles were laid out by all the rich courts of Europe and by Peter the Great in Russia. Although by the end of the eighteenth century a form of English landscape gardening (sometimes combined with strong Oriental overtones and called *jardins anglo-chinois)* was often adopted, many of the greatest layouts retained their formal features while adjacent parkland was "romanticized." Versailles, with all its cold formality, has an English garden, and

Sanssouci at Potsdam retains its magnificent terraces in contrast to the contoured parkland that stretches to one side.

THE FORMAL GARDEN INTERPRETED IN AMERICA

The geometric garden reached its highest expression during the Renaissance in Europe and traveled to America with the seventeenth-century settlers. A type of Renaissance formality, mainly utilitarian in purpose, with vegetables and orchards and a few flowers, dominated American gardening style for another two hundred years. The impeccable re-creation of gardens surrounding Colonial Williamsburg allows us to capture the spirit of these eighteenth-century gardens, where orchards of fruit and the kitchen garden beds were as essential as the more ornamental box-edged flower-filled parterres.

Even the great plantation gardens in Vir-

Left: *The Apollo Fountain at Versailles, designed by Jean Baptiste Tuby from 1668, represents the rising sun. Situated at the end of the great vista north of the château, it is a tribute to Louis XIV as the Sun King.*
Right: *Rousham in Oxfordshire was one of the earliest classical English landscapes. Laid out by William Kent in the 1730s, the garden incorporates views into the surrounding countryside.*

An eighteenth-century garden in France demonstrates the French interpretation of the new landscape movement in England. The jardin anglais *at Moulin-Joli incorporates buildings and bridges in its naturalistic design. (Vue Interieure d'un Jardin Anglais Appelle Moulin-Joli, 1786, Francois Denis Nee, after Charles Daubigny, National Gallery of Art, Washington, D.C., Mark J. Millard Architectural Collection—1985.61)*

ginia and the rest of the South had a *raison d'être*. At Middleton Place in South Carolina, one of the few eighteenth-century layouts to survive the depredations of the Civil War, the mirror-image butterfly ponds were an essential part of the rice-growing economy. The garden lies above the Ashley River and was laid out during the 1740s; one hundred slaves took ten years to complete the project. With its steep formal terraces, the simple design follows pure Italian lines.

VICTORIAN ITALIANATE AND ARTS AND CRAFTS IN EUROPE AND AMERICA

By the early nineteenth century the down-to-earth English gardener had tired of the flowerless eighteenth-century landscape. As new plants poured in from all around the world, garden fashions readapted for their reception; terraces and flower beds were reinstated in formal style near the house or on the broad, flat lawns. Colorful tender plants from such places as South America were grown in the new glasshouses, and schemes in beds were changed twice or three times in a year to give variety. The brash color themes depended mainly on primary hues, with concentric circles of yellow calceolarias, blue lobelias, and scarlet geraniums being commonplace. Toward the last half of the century flower beds were further decorated with colored foliage plants, massed in patterns as "mosaiculture"; in public parks in Paris and London large-leaved tropical plants were used for exotic-looking summer bedding.

By the middle of the nineteenth century, houses and gardens were remodeled in what is called Italianate style. Monumental terraces, balustrading, broad steps, elaborate bedding-out schemes, and box-and-gravel parterres framed the large houses. These layouts were frankly "historicist" in tone, designed to give an impression of period antiquity to suit the style of a "new" Gothic or Jacobean-style house. Charles Barry was often the architect of the house and W. A. Nesfield was an advocate of the strict parterre pattern where curving lines of box (only four inches [10 centimeters] high), sometimes in armorial patterns, were decorated with colored gravels instead of seasonal flowers. At Broughton Hall in Yorkshire one of Nesfield's box-and-gravel parterres still survives. The National Trust has reinstated bright-flowered bedding schemes on properties such as Kingston Lacey and Lyme Park, and there are annual parterres at Kew and Hampton Park as well as in many municipal gardens.

The crudity of these formal Victorian bedding schemes signed their death warrant. By the 1870s a new prophet, William Robinson, preached a different sermon. Defying fashion he advocated the use of hardy natives and introduced plants which would naturalize and spread at waterside or at the edge of woodland. His influence on planting styles was immense, but it was his near-contemporary Gertrude Jekyll, trained as a painter, who interpreted some of his ideas for the flower garden. She loved to work inside a formal framework created by an architect. The Arts and Crafts Movement led by William Morris encouraged a return to old values in art and architecture and the use of the vernacular in building materials. This exactly suited Miss Jekyll; inside a garden structure that owed much to the architect (she worked with Sir Edwin Lutyens and many other well-known contemporaries) her plants were allowed to grow in luxuriant profusion in traditionally shaped beds, with shrubs, perennials, bulbs, annuals, and biennials often arranged in quite strict formal color sequence to carry the garden through the whole summer. Each bed or border was as carefully composed as a painting, with flowers arranged exactly as the artist would handle his pigments, to create a series of static pictures to be viewed on a garden tour. Few of Miss Jekyll's own complicated designs can be seen today; the most interesting example is Hestercombe in Somerset, where Lutyens constructed formal walls and rills inside which she laid out borders in definite color schemes. It dates to just before World War I and recently has been restored to its former glory.

The gardens at Hidcote, Sissinghurst Castle, and the more modest Tintinhull are in Miss Jekyll's tradition, each a subtle blend between a formal layout and a more informal planting. The beds and borders, framed by architecture, are tightly packed with free-

The garden at George Washington's home at Mount Vernon, laid out at the end of the eighteenth century, was still formal, with an emphasis on useful fruit and vegetables as well as flowers.

The gardens of Shrublands Park in Suffolk, with steep terraces that descend to a lower valley, were laid out in the Italianate style, with monumental stonework and elaborate summer bedding. This chromolithograph from E. Adveno Brooke (1857) shows the view from the upper terrace. (The Royal Horticultural Society, Lindley Library)

growing "naturalistic" plantings. This style remains as "modern" today as when it was first conceived in Edwardian England.

In North America many of the great "country places" laid out by the barons of industry at the turn of the century were modeled on the Italianate style from Europe. But other more democratic forces were at work. America inspired Western civilization in the development of public gardens for use by urban populations. Frederick Law Olmsted's plans for Central Park in New York depended on the "landscape" ideals rather than geometric formality. In private gardening the democratic ideal led to the "open plan" front garden where sweeps of lawn and scattered trees stretched the length of city blocks. "Walls, high fences, belts of trees and shrubbery" can be simply means "by which we show how unchristian and unneighbourly we can be," wrote Frank J. Scott in *The Art of Beautifying Suburban Home Grounds of Small Extent* in 1870.

Even today the formal garden in America is typified by vast monumental layouts, where Italian and French styles blend to produce terraces, parterres, water basins and fountains, and avenues stretching into the distance. Longwood in Pennsylvania (1906), Vizcaya in Florida (1914), and Nemours in Delaware (1932) are splendid examples of contemporary gardening techniques fully exploited inside a formal theme. At Ladew in Maryland the topiary gardens were laid out between 1929 and 1971 with grand allées and topiary figures. In the Conservatory Gardens in New York (designed inside Central Park in the 1930s) the "frame" is Italianate, although much of the restored planting is in a more relaxed Jekyllian style. Allées of crab apples and yew hedging define the space, and formal bedding out of tulips gives way in season to massed chrysanthemums. "English" mixed borders are arranged in gentle harmonious color schemes.

Thus have the "formal" and "natural" styles merged, typified by the work of such great garden artists as Miss Jekyll in England; Beatrice Farrand, Fletcher Steele, and Thomas Church in the United States; and their modern disciples. Each of these designers, in his or her own way, emphasized the importance of the strictly geometric and structural Renaissance ideal and then proceeded to adapt

Right: *The gardens at Hestercombe were designed as a partnership between Sir Edwin Lutyens and Gertrude Jekyll before the First World War. Lutyens built the walls, steps, and paths wtih local stone to make a formal framework inside, and Miss Jekyll planted borders and flower beds in different color schemes. The garden, shown here in spring, has recently been restored using Jekyll's original plans.*

Bottom right: *The view at Tintinhull taken from the attic window shows the long axial path, edged with domes of clipped box, which stretches to the bottom of the garden. To the north a series of lateral compartments are divided up to make separate garden "rooms" for seasonal color schemes.*

Above: *At Hidcote all the borders, backed by a framework of dark hedges, are tightly backed with flowers to give an informal cottage garden effect.*
Left: *The flower garden at Tintinhull is divided up into a series of compartments in the style of Hidcote. Tall hedges and walls make a background to flowers. In the iris border the gentle colors of alliums and love-in-a-mist blend in the eye.*

it for each garden in its setting. This has led to the creation of the greatest gardens the world has ever known: Sissinghurst Castle in Kent, Hidcote in Gloucestershire, Mount Stewart in Ireland, and Crathes in Scotland, the smaller Tintinhull in Somerset, and Chilcombe in Dorset, with their strong twentieth-century look of billowing plants, tightly packed in flower beds, spilling out to break and blur the formal rhythms. In the United States the gardens at Old Westbury on Long Island, the Rockefeller garden on Mount Desert Island in Maine (with its interesting Oriental overtones), Filoli in California, the Herb Garden in the National Arboretum in Washington, D.C., and the Conservatory Garden in Central Park in New York are splendid examples of this modern idiom.

TODAY

We have come a long way since the formal garden first evolved. The history of garden development chronicles the gardens of the great. Today we are more concerned with the ordinary man's garden and his personal philosophy for living. Nevertheless, although garden styles reflect personal taste, good design is still a matter of principle. Even the best naturalistic gardeners draw heavily on fundamental formal principles that are most easily studied in the more architectural gardens. It is significant that toward the end of his life, Thomas Church (died 1978), inspired by recollections of the Italian and French gardens he had visited in Europe in his youth,

HIDCOTE MANOR

The gardens at Hidcote in the Cotswolds are today sheltered by a ring of thick woodland. When Lawrence Johnston came here in the early years of the century, the house (there was no garden) lay exposed on a windswept hill with seemingly little horticultural promise. Johnston, an American much traveled in Europe, had been influenced by the classic "formal" layouts found in villa gardens in Italy. At Hidcote, moving outward from the house, he designed the well-proportioned garden compartments and allées of hornbeam to reveal axial views to succeeding planting schemes as well as grassed allées from which there were vistas over the countryside. Evergreen oaks were imported to provide shelter, and the series of hedged "rooms" developed in which plants from all over the world could luxuriate with adequate protection from the wind. Johnston, as well as having a fine eye for design, was a great plant collector, and Hidcote is also notable for specific color schemes—a white-flowered garden set with topiary yew, a garden of yellow and bronze for his mother, the famous red borders that stretch away from the house—and for immaculate "tapestry" hedges that frame the tightly packed freestyle planting. Before the First World War Hidcote, now copied by gardeners all over the world, was revolutionary. It was a classic Italian garden with the addition of soft and luxuriant plant shapes. Vita Sackville-West of Sissinghurst Castle described Hidcote as a "jungle of beauty; a jungle controlled by a single mind." In season, roses, peonies, irises, and woodland plants all jostle in the flower beds to convey unsophisticated jungle detail, but the formal layout provides the essential background framework. Lawrence Johnston also made an inspiring garden on the French Riviera where, in that favored climate, he could experiment with more tender plants.

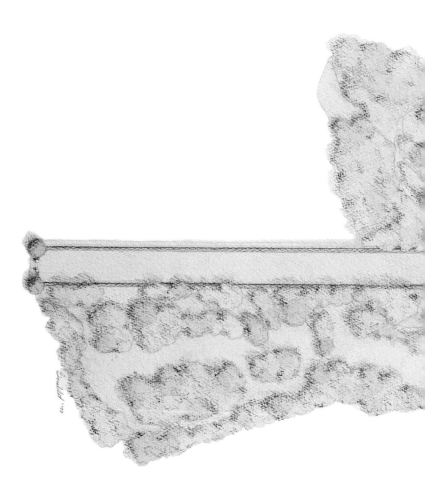

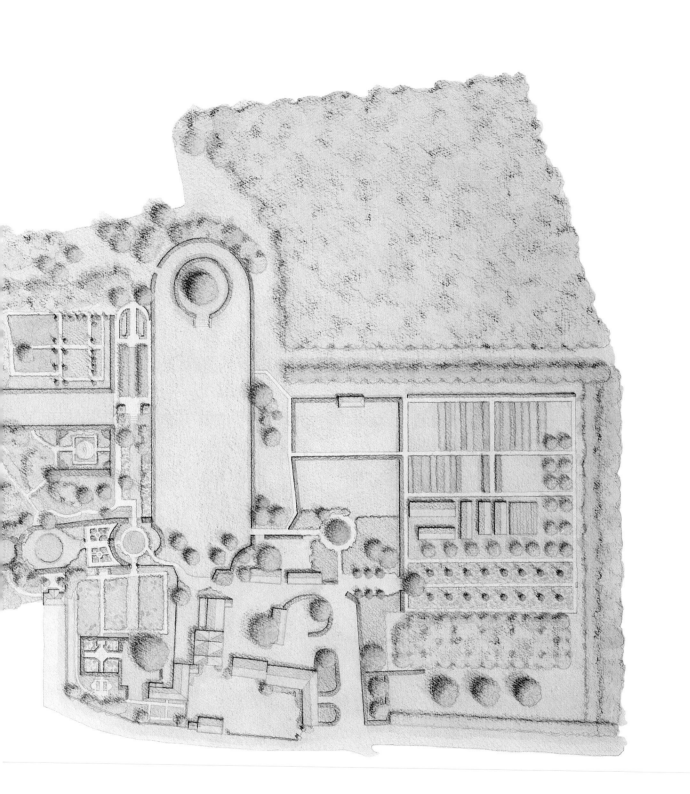

returned to creating gardens with strong Renaissance formulas. His own genius allowed him to translate this style to the California landscape in which he worked and adapt it to the outdoor style of living of his clients and the surrounding landscape. Pliny the Younger's descriptions in the first century of how his two gardens were laid out for sun and shade, evening and morning enjoyment, and more distant views and prospects, together with outdoor dining rooms and enclosed and heated swimming pools, sound almost familiar, expressing "modern" ideals for living an outdoor life within the garden. At the Paul Getty Museum in Malibu, the modern garden layout is based on villa gardens from both Pompeii and Herculaneum. In the California climate, hedges of Mediterranean box and

myrtle are laid out in formal style between high-flanking peristyle columns to capture the spirit of the Roman villa garden.

In every age gardening as an art has emerged as a compromise between the ideal and what is practical; now we face new challenges both for living and for survival. The small private garden has become a personal oasis. Between the concrete jungles of buildings and motorways the garden formalist searches for a defined structure dependent on old-fashioned design principles. As a gardener he or she seeks simultaneously to reconcile and restore an element of the lost wilderness, while retaining beloved principles of good design that link house and garden. The informal naturalistic gardener discovers that it is not enough to re-create nature in his backyard. A

At Mount Stewart in Northern Ireland the formal Italian garden is laid out in a pattern of beds on a terrace below the house. A central pond is surrounded by schemes in different colors.

In New York's Central Park the Conservatory Garden is laid out in an Italianate style. In the central section clipped yew hedges, framing an open expanse of lawn, are flanked by crab apples, which flower in spring.

garden is a work of art and, like a landscape painting, requires "composing" where rules of light and shading, color, texture, and perspective introduce order. American garden historian Anne Leighton seems to hit the nail on the head when she writes: "A garden, to be a garden, must represent a different world, however small, from the real world, a source of comfort in turmoil, of excitement in dullness, security in wilderness, companionship in loneliness. Gardening offers a chance for man to regulate at least one aspect of his life, to control his environment and show himself as he wishes to be." Surely there is a message here for both the naturalistic gardener and the formalist?

*A view across the large
pool at Hidcote shows the
importance of the hedging,
which divides this garden
up into a series of
geometric compartments.*

CHAPTER THREE

TULIPS AND THE SPRING BULBS

"The first of the spring bulbs." For gardeners few phrases are so evocative. As winter drags its dreary way we long for that day when, bravely touring the otherwise brown and sleeping garden, we see, just where we expected them, the first snowdrops spearing the ground. Less than a week later, if the winter weather has not been too unkind, each pair of leaves will have been pushed apart by a bud. Almost at once it bends over, throws back its pure white petals while the other triad holds together as a green-tipped bell to protect the stamens and stigma. Now the elements can do what they like. A foot of snow can arrest future growth for a couple of months, but when at last it melts, those snowdrops will have been preserved like flies in amber, but alive, unharmed. And joining them will be the flat green leaf sprouts of daffodils, orange-red tulip shoots, the bulletlike buds of crown imperials, all ready to burst upon the spring like Fourth of July fireworks in summer.

THE GEOGRAPHY AND
ANATOMY OF BULBS

Bulbs grow wild in many parts of the world, but they are especially common in areas that enjoy what is usually referred to as a Mediterranean climate. Typically, as we used to have to chant in unison in early geography lessons in school, the pattern consists of "warm wet winters and hot dry summers." Though northerners naturally crave the sun, their holidays, taken in Greece, Spain, or California, can, if they are also gardeners, be positively distressing. It is a great worry to be surrounded by plants that, if not continually watered, are burned to the same umber-colored crisp. The wild plants there, unlike Noël Coward's mad dogs and Englishmen, do not go out in the midday sun ("the smallest Malay rabbit/deplores this foolish habit") and have evolved adaptations to avoid it. Many are annuals that spend their summers as seeds; shrubs and trees frequently have shiny or gray leaves that reflect sun and heat or pores that are covered in fur or arranged within rolled leaves to slow the process of evaporation. Herbaceous perennials go underground and sensibly lie doggo until it is safe to emerge. They survive there by means of a specialized resting organ—with crocus, as corms; flag iris, as rhizomes; cyclamen, as tubers, or, as bulbs, as is the case with tulip, narcissus, snowdrops, and many other flowers. All of these organs are morphological variations on the theme of adaptation to environment; all are wonderfully effective.

A corm is composed of a compressed, swollen stem on top of which sits the spring bud or buds that will grow aboveground. That sudden spurt of growth is fueled by the corm's food store, which is entirely used up in the process; then, reciprocally, the leaves work to build carbohydrates and sugars to make a new corm on top of the spent husks of the old. Cleverly adapted contractile roots then pull it down to the optimum depth for summer survival and the seasonal cycle is complete. It is the pattern for success in the eighty species of crocus strewn in a brilliant band from Spain to Afghanistan.

Rhizomes are also swollen stems, but they grow horizontally on or just below the soil surface, the terminal and side buds turning up to spear the ground. Though they rest in summer, dormancy is never complete, which is why bearded iris are replanted immediately after being lifted and divided in July or August; one never sees a box of these dried off on a garden center shelf. Similarly, cooks know well that ginger "roots" (actually rhizomes) bought in greengrocers are much more flavorful when still plump.

Tubers can be swollen stems or swollen roots, with significant differences for gardeners. Root tubers—dahlias, for example—are just that; they have no buds, nor means of producing any, so they must always be attached to an old piece of the crown or stem if a new plant is to be produced. Stem tubers carry buds themselves as anyone peeling a potato or planting a cyclamen can see.

In many ways true bulbs are the classic storage organ, making in one year almost all that is needed for the next. In essence a bulb is a stem with its leaves and buds in its axils squeezed and compressed like a jack-in-the-box pushed back into its box, the stem reduced to a disc, the leaves to swollen, overlapping plates, the developing side buds causing the bulb to divide.

Only by planting a rosebush or shrub actually in flower is one certain of the show one has paid for. Seeds have the genetic potential to produce what is shown on the packet; bulbs actually possess it. A resting summer tulip bulb cut longitudinally shows the flower, its stamens already tinged with color, incipient seeds cluster in the ovary, all within enfolding petals that are like wings of a butterfly still in its chrysalis. These and next spring's foliage leaves are enclosed in several fleshy layers and a dry external tunic, shiny as a newly fallen horse chestnut. All are attached to a basal disc, a flattened piece of stem also holding the tiny bud that will build up into next year's bulb as the current one's food store is used up, its job completed. Here, in August, is next year's show.

The trigger that tells these dormant plants to start up their lives again is the first rain shower of autumn. Some bulbs (using the word generically to denote all types) immediately push up flowers through the parched ground—such is the case with autumn crocuses, colchicums, and sternbergias. Their leaves follow later, often not until the following spring. With most, however, the effect of that first rain is less apparent until one digs up, probably by mistake, a clump of established bulbs. Root growth by late September is well established; their preparation for spring

Previous page: At the historic Chelsea Physic Garden in London the popular 'Blue Parrot' tulip adds interest to a mixed herbaceous border in May. The brown-tipped leaves and dark spots on the petals show a slight infection of "tulip fire" fungus disease, a common scourge of garden tulips. A dash of fungicide as the shoots emerged in March would have been wise. 'Blue Parrot' occurred about 1935 as a sport of 'Bleu Aimable'.

Right: *Winter snowdrops at last herald the approaching spring. Galanthus elwesii, often called the giant snowdrop, can grow over a foot (30½ centimeters) in height. The pair of gray-green leaves, one folded inside the other, are always distinctive, as are the inner petals, each of whose two green spots sometimes join. This fine species is native to Yugoslavia and the Ukraine, south to Turkey; it likes drier soil than the common snowdrop.*

Bottom: *Nowhere are spring bulbs grown in greater profusion than at the gardens of the Keukenhof in Holland. Under the canopies of flowering cherries every possible bulb is cultivated to perform in a stunning kaleidoscope of color.*

has begun. So long as this root system is in place, winter can do its worst and the bulbs come to no harm. They can wait.

The first of the spring bulbs become available for purchase by catalog each year in spring and summer. If one agrees with Oscar Wilde that the one thing not to be resisted is temptation, then it is a mistake for keen gardeners even to glance at one of these tantalizing lists. They offer a floral feast—often in full color so they are even more irresistible—from *Allium* to *Zephyranthes*, with almost every letter of the alphabet offering a further bulbous genus, each more lovely than the last. Ordering must take place at once, if one is not to be disappointed by others having snapped up just the variety one wanted, and also to ensure, remembering how soon natural root growth starts, that planting is completed well in advance of hard frost and freeze-up. Those precocious roots must get out in the soil first.

Bulb breeders do wonderful things to develop vast diversities of flower color and flower size, plant habit, and fruit production, but (genetic engineering, which is in its infancy, aside) they can only build upon what evolution has programmed each plant to do, and that, of course, is to succeed in its habitat. We can pot up certain "prepared" hyacinths or daffodils or tulips and with care have them in

flower for Christmas; with much greater effort, bulb firms can hold back the little early species in order, for example, to produce a display for the annual Chelsea Flower Show in the third week of May. But in each case amateurs and professionals alike have to work within the invariable behavior of these wonderful plants.

FLOWERING BULBS AND THE DUTCH MASTERS

Spring bulbs are a part of everyone's garden memories, whether they be the great tulip displays at Keukenhof in Holland or lining the Rideau Canal in Ottawa, a few daffodils around an old apple tree in grandmother's garden, or the swaths of crocuses along the backs of the colleges at Cambridge. They are also a part of our artistic culture.

Although Victorian proponents of the language of flowers included, simply because they had to puff up their nonsense as best they could, almost any plant they could think of (great yellow daffodil—chivalry; yellow tulip—hopeless love; *Scilla siberica*—pleasure without alloy), none of the spring bulbs have the Christian and indeed pre-Christian symbolism of the rose. While the Burgundian

Left: *The early dwarf bulbous irises, with their delicate petals and brilliant pollen guides, are among the most beautiful plants we can grow. The highly scented* Iris reticulata *is now very rare in its native northern Iranian habitat but is common in cultivation. Violet, purple, and Cambridge and Oxford blue cultivars all carry the bright golden splash on the falls.*
Right: Crocus *'Jeanne d'Arc' is one of the fine large-flowered types developed from* C. vernus, *a plant of Swiss mountain meadows, often pushing up at the edge of woodland. These early flowers have many uses—as pot plants for a cool windowsill, naturalized in short orchard grass, or interplanted among ground cover plants such as* Stachys byzantina.

courtiers, such as those in the Duc de Berry's *Très Riches Heures*, pace the flowery mead, Renaissance Madonnas gaze serenely from bowers of roses.

Not a tulip is to be seen until, suddenly it seems, the Dutch and Flemish began to paint those seasonally impossible flower pieces—spring, high summer, and autumn—combining great cornucopias of blossom, often with enough caterpillars, snails, and beetles to gobble up the whole bunch by the next morning.

Brueghel is one of the many names of this period to conjure with; those bucolic scenes that made Peter famous—and earned him the nickname Peasant Brueghel—are familiar to us all. But as if sated with all that exhausting, drunken merrymaking, his son Jan the Elder became known as Velvet Brueghel, as well as Flower Brueghel, and stands at the beginning of the age of the painted flower piece. Son and grandson continued the line.

An almost exact contemporary began yet another dynasty of Flemish flower painters; Ambrosius Bosschaert painted one of the best-loved flower pieces of all time in the last year of his life, 1621. Its design is derived from the Italian Madonna, but was recast as if the object to be worshiped were the wonders of nature, rather than the Virgin. Instead of her figure, a great vase stands in an arched embrasure, framed in an ideal landscape (with distant Gothic spires rather than Renaissance domes and campanili and poplars rather than cypresses). The bouquet includes almost every spring bulb then known in Holland—feathered tulip, fritillary, bluebell, grape hyacinth, two sorts each of narcissus and iris, anemone, turban ranunculus, and lily of the valley. Then, as if summer came early that year, while the canvas was still on its easel, and Bosschaert could not resist adding them, we see roses, adonis, carnations, violas, and even a marigold.

As the genre moved on in time and place to France and Spain, more and more exotic flowers were included in the arrangements, often still bulbous plants—amaryllis from South Africa and hippeastrum from Brazil, tuberoses, and montbretias. The scene changed from the exuberant to the specific during the eighteenth century, as the age of scientific botany was recorded, plant by impeccable plant. Redouté's incredible *Les Liliacées* represents the pinnacle of this art. Commissioned by the Empress Josephine, five hundred "lilies"—monocotyledonous plants and hence among them all our spring bulbs —are depicted.

Clearly what we see in these flower pieces is the celebration of gardens suddenly filling with flowers from across the world. Portuguese voyagers, Spanish conquistadores, British adventurers, and Dutch merchants exploded outward from Europe. In less than three hundred years a frighteningly flat earth became like a great golden apple, a known globe ripe for the picking. And though travelers' tales concentrated upon El Dorado and galleons gunwale-down with precious jewels, the real riches were those of the natural world, the plants.

THE CULT OF THE TULIP

Unlike many popular plants of today, especially summer annuals, tulips were not plants of the New World, nor were they "discovered" by Europeans. This wonderful flowering plant, new to sixteenth-century Western science, new to gardeners, soon to cause a sensation in the money markets of Europe, was a product of an older world. In China the indigenous *Tulipa edulis* was an unremarkable article of food. In Central Asia the yellow-

Opposite page: *Dozens of fritillary species are strewn around the Northern Hemisphere in both the Old and New Worlds. The great orange crown imperial* (Fritillaria imperialis) *is often a central feature in seventeenth- and eighteenth-century painted flower pieces and the snake's-head, or checkered lily,* F. meleagris, *is also frequently depicted with its demurely nodding flowers. It is the most widespread species growing wild in damp meadows throughout Europe.*
Right: *The Dutch had a word for their unique still life paintings,* Prokstilleven, *which means "show-off still lifes." Ambrosius Bosschaert was one of the first flower painters in the northern Netherlands, born in Antwerp in 1573. Unlike Jean Brueghel, Bosschaert outlined every flower but without harshness. Most consider this his masterpiece. (Scala/Art Resource, New York)*

and-white starry *T. tarda*, the vermilion *T. praestans*, and a host of others then (as they still do) flaunted their beauty on arid hillsides and in rough scrub in a range of colors, shapes, and sizes that centuries of breeding have hardly surpassed. South of Samarkand on the Old Silk Road, the historic corridor that linked East and West, grows *T. fosteriana*, perhaps the most spectacular of all spring bulbs. Its huge shining scarlet flowers, bright as the bolts of Chinese silk the camel caravans carried past, open flat almost to the size of a dinner plate.

It is inconceivable that merchants and traders were not instrumental in transporting this eye-catching plant and its splendid rela-tions to any place where people made gardens. But it has to be surmise. The tulips that were introduced to Europe by the Belgian diplomat Augier Ghislain de Busbecq, envoy of the Holy Roman Emperor to the court of Sulei-man the Magnificent in the 1550s, were al-ready sophisticated garden plants.

De Busbecq records seeing these flowers when he was on his way to Constantinople (modern Istanbul) in 1554. He happened to know Carolus Clusius, one of the founding fathers of modern botany, to whom it is known he sent tulip seeds. Most tulips take about five years to flower from seed, so the first reference in English appears at about the right time. Richard Hakluyt, in his famous *Voyages*, re-

Above: *"Broken" or "bizarre" tulips are now usually called Rembrandts. Their flamed colors are caused by a virus present in the bulb. These extraordinary variations—as "self" or single colors became "broken"—were avidly collected by seventeenth-century growers throughout Europe.*

Left: *The tulip 'Lak van Ryn' was introduced in Holland in 1630; it shows the pointed petals popular in Constantinople, whence the first tulips had come only fifty years earlier. In Europe more rounded petals became fashionable as tulip breeding extended the range of colors and types.*

corded in 1582: "Within these four years there have been brought into England from Vienna where Clusius was working for the Emperor Maximilian, in Austria, divers kinds of flowers called Tulipas, procured thither a little before, from Constantinople by an excellent man called M. Carolus Clusius." This "excellent man" (later commemorated by the lovely little lady tulip, *T. clusiana)* soon became professor of botany at Leiden, but his tulip collection was stolen and distributed around Holland. (The Clusius garden at the Botanic Garden in Leiden has just been restored to mark its four hundredth anniversary and, it could be said, four hundred years of tulip growing.)

By the 1630s Dutch admiration for tulips had developed into an obsession, with prices for individual bulbs reaching astronomical heights (one bulb of the scarlet-and-white 'Semper Augustus' changed hands for 5,000 florins). Tulipmania is the name given to the years 1634–37, when fortunes were made and lost with tulip bulbs, the article of intense speculation. The bubble burst and sanity returned with the tulip taking its more rightful place as a staple horticultural crop for which the Netherlands has been renowned ever since.

Indeed, it was not long before tulip bulbs were grown for export, even to the country from whence they originally had come. The cult of the tulip became just as extravagant at the Turkish court of Ahmed III in the first two decades of the eighteenth century as it had in the Netherlands the century before. A contemporary account written by the Grand Vizier Mehmed Lalizari (whose name means "lover of tulips") described 1,323 varieties bred in Aleppo, Shiraz, and Turkmenistan, east of the Silk Road in the midst of wild tulip country.

The cognoscenti always want something different. The sultans and grand viziers especially admired single colors and flowers with pointed petals. In Europe a rounded outline came to be preferred and the tendency of the single-colored ("breeder tulips") to "break" into feathered and flamed patterns was encouraged. We know that today these striped variants are the providential result of a viral infection. Now known as Rembrandt tulips, they are enjoying a gentle renaissance, especially as the restoration of "heritage" landscapes increases, after a century or so of neglect. They evoke wonderfully the world of nineteenth-century cottage gardens, standing straight like soldiers among a tumble of pinks and polyanthuses.

SPECIES AND HYBRID TULIPS

In our own century extensive plant-collecting in the Middle East and Central Asia and increased interest in growing "species" plants have led Dutch growers, now supplemented by developing bulb-growing industries in England, Oregon, and British Columbia, to offer tulips strangely different from convention. Instead of the perfectly matched military precision of rows of turbanlike flowers on single stems in May, gardeners are offered the original wildlings, such as the water-lily tulip from Turkestan, *Tulipa kaufmanniana*. This is a tulip of the earliest spring, appearing with the scillas and crocuses. Even in the wild its color varies considerably, but typical buds are strawberry pink with cream stripes. As they open, the pinkness pales (being only on the outside of the three outer petals) and the interior of the petals shows cream, deepening to rich golden yellow at their base. It looks like the pale feathering of dawn giving way to a sun-filled morning. And indeed, the flowers respond daily to temperature and light, closing at night and opening with the day they seem to mimic.

The tulip parade continues. Soon after the water-lily tulip comes *T. tarda*, native of the Tien Shan in Central Asia. Each bulb produces a cluster of rich, yellow-centered white flowers, looking like a plateful of little poached eggs. *Tulipa fosteriana* and its forms then follow. The scarlet petals have a black or yellow base and for three weeks nothing in the garden can compete with its brilliance. Foster's tulip and the closely related *T. greigii* (whose purple-striped leaves have so dominant a gene that this characteristic, strikingly ornamental long before the flowers appear, is always apparent in its offspring) have been combined to produce the race known as peacock tulips. Like their parents they seldom grow above a foot in height and have vivid flowers whose petals—scarlet, vermilion, or gold—have contrasting zones of black and yellow at the base. In full sun they open wide like great tropical butterflies, often eight inches across.

Spring sun is what tulips want; plant breeders can change size and add colors, but

they cannot alter the needs that have evolved through response to habitat. From Portugal to Persia, Italy to Isfahan, wild tulips are plants of thin grassland and rocky hillsides, and gardeners growing tulips anywhere in the world have little choice but to conform to their requirements. Fortunately these are not difficult to provide. As previously described, the bulbs we buy in fall have everything prepared inside them and the gardener's role is to ensure they are planted at least by the end of October, and planted deep, at least eight inches down.

At this depth clumps of species or near-species tulips can build up naturally with other herbaceous perennials in the border or quietly remain *in situ* with summer annuals planted above. Of course there are the few weeks of declining foliage (not to be removed until it turns yellow if the bulb developing for next year is to reach its full potential) among which summer annuals can be planted. But this temporary untidiness is a small price to pay to avoid the entirely unnecessary nonsense of lifting the bulbs—at least in the informal parts of the garden—every June, and some are always ruined in the lifting. Although the lovely wild tulips have established a strong following among keen gardeners in this century, the hybrid groups are still grown by the million.

They have developed from, and in some cases remain, very similar to those paragons on which fortunes were staked in seventeenth-century Holland, and fortunes spent in eighteenth-century Turkey.

In cool temperate climates their season starts in late April and, carefully using each of the hybrid groups in turn, a garden can enjoy tulips well into June. Like roses, whose season carries on immediately after, tulips offer every color, and combination of colors, but true blue. Tulips perhaps have the edge; no rose is quite as dark as 'Queen of Night', a late variety often called 'La Tulipe Noire'. But, rose defendants will say, what about fragrance? The delicious scent of many tulips comes as a great surprise to anyone who presumes its absence.

With such diversity of color, of season, of size, of shape of flower, it should be obvious that tulips offer enormous potential to the garden in terms of effective plant associations; the sum of two or more plants is often greatly in excess of the components. Too often tulips are left to carry a formal spring display on their own, but when combined with a background plant the effectiveness of the area is maintained over a much longer period. Purest white lily-flowered tulip 'White Triumphator' may be

Opposite page: Tulipa kaufmanniana *is one of the wild tulips that grow in the arid steppes of Central Asia, where it flowers in April and May. In cultivation it is the earliest of all tulips, often appearing in late February in mild areas. Narrow buds open to a wide flat star that gives its colloquial name—the water-lily tulip. Hybrids such as this have broader petals than the species.* Above: *Purple stripes on the leaves are typical of* Tulipa greigii *from Central Asia. This characteristic is transferred to its hybrids and adds interest before the flowers open. Here they are grown with dwarf double daisies, resulting in a carpet of brilliant color for many weeks in spring.*

combined with forget-me-nots perhaps, or, in a white garden, *Arabis*. Fragrant scarlet 'Apeldoorn' can be cooled by a ground cover of pale violas. The permutations are endless.

In informal parts of the garden, there are tulips just made, it would seem, to provide interest and color to areas whose main emphasis comes later, to enhance spring-flowering shrubs and early nonbulbous herbaceous perennials. That latter phrase is worth repeating because it emphasizes the fact that all the spring bulbs are themselves, if suited to their site, fully functioning herbaceous perennials and take their place in the permanent garden scene.

DAFFODILS

Whereas tulips seem to have burst upon the European garden with all the brilliance and surprise of an unrecorded comet, other spring bulbs insinuated themselves into our ideals of spring beauty much more subtly. John Parkinson's famous *Paradisus in Sole Paradisum Terrestris* of 1629 (perhaps the first true gardening book; the punning title translates as "Park-in-son's earthly paradise") demonstrates this graphically. He begins the book with one of the stock plants depicted in the

Dutch and Flemish flower pieces of the seventeenth century: "The Crowne Imperial for his stately beautifulness, deserveth the first place in this our Garden of Delight to be here entreated before all other lillies. . . ." The other spring bulbs follow—alliums, stars-of-Bethlehem, crocuses, irises, snowflakes, and, above all, daffodils. In comparison to tulips, which got about twenty of his folio pages, daffodils received over forty. However, in a pre-Linnaean world, plant classification was primitive and Parkinson included as daffodils plants that have long been separated into their own genera and even assigned to different plant families. The "Red Indian Daffodil" is the still unusual and seldom seen sprekelia; the woodcut of the "early Daffodil of Trebizond" looks very much like a sternbergia.

Daffodils proper, both the long-trumpet types and those with trumpets reduced to tiny corona, have a mainly western Mediterranean distribution. Even Britain, at the far northwestern corner of Europe, has its own little daffodil, often called Lent lily or the Tenby daffodil *(Narcissus obvallaris)* which grows wild in Wales. There are twenty-five or so distinct species, as well as a number of hybrids that occur in the wild in areas where species overlap. Their habitats also vary widely: One

may pick bunches of *N. tazetta* at Christmastime from rocky slopes in Crete. The high sea cliffs at Cabo da Roca in Portugal, mainland Europe's most western point, are starred each February with the little hoop-petticoat daffodil. Pheasant-eye narcissus in the alpine valleys in Switzerland do not flower until June.

BULBS IN THE GARDEN

Although Parkinson described all the garden flowers he knew, as well as their methods of cultivation, he offered little about their use, how they make a garden. Parkinson's near-contemporary Crispin Vander Pass in his *Hortus Floridus* of 1614 shows why. *Hortus* contains fine engravings of individual daffodils, tulips, and other spring bulbs, and also shows views of contemporary Dutch gardens. In one we look across a balustraded terrace down on to a formal parterre: A Malvoliolike figure in a slouch hat leans over the balustrade watching a lady in a farthingale who admires a bed of tulips. Only in this one bed are the plants close together, making a show. Everywhere else hyacinths, crocuses, daffodils, martagon lilies, and crown imperials are dotted about without any apparent concern for their size or complementary arrangement. This type of "design" is indeed a cabinet of living curiosities, the garden equivalent of John Tradescant's Ark. The spring bulbs are treated like rare marvels, not yet a part, in our terms, of a complete, planned garden.

No doubt one reason is cost: Though an entirely new daffodil with perhaps significant stud potential for further breeding can command a high price, at no time in history have flower bulbs been cheaper (relative to earnings) than today. At no time has the ability to bulk up desirable new varieties, to the point at which they become quickly offered in the bulb catalogs of the world, been so effective. This fact, associated with our present ideals of garden design, confirms the late twentieth century as a golden age for these plants. That enigmatic-faced Flora figure in Botticelli's "La Primavera," drifting into the scene with flowers in her hair, would surely be delighted.

Few other groups of plants are able to span the requirements of both formal and informal planting schemes. Tulips, straight as soldiers, and hyacinths, solid and self-important, have been exactly bred, as in a mold, for height, color, and flowering period. Evenly spaced and underplanted with arabis or aubrietia, daisies or wall-flowers, patterns like living Persian carpets can be contrived. Edged with clipped boxwood or santolina, the beds become

Left: *The only Southern Hemisphere spring bulb at all commonly seen in northern gardens,* Ipheion uniflorum *is native to Argentina and Uraguay. The starry flowers are typically palest porcelain blue but 'Froyle Mill' and 'Wisley Blue' are fine darker forms. All are delicately violet scented, but the leaves smell of onions if crushed.* Ipheion *can be naturalized in grass as shown here or grown in the rock garden.*

Bottom left: *Looking much like our cultivated Roman hyacinth, the original* Hyacinthus orientalis *comes from western Asia. Since the seventeenth century it has been selected and bred to produce tightly packed spikes of heavily scented flowers in blue, white, pink, salmon, or yellow. The double forms seen in many early paintings are now very rare.*

even more formal; designs can be planned equally well for a tiny town plot or raised planter or extended to fill the terrace parterres of a grand country house.

Most of the other spring bulbs seem more suited to informal groupings: These may be apparently uncontrived as in the swaths of daffodils and crocuses naturalized in the rough grass of an old orchard. So too are bulbs available for combining in simple or sophisticated associations in every part of the garden. Chionodoxas and hardy cyclamen, aconites and anemones, scillas and fritillarias, snowdrops and snowflakes, all provide their special pleasures.

THE LITTLE SPRING BULBS

This celebration of spring bulbs has so far emphasized tulips and daffodils, but, though central to the season of "La Primavera," they neither open nor close it. Indeed, so variable are climatic and weather patterns in which spring bulbs are grown that even in the Northern Hemisphere the season spans six months. And beyond that there are outliers. In England no January unfolds, however foul the season, without the first snowdrops appearing; but in gardens of keen snowdrop collectors, who hope to grow the dozen different wild species and twice as many named forms, two Grecian snowdrops—*Galanthus reginae-olgae* from the Taygetus Mountains and *G. corcyrensis* from Corfu—will have appeared in October or November.

To the casual passerby, one snowdrop is just like another, but there is a delicate diversity that only the close observer can enjoy. The common snowdrop, *G. nivalis*, wild in woodland glades and by shady stream sides all over Europe, possesses the basics—the gray-green leaves and the six white petals (the inner ones with green markings). Among the geographical forms and the garden mutants 'Viridapicis' has green-spotted outer petals; so does 'Scharlokii', in addition to two long spathes standing up behind the flowerlike rabbit's ears. 'Lutescens' is a strange transluscent horn-yellow color, and 'Straffan' flowers very late. The leaves of *G. ikariae*, from northern Turkey, are bright green and *G. elwesii*, another Turk, grows as high as nine inches (23 centimeters). Sometimes called the giant snowdrop, it is the perfect choice for those who find other species too diminutive. Snowdrops

strongly resent having their bulbs entirely dried off; long supermarket shelf life is not one of their attributes, and the contents of those sad little packets seldom give results to encourage further trial. So often people complain that only half the bulbs planted emerge to see the spring and half again actually flower in the first year. Better by far, and not, if one compares results, any more expensive, is to buy snowdrops offered by specialist growers "in the green," leafy and just after flowering. Better still is to beg a clump from a friend, separate them carefully into twos and threes, and one is confident in expecting "the first of the spring bulbs" the very next year.

Long before the last of the snowdrops are over, the first of the crocuses, are out. Those in the mountains open their flowers as soon as the snow retreats, often appearing in the lee of a sheltering rock while all is still white around. These species when brought into cultivation are among the first harbingers of spring. *Crocus biflorus*, the cloth-of-silver crocus from Italy and the Balkans, often opens the pageant with its pale lilac petals, painted on the outside with darker stripes. Its Caucasian cousin, *C. susianus*, is known as the cloth-of-gold crocus: Here the petals are deep yellow, veined with bronze and even darker feathering on the outside; each corm produces several flowers.

The bigger garden forms, such as the old Dutch Yellow, in cultivation since the seventeenth century, and those derived from *C. vernus*, such as the purple-striped 'Pickwick' and lavender 'Little Dorrit' (Dickensian names hint at nineteenth-century origins), flower late in a spectacular but shorter show. Naturalized in orchard grass or clustering under shrubs, these old cultivars increase reliably over the years, needing no attention but occasional division when the clumps have more leaf than flower. They possess only one flaw: In North America squirrels and chipmunks have a fatal attraction for the corms. A thousand planted may, without preventive measures, be followed by a disappointing spring. In England the yellow crocus flowers are used by house sparrows as a butt for their avian frustrations—petals are torn to shreds and scattered to the winds. Nothing is more maddening to the gardener nor more difficult to deal with, though on a small scale planting beneath wire netting and black cotton strung above the flowers is effective.

While squirrels find crocus corms deli-

cious eating, man's use of crocuses is mainly aesthetic, with one economically important exception: saffron. This delicately perfumed and brilliantly colored spice is the product of an autumn-flowering species, *C. sativus*. Cultivated from Spain to Kashmir, though not known in the wild, the saffron crocus has been shown recently to be a sterile triploid capable of reproduction only by division. This is perhaps as well because the three long scarlet stigmas in each flower, which would normally be vital to seed production, are the parts that are harvested, dried, and marketed around the world.

In areas where it is grown, saffron can be bought in the local markets, measured out filament by filament onto the most sensitive of jewelers' scales. It is the world's most expensive spice.

The three stigmas in crocus flowers and the three accompanying stamens give the clue to a botanical relationship that is not immediately obvious. The regular form of the crocus cup is related to a visually very different genus, *Iris*, which always maintains its heraldic fleur-de-lis shape. The family, Iridaceae, is of great horticultural importance, with well-known representatives native to all five areas of the world with a Mediterranean climate.

South Africa is particularly rich in species that have become important garden plants around the world—montbretias, freesias, Kaffir lilies, and gladioli. These, however, when grown north of the equator, are plants of summer, whereas most true irises (none of which are wild south of that line) belong to the early part of the year.

The rhizomatous tall bearded irises that have been so worked upon by hybridists flower too late to be included in an account of spring bulbs—and anyway they deserve more than a cursory mention—but the irises with proper bulbs have a very important part to play. All true Mediterraneans (so long as one extends the eastern boundary well into Asia Minor), they divide conveniently into two seasonal and geographical groups. Both include some of the most desirable plants we can grow in temperate climates.

Their season begins with the snowdrops in early February or even earlier; it is still winter, but such is their miraculous freshness we cannot consider them, unlike winter viburnum, winter sweet, or winter jasmine, as anything other than precursors of spring. In some years the little yellow *Iris danfordiae* opens first, in others the clear blue *I. histrioides* 'Major' beats it by a few days. They both

appear as sharp-pointed buds through the leaf litter or, if grown in a rock bed, the covering of stone chips. Once two or three inches (5 or 8 centimeters) high, they seem to wait in suspended animation for a mild spell that will bring out pollinating insects. A soft sunny morning arrives and the decision is made; the three "falls" hinge outward, the delicate standards wave above, and the shop is open for business. Leaves follow later.

These two Turkish species are soon joined by *I. reticulata* from further east. Rather taller, with rich violet flowers and a golden blaze on the falls, it is also deliciously violet-scented. Sadly this attribute is lost, or at least greatly reduced, in the garden varieties with paler blue ('Cantab' and 'Clairette') or purple flowers ('J. S. Dijt'). The scent is also, when they are growing in an open garden, a long way from the appreciative nose. This, combined with the delicacy of flowers easily bruised at such a blustery time of year, makes them ideal for cultivation in pots. They must, however, in no way be forced as too much heat will cause the buds to abort.

These diminutive irises appear infrequently in the flower pieces that celebrated the great garden tulips and daffodils; presumably they lacked the brilliance demanded by the courts of Constantinople. It is worth noting,

though, that the very first plant illustrated and described in *Curtis's Botanical Magazine* of 1787 is little *I. persica* from Lebanon and Syria. This is one of the so-called Juno irises (the two hundred *Iris* species are classified into eleven groups that help to link cultural requirements with origin). The picture in the *Bot. Mag.* (as it is affectionately known, still in existence after two hundred years of publication, though recently incorporated into the *Kew Magazine*) shows an exquisite and still rare little iris of kingfisher blue and yellow.

The little bulbous irises of Asia Minor are over by April. From the other end of the Mediterranean comes another group for the other end of spring. Several fine species, yellow or blue with contrasting color splashes on the falls, stand up to two feet (61 centimeters) tall among the hillside grasses of Spain and Portugal and across the Straits in Morocco. They were brought into cultivation early and have been crossed and recrossed to offer an amazing range of colors, from white to deep bronze, and all the blues and yellows in between. One type, known now as Dutch iris, is grown by the million for cut flowers throughout the world; another, the English iris, is a persistent garden plant, making fine leafy clumps in climates that do not kill off the young leaves that begin to appear in fall.

A formal garden enclosed by high yew hedges. The beds are edged with box that, even in the flowerless winter months, provide an attractive pattern. As spring advances, tulips and daffodils, backed by crown imperials (Fritillaria imperialis), give a progression of interest. In such a site the bulbs are usually lifted to ripen off elsewhere, but even here summer annuals can be planted among the yellowing foliage to take over when it disappears.

Above right: *Serendipity often provides the most satisfactory of plant associations. Here the early single tulip 'Princess Irene', veined like a Tiffany lamp, reflects the purple of* Iris pumila, *the earliest of all dwarf bearded irises. Spring bulbs offer endless possibilities for striking combinations of both form and color.*

Bottom right: *Bluebells are one of the joys of the English woodlands; they seem to bring patches of spring sky down to earth. But when sharing the garden with other spring bulbs, their thin, one-sided spikes of narrow bells are better replaced by the stonger* Hyacinthoides (Scilla) hispanica, *the Spanish bluebell. The flowers come in shades of blue, pink, or white.*

These bulbous irises span spring. Between them comes all its panoply. Deciduous trees change from thickets of bare branches into airy clouds of tenderest green before the pattern is lost in the billowing foliage of summer. Those with spectacular flowers—the magnolias; then cherries, crab apples, dogwoods, and redbuds—each have their weeks of predominance. Beneath their canopy are the spring shrubs—forsythia, daphne, and viburnum, and, in acid soils, camellias and rhododendrons. No niche stands empty; there is a plant for every place, in every place. Those forest floors that are as dark and cool as a medieval cathedral in summer have light enough before the trees' leaves unfold for a quick burst of spring growth before sun and water are switched off by the dominant tree growth.

Joining the common snowdrops are winter aconites and sheets of blue scillas. In Europe acres of woodland floor turn from leafy green to floral blue as the English bluebells put on their sudden show. In northeastern North America the phenomenon is repeated, but even more rapidly, when, within a few weeks, trout lilies push up their marbled leaves, unfold their petals, and sink again into summer sleep. Woodland bulbs have evolved their life cycle to capitalize upon an otherwise unused ecological niche, providing a parallel to those of the Mediterranean sea shore or Asia Minor's arid steppes. The significant factors, of course, are those miraculous food stores, annually used up and annually restored. Every year they ensure our gardens are reborn.

Above: Scilla siberica *grows in woods and on rocky slopes. It adapts to cool gardens around the world; here it is naturalized under sugar maples on the thin limestone soil of the Niagara Escarpment in southern Canada.*
Right: *The green-tipped bells of summer snowflake,* Leucojum aestivum, *are seen against the purity of* Magnolia stellata *'Centennial'. This is an April association at the Royal Botanical Gardens in Hamilton, Ontario.*

CHAPTER FOUR

JAPANESE GARDENS

AN ACCRETIONARY APPROACH

Here is a land, an archipelago whose area barely adds up to the size of the state of California. Since it is surrounded by sea, the idea of national borders is not well understood by the people who live there. And if you ask whether anyone has seen the country's borders, you will probably not encounter one who has. The Japanese archipelago does not really have any borderlines per se; there is only sea. From ancient times it was the sea that hemmed in and defined the country. The sea both isolated the land and linked it to the adjacent continent, which could be reached even in a light sailing vessel.

In prehistoric times the people who dwelled on the Japanese archipelago had no idea that there were other countries like their own beyond the seas. They were certain, at least, that no land existed within sailing distance to the east; in that direction there were cliffs and the rough waters of a mighty ocean,

hardly one to name Pacific. To the south and west, and later to the north, they believed there was land or islands, populated, they imagined, by godlike inhabitants. Naturally their attention turned in those directions.

Sometime in the third century B.C. the hunter-gatherers of the archipelago began to learn the techniques of wet-rice agriculture, and they eventually became settled, but the culture was quite primitive. If anything, it was animism that ruled. Dense primeval forests and numerous rivers covered the land, and when pitch-black by night or tossed by subtropical storms, they were believed to be alive with evil spirits, monsters of the mountains, specters of swamps and streams. To create places in which they could live in peace, safe from these fearsome spirits, the people made *niwa* in the space in front of their humble dwellings. *Niwa* means open space. There they planted trees and brought in stones. The trees had practical uses, acting as a break against wind and snow and providing fuel and building materials, but their most important function was as *yorishiro*, abodes for the gods. The stones brought from the hills, fields, or seasides to set in these *niwa* were not carved or cut; stones were considered sacred works of art created over the millennia by nature, and they could be used as potential dwellings of the gods only if left in their natural state.

The gods are invisible; one never knows where they are. It was thought that they lived in the mountains of some distant place, that they dwelled somewhere in the heavens or in some unseen land beyond the seas. Each of the gods of the Japanese pantheon had a specific role. Some chased away evil spirits, some assured a good harvest; some brought good health and long life. In any case, the *niwa* had to be a place purified to make it suitable to welcome visiting deities.

Of the trees intended for this purpose, nondeciduous varieties were usually favored, perhaps because trees that retained their foliage the year round seemed to possess greater life force. The visitations of some gods, like those invoked when the construction of a house begins, were brief; those of others, like the god of the New Year, were cyclical, but some were thought to stay in the garden, taking up permanent residence.

Here is a very contemporary scene: It has become necessary to tear down a well located in the garden of an old estate. The workers are against it; there might be a god residing in the well, and if there is, an accident, caused by a curse placed by the angered well god, could easily occur. So the party concerned calls in the priest of the local Shinto shrine to perform a ceremony bidding the well god to depart the premises.

The trees and stones in a garden can be found anywhere. People who do not know might think them just ordinary stones or trees. In order to indicate that a certain tree or stone is the abode of the gods, a *shimenawa*, or sacred straw rope laced with rice-paper festoons, is tied around it.

Another contemporary story: In building the garden for a certain research institute of advanced technology, its president asked a Shinto priest to perform a ceremony purifying the building site, inviting the descent of the gods with sweeps of a leafy tree branch. In this ceremony antiquity and modernity converged. The president of the institute explained to his employees why the ceremony was performed: "I do not necessarily believe in such ancient rituals, and I do not believe, of course, that gods descend from the heavens.

Previous page: *The Kyoto Gosho, or Imperial Palace, was moved to its final location in the eighteenth century. Once sacred spaces were filled with plants, trees, and ponds and transformed into the palace gardens. The Chinese-style bridge is a major visual feature, effecting a graceful linkage of elements.*
Bottom left: *This is one of two steep, cone-shaped "mountains" rising from the gravel sea at Kamakura shrine. The stark, by Western standards, environment exudes a pleasing serenity. In the background one can see the sacred rope or shmenawa.*

The Heian shrine was built in the late nineteenth century to commemorate the 1,100th anniversary of the founding of Kyoto. Typical of the Heian era (785–1184), the garden's design centers on a large pond. The beautiful plantings, however, indicate it is a garden created in modern times.

The reason I have asked the priest to beckon to the gods with his tree-branch wand is to symbolize the kind of attitude we should cultivate in our research: to be flexible in our thinking, to be ready to entertain any abandoned notion, to study all manner of ideas, no matter how unprofessional or amateurish they may be."

This anecdote illustrates how, although old ideas may be discarded, the forms of the past are often preserved. In the history of Japanese gardens, this way of thinking is a recurrent theme.

II

In 663 A.D. a Japanese army went to the aid of the Korean kingdom of Paekche in a war against the combined forces of T'ang China and the kingdom of Silla, but was routed at the naval battle of Hakusukinoe. This decisive defeat prompted the rapid rise of a state system

in Japan. The leader who had been chief of the most powerful clan of the archipelago was made "emperor" and the heads of the most powerful clans were organized into a bureaucratic aristocracy. They built their capital in the Yamato basin, a sheltered inland plain in the heart of the island of Honshu.

These people built gardens adjoining their fine homes, on whose grounds were invariably manmade ponds. These artificial waterworks were not called lakes, but seas. Why?

One reason stemmed from the idea of the "isles of eternity," a belief that had become widespread among the Japanese since the introduction of rice culture. The isles of eternity were an imaginary utopia thought to be located somewhere far, far to the south of the Japanese archipelago. They were inhabited by people of eternal youth and were places where harvests of grain and fruit were always abundant.

These gods were thought to visit Japan, bringing long life and wealth to mortals. (This was an age when rice production provided the

Yamato aristocrats with their livelihood and filled the country's coffers.) By building "isles of eternity" in the "seas" of their gardens, the people sought to bring them within reach and, they hoped, within control.

Another reason ponds were called seas was related to the fact that the builders of these gardens were high-ranking officials. Sometimes they were sent to other parts of the country to serve as governors or to perform specific missions. When they traveled by land they rode horseback and when they moved by the sea they boarded vessels that sailed along coastal routes. These trips provided them with the opportunity to see quite different landscapes than those in the landlocked Yamato basin. The ocean might sometimes be wild and terrifying, but to them it seemed beautiful and exotic.

Among the most wondrous of these seaside landscapes were the beautiful Sumiyoshi coast (bordering the north side of what is now Osaka Bay) where the Sumiyoshi Shrine was built to watch over the safety of mariners; the string of islets protruding from Miyazu Bay on the north side of Honshu known as *Ama-no-hash-idate* (literally, "staircase to heaven"); and the pine-crowned islands that dot the inlet at Shiogama on the eastern coast near the present-day city of Sendai. Though many Yamato aristo-

crats had never seen these sights for themselves, the stories they heard about them became the stuff of inspiration set down in poetry and song.

The lakes in the ancient estate gardens were not intended to be realistic; they were expressions of imaginary scenes that transcended any real landscape. Clusters of stones were cliffs buffeted by violent waves, and pebble-lined shores of the ponds were ports approached by returning fishing vessels.

Contact with the continent grew, and it was not long until Taoism, with its belief in immortal beings with wizardlike powers, was introduced from China. These teachings were eventually grafted onto the earlier beliefs in the "isles of eternity," and the Japanese were not long in drawing from Taoist teachings those ideas that had to do with the divine favors to be enjoyed in this world. The Japanese harvest from the bounty of Taoism was the practice of building islands in garden ponds symbolizing the abodes of the immortals and the belief that members of the household that had such islands in its garden would enjoy the same longevity as the immortals themselves.

The shape and style of the islands in these ponds did not differ much from those that symbolized the "isles of eternity." The form was quite the same for both, no more than

artfully arranged clusters of ordinary stones that could be found in any field or stream; the landscaping was quite like the natural scenery existing anywhere. Though some artificial elements were added, artificiality was for the most part eschewed. The more "natural" the scene, the more pleasing.

This was the concept of the garden evolved by a rice-growing society. The cycle of rice cultivation depended on many factors completely beyond human control—sun, rain, flood, and the soil determined whether the harvest would be abundant or lean, not human powers, and this reinforced the people's sense of awe and acceptance of nature.

In the mid-sixth century Buddhism was introduced to Japan. At first the animistic Japanese believed that the Buddha was just another of the myriad deities in their indigenous pantheon. The eventual realization that the Buddha was something of quite a different order was a major culture shock. Native beliefs had no scripture, no images, at that stage not even shrines in which the gods were worshiped.

The ancient Japanese showed some interest in the Buddhist sutras and teachings, but what fascinated them most was the highly developed culture introduced along with the new religion—the red-lacquered Buddha halls, the

Opposite page: *The "isles of eternity" in the pond garden at the famed Ryōan-ji (Dragon Peace Temple). This once private estate became a temple of the Rinzai sect of Zen Buddhism in the fifteenth century.*
Right: *The Phoenix Hall at Byodo-in dates back to the eleventh century. Named for the mythological bird that rises out of its own ashes, it is reflected in the pond in front of it.*

Left: The garden at Saihō-ji was conceived as a serene environment to aid in contemplation. The garden is especially beautiful in May and June, after the spring rains.

Right: Saihō-ji, also known as Kokedera and the Moss Temple, features over forty varieties of moss. Shade, humidity, and heavy, moist clay soil have combined to create conditions ideal for the velvety carpet of moss that has grown there for hundreds of years.

Following pages: The Golden Pond at Saihō-ji. From the work done on it in the latter part of the fourteenth century, Saihō-ji derived its form as a "paradise garden." With its lake garden, it was to reflect the Buddhist deity Amida's palace in heaven.

sophisticated architectural techniques used to build them, the gilt-covered Buddhist images shining resplendently and mysteriously within, the delicately wrought altar fittings, the orthography of the sutras, and the brilliant ceremonies accompanied by music and dance.

Still resisting the onslaught of Buddhism, the people built shrines for the traditional indigenous gods in their *niwa*, and to show that the space of these *niwa* was pure, they spread their precincts with white gravel. There is little evidence that early Buddhism had much impact on the style of gardens in Japan, although there is one record of red-lacquered bridges being built in gardens. These lacquered bridges did not exactly harmonize with the other elements in the garden, but they provided an element of the exotic that the people found pleasing. With the introduction in the ninth century of esoteric teachings, Buddhism finally became accepted among Japanese as a religion offering salvation to the soul. Esoteric Buddhism—through the mandala— taught them now to express their worldview in schematic form by arrangement of elements of shape and color. And these mandala provided the inspiration for the design of a new type of garden built within the precincts of temples or at the villas of the nobility: the paradise garden.

The aristocrats of the tenth and eleventh centuries were haunted by the teaching that two thousand years after the death of the historical Buddha, Shakyamuni, the Buddhist law would decline and society would fall into chaos. They believed the two-thousandth year was 1052—in their own time. Some diverted themselves in the shadow of this cataclysm by trying to re-create in this world their visions of paradise. In Uji, on the southeast side of Kyoto, Fujiwara no Michinaga (966–1027), who built the fortunes of his family line of imperial regents, had a villa above the river. There his son and successor, Yorimichi (990–1074), built a paradise garden and hall that became a Buddhist temple in 1052. The chapel that is the center of the temple, the Hōōdō or Phoenix Hall, was completed in 1053.

Today, more than eight centuries later, tourists troop through the hall and tour the paths around the pond before it; what they see are but shabby relics of what was once a paradise on earth. Only in the evening, after the people depart and the gates are closed, do glimpses of the illusion Yorimichi treasured flicker in the fading rays of the sun as it slants into the west.

Seated placidly in the center of the Phoenix Hall is an image of Amitabha, who reigns over the Western Paradise. When the oil

The raked gravel waves in "The Sea of Silver Sand" at Ginkaku-ji are most beautiful in the moonlight.

lamps are lit for an evening service, the gilt image glimmers in the shadows of the hall, the flames of the lamps hung around the lake glow brightly, shimmering on the surface of the pond that symbolizes the "seven-treasures pond" of paradise—the Pure Land. In the chapel, music and dance begin, and the glowing building casts an eerie silhouette against the dark of the night.

Yorimichi and his contemporaries imagined that upon their deaths a silken, five-colored cord would extend from their own hands to the hand of Amitabha, and heavenly emissaries from paradise mounted on flying clouds would come to guide them back to the Pure Land. In a sense the paradise garden really manifested itself only after dark. It was the splendidly prepared backdrop within which the ancient aristocrats could indulge the aesthetic and mystical pastimes that kept their ever-present dread of death at bay.

One of the first paradise gardens to be created was that at Saihō-ji temple, where construction began in 1339, and whose fate reflects the tumultuous centuries since. In the Ōnin Civil War that broke out in Kyoto in 1469, the Buddhist halls and the garden at Saihō-ji were burned, leaving its original beauty in ruins. A succession of ravages, human and natural, plagued the temple through the centuries, and it fell into prolonged neglect in the late nineteenth century for lack of financial resources for repair and upkeep. It was during this, the nadir of Saihō-ji's fortunes, that the damp climate nourished the growth of a rich and velvety cover of moss over its entire grounds. Thus was created the garden we know today, the moss garden that is more famous than the temple itself, once called Temple of the Western Paradise and now popularly known as the Moss Temple.

III

Among the eleventh-century nobility was one Tachibana no Toshitsuna. He was the son of the powerful Fujiwara no Michinaga, but his mother was of lowly status, a circumstance that precluded Toshitsuna from access to positions of political power. Instead he became a man of culture and the arts, in particular a critic of garden culture; he served as the emperor's chief advisor on gardens and authored Japan's oldest text on gardens, *Sakutei-ki*.

In the second chapter of the *Sakutei-ki* is a discussion of *feng-shui*, Chinese geomancy of spatial layout relating to the directions. According to its tenets, a house should ideally be positioned with a stream or river to the east, a pond to the south, a road or highway to the west, and a hill to the north. In these directions it was believed dwelled, respectively, the blue dragon, red phoenix, white tiger, and black tortoise, deities that would protect the house and secure for its inhabitants the blessings of high rank, happiness, good health, and long life.

But if it was not possible to create such conditions, Toshitsuna was quick to add, the presence of the guardian deities could be secured by planting nine willow trees to the east, nine Judas trees to the south, seven maples to the west, and three cypresses to the north. The rest of the garden could be planted with any kind of tree in any arrangement. While giving due tribute to Chinese geomancy, Toshitsuna went on to interpret and elaborate on it according to his own reasoning and fancy, and he succeeded in devising what he thought was an original garden concept.

Toshitsuna was not the first or the last to adopt this approach in the introduction of other cultures; it became quite the norm to study carefully the ways and things imported from outside and then proceed regardless, following indigenous tastes and inclinations. Whether the result was a distortion or a misunderstanding of what was being interpreted, the approach appears to have given the Japanese a free hand in garden design.

Who were the actual garden designers of ancient times? From the tenth to the fourteenth century most were Buddhist priests. Generally known as *ishitate-sō* (literally, "stone-setting priests"), they were commissioned by the emperor, the nobility, the temples, and later the warrior elite to build landscape gardens. The major reason priests came to be involved in garden design was that the shape and features of gardens at that time were all determined to some degree by the ideas and precepts of Buddhism, and the priests were more conversant in that kind of information than others. Among the most active of the *ishitate-sō* were those affiliated with the esoteric temple Ninna-ji in Kyoto. The secrets of their accumulated know-how were passed down from master to disciple and recorded in a scroll text called the *Senzui narabini yagyō no zu*.

The *ishitate-sō* were priests of relatively humble status, mostly from the middle or

lower ranks of the clergy, for, according to the social norms of the time, those who labored with the soil (with the exception of farmers) in such tasks as road and bridge building and well digging were considered lowly. Persons of social standing were not supposed to engage in such work. Gardening, inasmuch as it involved working with the soil, fell into the same category.

In the fourteenth century a high-ranking priest appeared who did much to raise the status of gardens and gardening from the new philosophical viewpoint of Zen Buddhism, Musō Soseki (1275–1351). Soseki enjoyed the esteem of Emperor Godaigo (1288–1339), Shogun Ashikaga no Takauji (1305–58), and the newly risen warrior elite, and he was accorded the most illustrious title a priest could receive, *kokushi*. He shocked the establishment with his belief that gardening was a form of Zen training, and he designed a number of important gardens. Zen taught that all aspects of daily life—eating, sleeping, drink-

ing tea, cleaning, defecating, cultivating gardens, and raising vegetables, in short all forms of physical labor—provided the basis for spiritual discipline. It was not surprising then that its priests considered garden building a particular challenge in their way of life. Certain prelates of the old established schools of Buddhism, however, were ill disposed toward Soseki's work with gardens. One writing of the famous Shingon priest and scholar Gōhō (1306–62) censured him with the words, "Making gardens—and calling it 'Zen training'—is not befitting a priest of respected standing!" But times were changing; a new wave of influence was washing into the world of the Japanese garden.

IV

The rise of Zen Buddhism in the fifteenth century provided an important turning point for Japanese garden philosophy. Essentially,

it served as the philosophical medium through which the religious elements of gardens—until then central to their role—could be dispensed with, for Zen rejected all forms of religious art.

Zen taught that all things—every blade of grass, every tree, grain of sand, or stone—represented a this-worldly manifestation of the Buddha nature, that the sound of the wind and the chirping of birds were voices chanting the sutras, and that in the light of the sun and the glow of the moon shone the virtues of the Buddha. Since nature and the Buddha were one, there was no need for expressly religious symbols, and, freed from religious dogma, garden designers could pursue all sorts of forms.

As a result, Zen gardens sought to do away with as many of the multifarious features of gardens as possible, to pare them down to the essentials, thereby placing people directly in touch with fundamental universal truths.

What was needed to attain enlightenment *(satori)* was not thought, said Zen priests, but insight, intuition. Nature's decorative apparel should be, as far as possible, taken aside, leaving only the rudiments: stones and sand, and, if deemed necessary, perhaps a closely pruned shrub. Rocks and clusters of stones provided the framework of the garden, representing the order of nature; sand or gravel represented streams or the sea, evoking the everchanging mutability of things *(mujō)*. Zen taught that transience was a quality of eternity, but water itself was unnecessary. These gardens are known as *karesansui*, or "dry landscape gardens." Expressed another way, the stones stand for stability and permanence; the sand for dynamism, evanescence—this, says Zen, is the epitome of our real world.

The size of a garden was of little importance in Zen, for the universe could be expressed as easily in a small space as in a spacious one. "Small is beautiful," and, after

Ryōan-ji represents a superior example of a dry landscape garden; water and landscape elements are represented by rocks and raked gravel. No plants are used. (The moss around the rocks is a happy accident of nature.)

all, the expression and manifestation of universal truth unfolding in a small garden is relatively easier to grasp.

By the end of the fifteenth century, the civil wars that were to bring an end to the medieval age had begun. It was during this time that the dry garden at Ryōan-ji temple was built. In a serene sea of gray pebbles are fifteen stones clustered in five islandlike groups. Some people think these stones symbolize a tiger and her cubs crossing a river. It is a garden that has fascinated many people with its abstract, symbolic design, but for most it remains mystifying. As far as I can see, it is not a garden intended to convey any fixed concept or message, but one open to all kinds of interpretations. In this sense it embodies the potential of new imagination, new creativity. We do know, nonetheless, that most Zen temple gardens were made by Zen masters as *koan*, or spiritual riddles, to challenge their disciples. Perhaps the *karesansui* garden at

Ryōan-ji was among them.

By the time these dry landscape gardens were being built, the *ishitate-sō* had mostly left the gardening profession. In their place were their former assistants, who were members of society's lowest stratum, especially the lowest of the low, the *kawaramono*. They lived on the banks of the Kamo and Katsura rivers, and their traditional occupation was the skinning and tanning of the hides of dead horses and cattle, work that was abhorred because of the Buddhist injunction against killing. Working as assistants to the *ishitate-sō* had been among the obligations imposed by society on the *kawaramono*.

The riverbanks where these people lived could be dreadful places. In times of flood their houses would be swept away, and when, in 1461, there was widespread famine in the city, it is recorded that tens of thousands of bodies were left on the riverbanks for the outcasts to dispose of. The vast majority of the

A purely symbolic, abstract garden in front of the main hall at Daisen-en. Made only of white gravel raked into patterns, this is one of two white gravel mounds contained within it.

Left: *Stepping-stones have dual functions in the gardens of Japan: They are both practical and ornamental. At Konchi-in, this path configuration is* hizumi, *or a shallow curve.*

Right: *The garden at Daisen-en occupies a narrow strip of ground—twelve feet (3½ meters) wide by forty-seven feet (a little more than 14 meters) long. One of the most famous gardens of Japan, it satisfies the imagination and uses small space to great effect.*

Above: *This waiting booth for the teahouse at Katsura is flanked by two Kasuga-type (Korean temple light) stone lanterns that serve as objects of admiration within this harmonious setting.*
Left: *Within the three-dimensional miniaturizations of an idealized landscape at Daisen-en, this now famous grouping of rocks implies a mountain scene, with a (dry) waterfall cascading down to its right. As in Tenryu-ji, the garden design at Daisen-en is based on Chinese landscape paintings.*

kawaramono were nameless, but one, Zen'ami, is mentioned in the diaries of Zen priests of the day. Zen'ami, though a person of great talents, belonged to this lowest class, so it is not surprising that he contrived in any way possible to augment his social standing. Eventually he managed to obtain the title *-ami*. In this period the title *-ami* could be acquired by becoming a follower of the Jishu sect of Buddhism and making a quite sizable donation of money. It served as a kind of passport for people who were otherwise unable to exercise their talents or engage in cultural activities because of their status. Having acquired this title, Zen'ami was able to engage in the design and management of temple gardens without relying on the influence of an *ishitate-sō*. He became a highly respected garden designer whose greatest patron was Shogun Ashikaga no Yoshimasa, and he participated in the repair of the imperial palace gardens.

V

At four o'clock in the morning of the fourteenth day of the tenth month, 1591, the Nara tradesman Matsuya Hisayoshi and his friend Takeda Sōgu called at the residence of Ogaya Dōka in the western suburbs of Nara. They had been invited to an early-morning tea ceremony. It was the tenth month, but by the lunar calendar, and winter had already set in. It was cold and still before daybreak. As they entered Dōka's tea garden, they found stone lanterns positioned among the trees to cast a dim light upon the stepping-stones leading to the teahouse.

Matsuya's journal of his tea ceremony parties records tersely on this occasion: *roji ni tōrō ari* ("lanterns in the garden"), and this is the earliest written record of the use of stone lanterns in Japanese gardens. Until then, stone lanterns had been used in temples and ceme-

Left: *Honami Koetsu was a great tea master and a highly accomplished potter and calligrapher. When he retired at the age of seventy-six, he moved to the Taikyo-an in northern Kyoto, now called Koetsu-ji. Pictured here is the entrance walkway to the garden, which features several teahouses.*

Bottom right: *Stepping-stones are rarely set out in straight lines, which are considered hard to align, difficult to walk on, and, simply, unattractive. As in most aspects of Japanese garden design, the stepping-stone patterns are modeled on real phenomena in nature. This pattern is* magari, *or a wide curve.*

teries as a fixture of Buddhist services, but they had not been found in gardens. It was the tea masters who brought them into their tea gardens.

It has long been said in Japan that there are beautiful flowers, but that the *beauty of the flower* is unknown; in other words, Japanese tradition did not possess an abstract notion of beauty. It was the sixteenth-century aficionados of the tea ceremony *(chanoyū)* who espoused for the first time an original aesthetic in the form of the concepts of *wabi* and *sabi*. These ideas were difficult to explain in words, but one dimension of this aesthetic was a sensitivity and feeling for beauty in all kinds of things, whether they were originally intended for some other purpose or had been discarded by others. The stone lanterns were among them.

Matsuya Hisayoshi's tea journal calls his garden a *roji*, but the original meaning of *roji* was the narrow pathway or alley often found between two buildings, for the first tea gardens were simply passageways from the host's residence to the tea ceremony room. The important new feature of these gardens is that they were designed to be enjoyed by people *passing through* them. The role of the tea garden was not simply to lead guests to their destination, but to imbue them with the special state of mind that is conducive to enjoyment of the cultural pursuit that is *chanoyū*. This was the beginning of the concept of spatial sequence in Japanese gardens.

Another innovation original with the tea masters was the use of stepping-stones, *tobi-ishi*, which not only lead the visitor through the tea garden but create a specific aesthetic effect as well. Tea gardens are usually quite small, rarely more than three hundred square yards (275 square meters), but the stone lanterns and stepping-stones they introduced became indispensable elements of the Japanese garden. The concept of a sequence of spaces evolved, eventually to blossom on a large scale in the magnificent stroll gardens of the following century.

VI

On June 18, 1620, in Kyoto, the early-morning rain had lifted, leaving the sky blue and clear. In the imperial palace the splendid ceremonies of the marriage of the young Emperor Gomizuno-o to Kazuko, the daughter of the second Tokugawa shogun Ietada (1607–78), were unfolding, and the palace was filled with courtiers in resplendent kimono. Not among them, however, was Prince Toshihito (1579–1629), an uncle of Emperor Gomizuno-o, who had not been invited for political reasons.

A chronicle of the life of Prince Toshihito *(Toshihito shinō gonenreki)* recounts how the slighted uncle suppressed his anger and went off to absorb himself in the construction of his retreat in the village of Katsura on the south-

Left: *Katsura, the earliest known stroll garden still in existence, contains several teahouses and noteworthy stepping-stone arrangements. The placement of stones accords with the gait of people dressed in kimono.*

Bottom left: *The magnificently designed and crafted bamboo fence surrounding the periphery of Koetsu-ji is attributed to Koetsu himself. A gate of diagonally lashed bamboo is used for the gate.*

Bottom right: *Stone lanterns were originally used as votive lamps in front of the halls of Buddhist temples. In the sixteenth century, when tea masters began to employ them in their gardens, stone lanterns lost their religious association and became decorative features by day and provided mood-making illumination by night. This lantern, at Koetsu-ji, is of the Kasuga type, or a Korean temple light.*

west side of the city. The villa and the garden as we know them today were completed by Toshihito's son Toshitada sometime around 1645, and the garden is the oldest stroll garden still in existence. Had Prince Toshihito been free to exercise his talents within the structure of political power, he would no doubt have become embroiled in the struggles between the Tokugawa government in Edo and the emperor in Kyoto, and might not have had either the time or the mental composure to create such a superlative garden.

In the peaceful years between the seventeenth and nineteenth centuries a large number of stroll gardens were built. When Emperor Gomizuno-o, after years of resisting the Tokugawa shogunate's strategies to undermine imperial power, abdicated the throne in protest, he built the famous Shugaku-in stroll garden. The provincial lords, pacified under the iron hand of the new Tokugawa regime, channeled their resources to peaceful pursuits and built many fine stroll gardens throughout

the country, some of which remain today, including Ritsurin-sō (in Takamatsu), Kōraku-en (in Okayama), and Keroku-en (in Kanazawa). After the middle of the nineteenth century, with the shifting of Japan's gears into the modern age, high-ranking government officials and wealthy magnates built such distinguished stroll gardens as Murin-an and Shinshin-an (both in Kyoto), and Chinzan-sō (in Tokyo).

The stroll garden invariably has a large pond encircled by a footpath linking the garden's attractions—a waterfall, tea ceremony house, a rustic cottage, stone lanterns, and streams. These features and the path linking them are designed in such a way as to create a kind of music for those strolling in the garden—exhilarating vistas in sunlit space giving way to pensive corridors of sun-dappled woods, open dells leading toward quiet paths, rustling thickets of dense greenery succeeded by beds of blossoming flowers—a rhythmical sequence in which the visitor is

caught up and transported into the pleasures of the landscape. Strollers along the path can be glimpsed as they proceed—into a bamboo grove, a wood, the teahouse—creating an "appearing-disappearing" effect deliberately planned by the garden designer.

This, in brief, is the history of garden culture since ancient times in Japan. The Japanese never rejected older forms of garden culture nor tried to eliminate them. They might have altered their original meaning or completely forgotten the ideas that sustained them, but they never discarded the forms. New garden culture did not replace the old; it was simply added, in an ongoing, accretionary process.

The process merely continued when the garden culture of Western Europe was introduced in the latter part of the nineteenth century. The Japanese did not pour great energy into the introduction of new or foreign ideas in landscape gardening, for the history of gardens was not one of rejection of the past and did not advocate decisive change.

Japanese gardens are a mixture of old and new, East and West. Some say the result is a hodgepodge and that Japan's unique garden culture has been deprived of creative vitality because it is so innocent of rejection. Others suspect that this accretionary approach may provide an important condition for the creation of a new, original phase of development.

After traveling around the world for three years I realized one thing upon my return: Nothing more momentous than a small earthquake has shaken the world of the Japanese gardener. The gardeners of Japan today do not try, any more than their predecessors going back to the third century B.C., either to compete for novel concepts of creativity or to assert their individuality. It seems to me that the age of the accretionary approach to garden culture is drawing to a close, yet I trust in the old saying, "Tomorrow's wind shall blow."

Above: *The pond at Shinshin-an is floored with a rich gray clay that greatly enhances the intended reflective characteristics of the pond. Ponds are traditionally modeled on natural bodies of water, shorelines, or Chinese written characters. The cursive forms of certain characters— particularly those for "mind," "river," and "water"—are especially common pond shapes.* Right: *Shinshin-an is a refined contemporary Japanese garden. A detailed examination reveals, however, evidence of the influence and evolution of hundreds of years of Japanese garden design.*

The stark beauty of tree trunks in a sea of gravel is one of many excellent features at Shinshin-an that help create a highly aesthetic and satisfying garden experience.

CHAPTER FIVE

FLOWERS AND FLOWER GARDENS

To those of us who find flowers enchanting, who spend hours and even years in their company, a garden without flowers is a contradiction in terms. Not for us those static green spaces in which geometry and the stern hand of man triumph over nature. Our gardens are rowdy with bloom; they spume and froth and bubble over with flowers, changing with the weather, the season, and the moon. In our gardens, flowers not only hold center stage, they play every part, take on every role, fulfill our every expectation—at least, at first.

When we begin to garden, we ask quite little from our plants. Uncertain of our skills, we are not particularly surprised by failure and are elated by any success. We are awed by all that happens to the little plants and seeds we nurture so tenderly. We spend more and more time in the garden, ardent in pursuit of this heady experience, fascinated by floral charms. Lost in admiration for our flowers,

we do not notice the tensions that accumulate so rapidly in modern life. We are refreshed by our flowers' quintessential freshness. We return to them again and again, seeking comfort and peace.

What we find, if we stick with it, are both comfort and challenge, for as we gain experience and skill, those first and simplest garden pleasures lose their piercing, time-stopping quality. The more we know, the more we want both for and from our flowery gardens. Perhaps one day we become aware that the garden is indeed pretty, yet it somehow lacks substance. The glories of spring begin to seem a bit forlorn, dotted in random groups throughout the early, empty border, and later their fading foliage looks decidedly hideous among summer's burgeoning splendors with nowhere to hide. Our first combinations, joyful and innocent, now strike us as trite or insignificant, yet adding more unusual plants doesn't help.

Worst of all, our rapidly increasing collection of border beauties stubbornly refuses to coalesce; put the plants where we will, they will not make a proper garden.

Eventually, and quite reluctantly, we are forced to admit that gardens dedicated entirely to flowers can be as unsatisfactory as any blossomless expanse of greenery. It becomes clear that although we may consider strictly foliar gardens barren, our frail and fleeting flowers might easily be seen as flimsy and formless unless they get some significant architectural support, whether from evergreen plants, formal hedges, or stonework. A hard truth emerges—flowers need a setting to give their best.

LEARNING BY OBSERVING

Discovering just how to craft a worthy framework against which to display our beloved flowers can challenge the most willing of gardeners. First, we might visit every available garden, public and private, and take notes about what we like (and dislike). Next, we may browse through dozens of garden books, studying the pictures and sifting the often contradictory practical information therein. Finally, we apply the lessons thus gleaned in our own gardens and evaluate the results as they mature. (If this sounds like a time-consuming process, it is indeed, yet this process is the heart and soul, the blood and guts of garden making.) Since outstanding, multiseasonal flower gardens are not to be found on every block, before long gardeners seeking advanced courses are forced to look further afield.

In North America, some of the most exciting and successful gardens are small, private ones that are rarely open to view. Fortunately, there are an increasing number of wonderful public gardens where gardeners can reap invaluable lessons to take back home. Wave Hill in the Bronx borough of New York City, the North Carolina State University Arboretum in Raleigh, the Children's Orthopedic Hospital in Seattle, Washington, and the Western Hills Nursery in Occidental, California, all boast extraordinary flower gardens. In England, where gardening is a national pastime, hundreds of private gardens, large and small, are regularly open to visitors. Even when only seen through photographs, the fabled flower gardens of England impress us with their strength of identity. They draw

the flower lover irresistibly, as does Monet's recently restored Giverny across the water in France.

When we look more closely at any of these exceptional gardens, we find that each offers seminal lessons in garden making. Although all are quite different in character, setting, size, and style, they are united by principles that hold true everywhere. Roughly speaking, these can be reduced to four factors—context, coherence, color, and abundance.

Context refers to the relationship of a garden to its setting, which can involve sensitive echoing or mirroring of the salient characteristics of a regional landscape as well as those of the immediate neighborhood and the house itself. The relative proportion and scale of the garden layout and plantings also enter in, so that a small, rustic farmhouse would have a simple cottage garden rather than acres of elaborate, symmetrical bedding out, whereas an angular modern condominium on a busy street might be surrounded by a tough, pollution-tolerant grass garden.

Coherence refers to the visual integrity of the garden, as well as the smoothness of tran-

Previous page: *In the gardens at Hatfield House, the formal design elements of lawn, hedge, and wall serve to showcase a joyful abundance of flowers.*
Left: *Pure color captures the eye, but it is the careful balance of texture, form, and line that holds our attention in this stimulating vignette found at the North Carolina State University Arboretum.*
Right: *Edith Eddleman's perennial borders at the North Carolina State University Arboretum illustrate vital precepts of garden making for thousands of visitors each year.*

sition from one section to another. A coherent garden will maintain its distinctive character or overall flavor though the styles of various parts may be quite different, just as a singer's voice is recognizable whether she is singing opera or pop. With *color* in the garden, our goal is not only to have lots of it, for as long as possible, but to use it artistically, both to soothe and to stimulate. Controlled *abundance,* an intelligent generosity of spirit which dictates uncluttered design and luxuriant planting, characterizes all of the great flower gardens. In each of the following examples, these principles have been interpreted according to the personal taste and inclinations of the garden maker, indicating the endless range of possibilities open to us.

ENGLAND

HIDCOTE MANOR

In the early decades of this century an expatriate American, Lawrence Johnston, made a lastingly influential garden at Hidcote, one that is remarkable in many ways, several of which dramatically changed English garden style. First, Johnston divided his garden into a series of outdoor rooms or compartments by means of hedges, some plain and others made of several kinds of trees blended together. Each room has a theme, often based on a color scheme, some of which were highly unusual in Johnston's day. His red border was justly famous for its subtle handling of strong colors; flowers in every tint of red are mingled with purple and red foliage plants. The effect is heavy and sensuous, for the intense colors smoulder like banked embers that erupt suddenly into flame. (In some circles, indeed, the red border was found mildly scandalous, neither conventionally pretty nor quite "nice.")

We generally think of English flower gardens as filled with perennials, and indeed many of them are found at Hidcote, but it is interesting to note that much of the red border's impact comes from half-hardy shrubs with red or dusky leaves. Even in mild England these must be wintered over in greenhouses and are not planted out until all danger of frost is past, usually in early to mid-May. This border, like

Above: *At Hidcote
Manor, topiary and
sculpturally pruned shrubs
take on the architectural
role traditionally played by
statuary.*
Right: *A view curtailed
by a lovely old gate lends a
dramatic air of mystery to
the garden entrance at
Rousham House in
Oxfordshire.*

the rest of Hidcote's gardens, is at its best from mid-June through mid-September. As autumn progresses, the tender plants are taken back to the greenhouses to winter over alongside cuttings of short-lived ornamental herbs and lovely but unreliable perennials.

The progression of the gardens is also of interest; near the house, the garden rooms are small and formal, increasing in size as one gets farther away. The plantings alter as well, from tidy and often symmetrical treatments near the house, through a series of less and less formal borders, and ending up with the distant "wild" gardens where vigorous shade-loving plants are naturalized near orchard and stream. These relaxed, almost rough areas appear in strong contrast to the clipped perfection of the largest and minimally planted formal areas that lie close at hand, and there is a piquant pleasure in passing through the arched doorways in the trim hedges that divide these disparate gardens.

While Johnston was making Hidcote, thousands of new plants were pouring into England as plant hunters searched the secret places of the earth for unknown species. Many a collector's garden became a sad jumble, but Johnston, though a keen plantsman, also had a strong sense of design. In order to make visual sense of his mixed bag of plants, he planted some of them in "natural" communities within the confines of his borders. In doing so, Johnston pioneered what is now known as the mixed border, where plants of every persuasion—shrubs, trees and vines, annuals, perennials, and bulbs—are planted together, naturalistically rather than in patterns. Though casual in appearance, there is nothing haphazard about these plantings, for each plant is placed according to its habit and needs, given companions that will emphasize its best points and minimize its weaknesses. Hidcote became famous as a garden in which one met choice and uncommon plants at every turn, each used thoughtfully and artistically.

Hidcote is also unusual in its architectural use of plants. Johnston favored foliage walls over those made of brick or stone, using both

Once inside the gate, the Rousham House garden is found to be full of flowers, their "sweet disorder" in sharp contrast to the geometrical layout, their brilliance enhanced by the background of somber yew hedging.

Hidcote's red border, made early in the twentieth century, was one of the first embodiments of the color theme gardens proposed by Gertrude Jekyll.

severe expanses of clipped yew or box and tapestry hedges woven of mixed rows of beech, plain and golden holly, and hornbeam. Topiary replaces statuary, and most of the paths are simply surfaced in unpatterned stone, cobbles, or brick. Although it is now a commonplace in English gardens, Johnston was among the first to exploit the contrast between the austerity of sheared hedges and edgings and a loose, billowing, romantic style of planting.

Although Hidcote was intended to be a summer garden, and was little used out of season, it retains much of its character through the winter. Where traditional herbaceous borders melt away entirely by late fall, Hidcote's borders, framed in their tapestry hedges, remain firmly delineated. Throughout the gardens, the many evergreen plants (mainly shrubs and perennials) maintain the integrity of the overall design even without benefit of blossoms. One can plainly trace at Hidcote the origins of the multiseasonal mixed borders that are now perhaps the most common form of flower gardening in England.

Although the mere ten acres of plantings makes this a small garden by English standards, to North American eyes it looks quite large. It is even more unusual in being made almost without reference to the house, enclosed and set away from it, probably because Hidcote Manor was—and is—condemned by the English as being "of no importance" or "without interest." In fact, it is considerably more charming than the average suburban split-level, but those whose houses lack charm entirely may find in this approach a practical solution to their aesthetic difficulties.

HESTERCOMBE

Hestercombe's garden is the finest extant example of an extremely influential partnership in which an artist and plantswoman, Gertrude Jekyll, planted beds and borders laid out by an architect, Edwin Lutyens. Lutyens was an advocate of firm, geometric border design, whereas Jekyll massed her plantings with controlled generosity. Flowers are everywhere in this small garden; bold-leaved peonies fill the central beds, roses hang in thick swags from the long pergola, catmints and shrubby salvias sweep in soft drifts through the borders. Mats of tiny Mexican daisies soften the line of the curving steps, honeysuckle laces the glowing stone walls, and blue-bladed irises edge the narrow stone rills that feed small pools of water lilies at the far end of the garden.

Based on Jekyll's famous color precepts that shaped the sensibilities of every succeeding generation, the borders build from cool, misty tints of blue and chalky yellows to peaks of flaming reds and oranges, all mellowed and mingled with gray foliage plants. Characteristically, Jekyll's plantings appear casual, yet are never sloppy or indefinite; every plant is placed with a specific point and purpose in mind. The color comes in overlapping waves, beginning in late spring and building through a succession of garden vignettes to a powerful climax in high summer. This, like Hidcote, is chiefly a summer garden, given definition through the colder months by the stonework and evergreen shrubs. Hestercombe's winter presence is modest, but a greater variety of evergreens and some winter-blooming plants would make it a delightful year-round garden.

Lutyens's design is beautifully balanced, rich in detail yet uncluttered overall. The long axes and radiating walks, the paths and pergola pillars are simple in shape, yet marvelously textured. Restrained mixtures of stone and tiles, flints and cobbles play up the lovely surfaces of each substance, softening the cumulative effect of so much hardness. Indeed, Lutyens's hardscape—the manmade architectural and structural elements of the garden design—has an almost organic quality that makes the plants look right at home. The contrasts here between the plantings and the stonework are gentle rather than stark, and the two work in balanced partnership. Although there is a good deal of stonework at Hestercombe, it does not dominate the flowers, but sets them off as a male dancer's strength emphasizes the grace and fragility of the prima ballerina.

Left: Designed by Sir Edwin Lutyens and planted by Gertrude Jekyll, Hestercombe exemplifies their fruitful relationship. Though highly architectural, the hardscape of the garden supports rather than overwhelms the controlled abundance that Jekyll popularized.
Right: Jekyll's color theories influenced twentieth-century gardening in England tremendously. At Tintinhull House, the strong reds and purples in the red border are tempered by chalk yellows and creams rather than stark whites, a contrast that Jekyll felt was so strong as to be distressing.

NORTH AMERICA

WAVE HILL

Although it is evocative of the gardens of the golden Twenties, Wave Hill is no historic recreation but a vital, ongoing garden of the present. Located on a twenty-eight-acre estate in the Bronx, it is owned by the city of New York but privately funded and administered. The flower garden is one of some dozen gardens, all intended both to entertain and educate the public. In design and style it refers to the English gardens of the 1920s—wide paths divide geometric beds that hold relaxed and abundant plantings—yet has a definite American flavor. The rectangular flower garden is framed by a handsomely detailed wooden fence, with a Victorian conservatory for a backdrop and an irregular row of evergreens forming a green wall at one side. The opposite side is open, with dramatic views of the Hudson River and the rugged cliffs of the Palisades to be glimpsed beyond the roses and clematis that drape the fence.

The floral palette at Wave Hill is outstanding, for this small garden holds a collector's trove of plants: antique flowers and English border plants, species irises and the latest American hybrids, old roses and newly discovered rarities grown from seed. Handsome herbs are everywhere, and beautiful vegetables, such as shaggy armed cardoons and red-backed rhubarb, look stunningly unfamiliar used as ornamentals. Plants of every persuasion are combined artfully, the strengths of one camouflaging the weaknesses of another. Even a commoner like the woolly gray lamb's ears is put thoughtfully to work; a nonflowering variety makes a running edging that plunges deep into the borders in wandering ribbons, drawing the eye in and down to discover small treasures tucked among the larger plants. This underscores the fact that these beds are not just puffy rectangular pillows but plantings with a distinctive topography. Though most of the tallest plants are ranged comfortably in the centers of beds (made to be viewed from all sides), a few are placed right up front. Where this happens, the angular, pencil-slim stems of *Verbena bonariensis* may rise five feet (1½ meters), making an airy veil through which the rest of the plants look enticingly unfamiliar.

Though intended to delight and instruct the public, Wave Hill's gardens intentionally have the look and feel of private ones. A winding walk connects the flower garden to a nearby wild garden, where paths deliberately have been kept narrow. This forces people to walk

Above: *Wave Hill is a splendid example of a public institution that maintains a strong and individualistic identity. Its series of teaching gardens serve both to delight and instruct the visitor.*
Right: *The sumptuous flower borders at Wave Hill draw us in while the glimpse of distant views across the Hudson River provides a most pleasing framework for the garden from almost any vantage point.*

slowly, alone or in pairs, and to pay attention to the complex plantings in which native American wildflowers mingle with shade lovers from all over the world. Even when the first rush of spring bloom is over, this garden holds together in a tightly woven tapestry of foliage textures and tints, punctuated by a variety of later bloomers. Like the flower garden, this is not a walk-through showplace to be taken in at a brisk pace, but a garden to savor at leisure. Marco Stufano, Wave Hill's director of horticulture, explains that the scale and proportion of a garden dictate its impact and flavor; both the small, casually planted flower garden and the wild garden feel intimate, for everything is close at hand. If the paths were wider, the beds larger and planted on a grander scale, both gardens would seem coldly institutional rather than warmly personal.

The flower garden is still young, yet it already provides months of ever-changing color. In 1985 Stufano and the late John Nally (who was Wave Hill's curator of plants) decided to replace an elderly rose garden with a stimulating array of flowers set among vivid foliage plants. Both talented plantsmen, the two worked closely, amassing a huge palette of plants to draw from and consulting constantly as to which plants would go where. Now, the maturing garden seems made to a single vision. Soft runs of lavenders and blues, pinks and silvers predominate, yet "difficult" colors are not ignored. Magenta is tempered with lavender, rose, and silver, while deep, murky reds are lightened by pewtery blue and gray foliage. Each unfolding succession of flowers is framed as much by the rich range of foliages, varying in color and shape, texture, and surface quality, as by the walls and hedges. Repeats of plants with similar form, color, and texture, and the generous use of theme plants, like the silvery, carpeting lamb's ears, further unify the mixed borders.

Wonderful as the garden looks, its effects are continually being reevaluated and refined.

A RED BORDER

Patterned after the deep-toned borders at Wave Hill, this vivid scheme employs red chard, purple perilla, burgundy okra, and other ornamental vegetables with flowers in every shade of red. Perennials, flowering vines, and shrubs unite in a changing succession of combinations which carry the garden from late spring well into autumn. Flame bright cardinal flowers, ember-toned roses, and daylilies of ruby, amethyst, and garnet glow amid a tapestry of ruddy grasses and foliage plants. Ruffles of velvety gray lamb's ears spread in understated counterpoint about each section to unify the scene. All of the clematis are trained onto tripods. Each bed is planned fifteen-foot (4½-meter) square, with the intersecting paths five feet (1½ meters) wide.

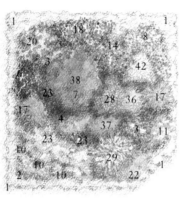
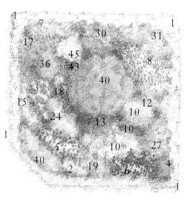
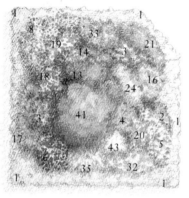
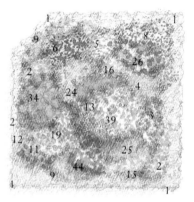

PLANT	# USED
1. *Stachys byzantina* 'Silver Carpet'	80 (in groups of 20)
2. *Viola* 'Arkwright Beauty'	15 (in groups of 3)
3. *Echinacea purpurea*	18 (in groups of 3)
4. *Foeniculum vulgare*—a bronze variety	8 (2, 2, 2, 2)
5. *Lobelia fulgens* 'Bee's Flame'	11 (3, 3, 5)
6. *Penstemon* 'Husker Red'	9 (2, 2, 2, 3)
7. *Ajuga* 'Burgundy Glow'	14 (7, 7)
8. *Geum* 'Red Wings'	12 (in groups of 3)
9. *Sedum* 'Vera Jameson'	7 (3, 4)
10. Cardoon	6 (6 times)
11. *Hemerocallis* 'Little Grapette'	6 (3, 3)
12. *Sedum* 'Rose Glow'	8 (3, 5)
13. *Atriplex hortensis* (Red orach)	12 (6, 6)
14. *Monarda didyma* 'Adam'	6 (3, 3)
15. *Fuchsia magellanica* 'Tom Thumb'	6 (3, 3)
16. *F.* x *exoniensis*	6 (3, 3)
17. *Imperata cylindrica* (Blood grass)	12 (in groups of 3)
18. *Aster* x *frikartii* 'Monch'	6 (2, 2, 2)
19. *Salvia rutilans*, synonym *S. elegans* (Pineapple sage)	6 (2, 2, 2)
20. *S. sclarea* (Clary sage)	4 (2, 2)
21. *Sedum album* 'Nigrum'	5
22. *S.* 'Meteor'	5
23. *Canna* 'Giant King Humbert'	5 (2, 1, 2)
24. *Artemisia* 'Powis Castle'	3 (3 times)
25. *Perilla frutescens*—a purple variety	6
26. *Hemerocallis* 'Pardon Me'	2
27. Red chard	3
28. 'Burgundy' okra	3
29. *Crocosmia* 'Lucifer'	12
30. 'Rubine' Brussels sprouts	5
31. *Sedum* 'Autumn Joy'	3
32. *Hemerocallis* 'Admiral'	2
33. *Gaillardia* 'Goblin'	3
34. Rhubarb	2
35. *Cimicifuga simplex* 'Atropurpurea'	1
36. *Salvia officinalis* 'Purpurea' (Purple sage)	2 (2 times)
37. *Rodgersia henrici*	1
38. *Gleditsia triacanthos* 'Rubylace'	1
39. *Rosa glauca*	1
40. *Berberis* 'Rose Glow'	2 (2 times)
41. *Cotinus coggygria* 'Royal Purple'	1
42. *Clematis* 'Niobe'	1
43. *C.* 'Richard Pennell'	1
44. *C.* 'Duchess of Albany'	1
45. *C.* 'Mme. Julia Correvon'	1

AMERICAN NATIVES BORDER

Inspired by Edith Eddleman's masterful borders at the North Carolina State University, this American natives border showcases spectacular yet easy-to-care-for American beauties. Lily-flowered yuccas and fine-textured grasses with feathery bloom spikes provide contrast among the broader leaves of perennials, which themselves offer an exciting diversity of foliar form and color. The plant list includes North American natives that will perform well in many parts of the continent as well as in much of northern Europe. Naturally, local species may be freely substituted, and many of these plant families are well represented throughout North America. Virtually any of the many asters or goldenrods, evening primroses, or coralbells (Heuchera) would fit comfortably into this setting, making the color flow warmer or cooler as may be preferred. The border is thirty-five feet (10½ meters) long by twenty feet (6 meters) at its deepest and ten feet (3 meters) at its shallowest.

PLANT	# USED
1. *Heuchera americana* (Coralbells)	5
2. *H. micrantha* (Coralbells)	5
3. *H. villosa* (Coralbells)	5
4. *Uvularia grandiflora* (Merrybells)	10
5. *Artemisia* 'Silver King'	11 (3, 3, 5)
6. *Coreopsis* 'Moonbeam'	9 (4, 5)
7. *Gaillardia* 'Mahogany'	9 (4, 5)
8. *Helenium* 'Brilliant'	11 (5, 6)
9. New England asters— purple, lavender, blue, rose, and pink	in groups of 6 to 8 each
10. *Echinacea pallida* (Coneflower)	7
11. *E. purpurea* 'Magnus'	3
12. *Oenothera tetragona* 'Fireworks'	5
13. *O. missourensis* (Evening primrose)	5
14. *Amsonia tabernaemontana* (Blue stars)	5
15. *Monarda didyma* 'Mahogany'	6
16. *M. d.* 'Violet Queen'	5
17. *Gaura lindheimeri*	5 (5 times)
18. *Boltonia asteroides* 'Pink Beauty'	6 (3, 3)
19. *B. asteroides*	3
20. *Heliopsis scabra* 'Summer Sun'	5
21. *Chelone obliqua* (Turtlehead)	5
22. *Eupatorium purpureum* (Joe-pye weed)	6 (3, 3)
23. *Veronicastrum virginicum*	6
24. *Cimicifuga racemosa* (Bugbane)	3
25. *C. cordifolia* (Bugbane)	3
26. *Thermopsis caroliniana*	3
27. *Yucca glauca*	3
28. *Y. flaccida*	2 (2 times)
29. *Y. filamentosa* 'Gold Sword'	1
30. *Aristolochia durior* (Dutchman's pipe)	1
31. *Polystichum munitum* (Sword fern)	6 (3, 3)
32. *Filipendula rubra* (Queen of the prairie)	3
33. *Asclepias tuberosa* (Butterfly weed)	6
34. *Gillenia trifoliata* (Bowman's root)	3
35. *Aruncus dioicus* (Goatsbeard)	3
36. *Solidago virgaurea* 'Crown of Rays'	6
37. *Rudbeckia* 'Nutmeg'	11 (5, 6)
38. *Eschscholtzia* 'Thai Silk'	36–40 (in 3 groups)

Stufano believes that garden making is an ongoing process, and stresses that developing the kind of linked seasonal floral pictures seen at Wave Hill takes time and practice. Perhaps the most important lesson here is never to worry about making mistakes, which he considers to be an important learning tool. With unusual, often insouciant combinations, juxtaposing border perennials with ornamental vegetables and tender greenhouse plants, Stufano encourages gardeners to keep searching for the perfect plant to complete or complement each vignette. He urges fellow gardeners to experiment, to try new things, to take risks rather than to stick with the safe and proven.

NORTH CAROLINA STATE UNIVERSITY ARBORETUM

Edith Eddleman's perennial borders at the NCSU arboretum provide thousands of visitors with inspiration each year. The main border, begun in 1983, is on a scale rarely attempted these days, stretching three hundred feet (91½ meters) in length and fully eighteen feet (5½ meters) in depth. About half of the plants used in the main border are American natives, many from the Southeast. The remainder are exotics, including foreign species, cultivated hybrids, and border selections. All are artfully intermingled to provide color and often blossoms from March through December, for one of Eddleman's goals is to stretch the accepted limits of the garden season. An evergreen hedge frames the border and divides it from a white garden and an ornamental grass border, both designed on a generous scale. Naturally, few home gardeners will be inclined or able to duplicate such plantings, yet all leave these gardens with a renewed vision and a strong resolve to apply the lessons gained here in their own gardens.

Eddleman categorizes perennials by shape and habit, calling them spiky or vertical, rounded or oval, and creeping or weaving. In her borders, she weaves her complex and long-lasting combinations with care, balancing shape and texture as carefully as tint and tone. Foliage plants are used as lavishly as flowering ones, each a foil to the other. Flaring, sharp-edged yuccas and soaring fountain grasses contrast with bold, coarse hibiscus and delicate cloud grass, fine and threadlike. The exciting variety of foliage textures and forms entertains the eye as much as the flowers themselves. The border plants are arrayed in color flows that intensify from cool pastels at either end to the

The red-flushed, sinuous stems of unfurling yucca echo the red roses behind them in the North Carolina State University Arboretum borders, where insouciant combinations and sensitive color runs characterize the plantings.

Nearly half the plants used in the perennial borders at the North Carolina State University Arboretum are American natives. These include a number of flowering grasses that make exciting contrasts of form and texture to the larger leaved perennials.

hot, glowing center. Here, strong yellows and golds meet reds and oranges, deep purples and electric blues in joyful exuberance, and plants with leaves of silver and soft gray-green unite the whole.

Continually seeking out and growing American natives, Eddleman has collected fine forms of indigenous plants from sources all over the world. She finds it ironic that many of her American treasures have come to her from Germany, England, and the Netherlands, and draws an important lesson from this. Exotic plants are often prized for rarity, given the best conditions, and viewed without prejudice. Eddleman tries to do the same when growing native plants new to her, recognizing that an unprepossessing plant languishing, starved and dry, by the roadside can respond with spectacular results when given a place in the garden proper. She has also learned to appreciate the elasticity of American plants, finding that many are tolerant of a wide range of conditions, despite their preferences in the wild. Thus, she successfully grows wetland plants such as *Lobelia cardinalis*, the cardinal flower, a special pink form of *Boltonia asteroides* that she discovered as a seedling in a local nursery, and *Vernonia* (ironweed) in her comparatively dry border.

Eddleman has developed an extraordinary plant palette that celebrates the tremendous range and versatility of American natives. Each of her theme gardens at NCSU gives gardeners the opportunity to similarly broaden their own palettes, both through observation of uncommon plants during the year, and through programs in which both private and commercial nursery propagators are invited to take cuttings, so that the best of the plants seen here may be widely disseminated.

FRANCE

GIVERNY

English gardens may be characterized by a tremendous range of flowering plants used naturalistically within a geometrical layout against a firm and generally evergreen framework. American gardens are distinguished by an appreciation of the native flora, a willingness to adapt the critical precepts of the long-established English garden school, and a delight in playful experimentation. Monet's garden at Giverny, extremely simple both in form

and palette, is exemplary in his free and exhilarating use of color. Framed only by the paths and the rose arches that echo the curve of the hill behind the house, it owes everything to the lively, joyous presence of flowers.

Monet laid out his borders and beds with typically French precision, but where most French gardens would have formal evergreen hedges, Giverny has virtually none. The beds of Giverny are packed with tulips and forget-me-nots in May, irises, poppies, and rambling roses in June. Through high summer, lupines, daisies, and bachelor's buttons abound. By autumn, the color cools, and in winter the garden is fully at rest.

At Giverny there are few plants a horti-

culturist would give a dime for, yet the flowers are placed with a sympathy that amounts to genius. Here are all the homely flowers of field and cottage, arrayed in sumptuous color runs that wander from subtle browns and creams to soft gold into vibrant, triumphant orange, from the blued white of skim milk through the snapping electricity of pure cobalt, from chalk pink through singing clarion reds. The colors meld into and through each other, building into impressionistic scenes that startle us with their familiarity. Indeed, Monet's garden was designed as an outdoor workshop. Every flower in it earned its place by virtue of its paintability, and the plants are deliberately arranged so the afternoon light

Left: Though Monet's garden at Giverny is laid out with Gallic precision, the simple plantings are enlivened by the free and exhilarating use of color. Bottom right: The house at Giverny is the heart of the garden, which flows out from the main doorway in floral rivers. Vivid all spring, brilliant during the summer, and subtle through the fall, the garden is at rest during the winter months, when the artist worked in his studio.

will catch them in a certain way, or to create specific gradations of value and shade.

Though casual, even anarchic in appearance, Monet's plantings were no less deliberate than Jekyll's. The eye of the painter was loving but merciless; not sentiment but recognition of essential qualities puts hollyhocks, irises, and daylilies in this garden. He knew no color rules but his own; not for Monet the careful gradations according to intellectual plan—he was afraid of no color, no clash, no breach of taste. He saw beyond convention, looked past preconception, and in so doing, influenced the perceptions of all who followed him.

At Giverny we are reminded that although in most parts of North America we cannot begin to match the exceptionally rich plant palette of the English, we do not necessarily need to. Certainly, those of us who are de-

veloping year-round flower gardens will continue to gather in the widest possible selection of plants. However, if we desire no more than a summer packed full of flowers, we can learn to weave a changeable season of rainbows using only the most ordinary plants. Like Monet, we may work colorist marvels with these common creatures, as long as we, too, give their qualities and their relationships our full and thoughtful attention. Monet loved his flowers with a consuming, almost ferocious passion. He planned and painted his garden with the same concentrated attention, often setting aside his brush to scribble a few notes before returning to his canvas. Our art may be restricted to the garden, our only canvas our borders and beds, yet if we follow Monet's lead, his approach can work as successfully in our gardens as it does at Giverny.

Opposite page: *Monet's effects, refined through constant rearranging and replacement, were often achieved with the most common plants. Giverny today continues to demonstrate that a trained and passionate eye is at least as valuable to the garden maker as a collection of horticultural rarities.*

Above: *Monet's garden was an outdoor workshop, and his plant palette reflected his personal predilections more than the dictates of garden fashion. His legacy of experimental freedom has inspired countless gardeners to develop and express their own preferences in their own gardens.*

THE MIXED BORDER

In this mixed border, which is thirty feet (9 meters) by fifteen feet (4½ meters), the belt of woody plants that defines the border serves to frame and set off floral displays from earliest spring through fall, yet comes into its own in winter when perennials are at rest. In winter the drooping branches of the silver weeping pear shine like oiled silk, the dogwood thrusts slender twigs of lavender gray toward the leaden skies, and the vanilla scent of sweet box *(Sarcococca)* fills the air. Foliage plays a major role as glossy holly and glittering mahonia gleam among the duller leaves of kalmia and pieris, and shining mounds of purple heuchera are offset by dusky blue rue and catmint. Contrasts of form and structure are as important as those of color and texture, and plants of every description mingle to produce an endless cycle of vignettes.

PLANT	# USED
1. *Juniperus* 'Skyrocket'	2 (2 times)
2. *Mahonia bealei* (Leatherleaf)	1
3. *M. aquifolium* (Oregon grape)	1
4. *Pieris japonica* 'White Cascade'	1
5. *P.* 'Forest Flame'	1
6. *Ilex meserveae* 'Blue Princess' (Holly)	4 (2, 2)
7. *Kalmia latifolia* (Mountain laurel)	2 (2 times)
8. *Viburnum plicatum tomentosum* 'Mariesii'	1
9. *Daphne* x 'Somerset' or *D. odora*	1
10. *Sarcococca humilis* (Sweet box)	6
11. *S. confusa* or *S. ruscifolia* (Sweet box)	6
12. *Pyrus salicifolia pendula* (Weeping silver pear)	1
13. *Cornus florida* 'Cherokee Daybreak'	1
14. *Lamium maculatum* 'White Nancy'	30 (12, 18)
15. *Hosta* 'Krossa Regal'	5
16. *H.* 'Blue Umbrellas'	3
17. *Helleborus orientalis* (Lenten rose)	6 (3, 3)
18. *H. foetidus* (Stinking hellebore)	3
19. *H. niger* (Christmas rose)	3
20. *Iris foetidissima* (Gladwin iris)	5 (1, 1, 3)
21. *Crambe cordifolia* (Sea kale)	2 (1, 1)
22. *Nepeta* 'Six Hills Giant'	4 (4 times)
23. *Heuchera* 'Purple Palace'	4 (4 times)
24. *H.* 'June Bride'	9 (3, 3, 3)
25. *Ruta graveolens* 'Blue Beauty'	6 (6 times)
26. *Alchemilla mollis* (Lady's-mantle)	3 (3 times)
27. *Fothergilla gardenii*	2 (2 times)
28. *Sedum* 'Autumn Joy'	6 (3, 3)
29. *Helictotrichon sempervirens* (Blue oat grass)	2 (2 times)
30. *Callicarpa* 'Profusion'	2 (2 times)
31. *Achillea taygetea*	6
32. *A.* 'Salmon Beauty'	6
33. *Artemisia* 'Valerie Finnis'	6 (3, 3)
34. *Linum narbonense* (Blue flax)	2 (2 times)
35. *Coreopsis* 'Moonbeam'	6 (3, 3)
36. *Verbascum chaixii* 'Album' (White mullein)	3
37. *Caryopteris* 'Kew Blue'	5
38. *C.* 'Blue Mist'	3
39. *Potentilla fruticosa* 'Primrose Beauty'	3
40. *Lilium speciosum* 'Rubrum'	18 (6, 6, 6)
41. *Thymus citriodorus albomarginata* (Silver thyme)	18 (in groups of 3)
42. *Rhododendron yakusimanum* (Dwarf rhododendron)	2
43. *Lythrum salicaria* 'Morden's Pink'	5
44. *L. virgatum* 'Dropmore Purple'	5
45. *Thalictrum* 'Hewitt's Double'	3
46. *Tricyrtis hirta* 'Miyaki'	6
47. *Deutzia gracilis* 'Nikko' (Dwarf deutzia)	1
48. *Rosa* 'Just Joey'	1
49. *R.* 'Sterling Silver'	1
50. *Hydrangea serrata* 'Pink Beauty' (Dwarf hydrangea)	1
51. *Salvia superba* 'May Night'	3
52. *S. s.* 'East Friesland'	3
53. *Iris pallida albomarginata* (Variegated iris)	3
54. *Lychnis coronaria* (Rose campion)	5
55. *Physostegia virginiana* 'Variegata' (Variegated obedient plant)	5
56. *Lavatera* 'Barnsley'	1
57. *Hibiscus syriacus* 'Diana'	1
58. *Buddleia* x 'Lochinch'	1
59. *Clematis* 'Hagley Hybrid'	1
60. *C. viticella* 'Etoile Violette'	1

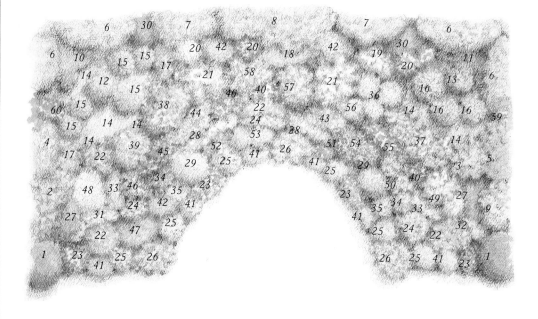

THE PAINTERLY GARDEN

Gardeners who love flowers and color and abundance can glean invaluable lessons from Monet for, with minor modifications, many an unfocused garden could have as distinctive a presence as Giverny. Lively but formless groupings gain strength when key plant combinations are echoed several times. Important color runs may be woven repeatedly, using different plants, if desired. Though a geometric setting will give any planting definition, stern lines may want softening with a free-form curve or two where architecture or landscape is informal. Here, the gentle colors of catmint quell what might otherwise be a riot of color into an orderly yet relaxed outpouring of bloom which continues from spring till frost. The border, on its longest sides, is thirty feet (9 meters) by forty feet (12 meters).

PLANT	# USED
1. *Nepeta* x *faassenii superba* (Catmint)	6 (6 times)
2. *Aster* x *frikartii*	6 (3, 3)
3. *Salvia officinalis* 'Purpurea' (Purple sage)	2 (2 times)
4. *Zinnia* 'State Fair'	(annual filler)
5. *Papaver orientale* (salmon and pink)	12 (4, 4, 4)
6. *Iris*, tall bearded, yellows and creams	12
7. *Iris*, tall bearded, lavender and blue	12
8. *Hemerocallis* 'Ice Carnival'	3
9. *Echinops* (Globe thistle)	4
10. *Perovskia* (Russian sage)	5 (5 times)
11. *Gaura lindheimeri*	3 (3 times)
12. *Stachys byzantina*	15
13. Strawberries	15 (2 patches)
14. *Allium schoenoprasum* (Chives)	15 (2 patches)
15. *Dianthus* 'Little Bobby'	5 (2 patches)
16. *D.* 'Painted Beauty'	7 (2 patches)
17. *D.* 'Garnet Star'	5 (2 patches)
18. *D.* 'Raspberry Tart'	7 (2 patches)
19. *Heuchera* 'Purple Palace'	4 (4 times)
20. *Coreopsis* 'Moonbeam'	12 (6, 6)
21. *Sedum* 'Autumn Joy'	5
22. *S.* 'Honeysong'	5
23. *Hemerocallis* 'Prairie Blue Eyes'	3
24. *Achillea* 'Moonlight'	6 (3, 3)
25. *A.* 'Hope'	3
26. *Kniphofia* 'Primrose Beauty'	6 (3, 3)
27. *Gaillardia* x *grandiflorum* 'Burgundy'	10 (5, 5)
28. *Thalictrum* 'Hewitt's Double'	2 (2 times)
29. *Monarda* 'Prairie Night'	6 (3, 3)
30. *Hosta* 'Sum and Substance'	3
31. *Cornus florida* 'Cherokee Sunset'	2
32. *Lysimachia nummularia* 'Aurea' (Golden creeping Jenny)	12
33. Tree peony (purple)	1
34. Tree peony (yellow)	1
35. *Miscanthus sinensis* 'Zebrinus' (Zebra grass)	1
36. *Stipa gigantea*	1
37. *Rosa* 'Just Joey'	1
38. *R.* 'Graham Thomas'	1
39. *R.* 'Climbing Butterscotch'	1
40. *R.* 'Golden Showers'	1
41. *R.* 'Amber Queen'	1
42. *R.* 'Harison's Yellow'	1
43. *R.* 'Peace'	1
44. *R.* 'Sonia'	1
45. *Clematis tangutica*	1
46. *C.* 'Will Goodwin'	1
47. *C.* 'Lady Betty Balfour'	1
48. Regal lilies (100) with fennel (maybe 5 of these)	3 groups
49. Asiatic lilies (100) with *Cosmos* 'Seashells' (make an even mixture, as the cosmos will carry on after the lilies go, overlapping just a bit)	2 groups

CONTEXT: GARDENING WHERE YOU LIVE

Most of the great gardens owe some of their merit to their setting, illustrating the positive value of context. Most of us, however, must garden where we live, whether or not it is an attractive and gardenworthy spot. Where the setting is unfortunate we can take another page from those great gardens, remembering that when the setting is inappropriate or ugly we can give the garden its own setting, creating a new reality where we choose to ignore the larger landscape. Making a delightful garden with connoisseur's plants nestled into the supportive framework of house (or castle), walls, and hedges is a bit like cooking with lobster, fresh cream, and a good vintage wine; it is pretty hard to go wrong. In North America,

however, the gardener is more likely to be dealing with a suburban tract house than a Sissinghurst. In making a garden, he or she may prefer to enclose it without reference to the house, as Major Johnston did at Hidcote, or even go so far as landscape designer Beatrix Farrand, who covered the walls of her country home in Maine with handsome trellising to support vines and climbing plants, obliterating the house rather than emphasizing it.

This is not to say that American settings are not inherently gardenworthy; there are gracious old houses and comfortable farms as well as airy beach cottages, rough-hewn cabins, and even sturdy urban workman's bungalows that are not without charm. However, whereas England is a small and long-settled country (about the size of Illinois) with a comparatively homogeneous climate and land-

Above: *This small, stone-flagged corner of the garden at the Priory in Kemerton, Worcestershire, provides an intimate sitting area where old-fashioned pinks and primroses can be admired at close range.*
Right: *A vegetable wall of clipped yew provides a sturdy architectural setting for clouds of flowers in the kitchen garden at Tintinhull. The relaxed planting includes self-sown seedlings that soften the lines of the doorway, helping to link the two adjacent gardens, and beckon the visitor invitingly onward.*

scape, North America is huge, fantastically varied in both climate and scenery, and still rough around the edges. Magnificent gardens await the making, gardens that echo the soaring firs and sharp mountains of the Pacific Northwest, the crashing coast of California, the umbrous, secret mountains and deserts of the Southwest, the lush, almost tropical Southeast. There will never be a single American garden style, for every region has its own flavor, its own set of plants that thrive, its gardeners who love the land and are sensitive to its beauties.

However that may be, those who don't love it are not bound to reflect a landscape they cannot admire. Unless we are willing to link our gardens to our landscapes, we do better to turn inward, making enclosed havens, our own personal paradises, for in the original Persian, the word "paradise" signifies an enclosed or walled garden. In England every garden, big and tiny, is enclosed with a wall and often a hedge as well. Open American lots need similar definition before they can offer the comfort and privacy that give English gardens their particular out-of-the-world quality. Although the massive evergreen hedges of the English estate gardens are too bulky to fit comfortably in little urban lots and suburban yards, gardeners might profit from studying Major Johnston's tapestry hedges in Hidcote.

Tapestry hedges have several advantages over plain ones. To the flower lover, hedges of blooming shrubs and small trees are of more interest than stolid yew. To the collector, they offer the chance to grow still more kinds of plants. Informal mixed hedges appeal to the busy gardener because they require less care and pruning than sheared hedges. Even in the smallest yard, all the beloved shrubs of spring—lilac and quince, forsythia and spiraea—which take up so much room in the flower beds can be mingled with evergreens around the perimeters of the property. In North America the overgrown shrubs now lumped at the feet of houses as foundation plantings can be moved to mark the outer, rather than the inner, limits of the property. The evergreens in the mixture—broad-leaved rhododendrons and mountain laurels, brooms and daphnes, andromedas and slim, columnar conifers—will delineate the garden in winter, form a protective barrier between us and our neighbors, and provide a substantive framework for our flowers in their seasons.

Every climate zone will have its favored plants, evergreen and otherwise, that may easily replace the ones mentioned. In North America the important thing is not to zealously copy the actual plantings of the English gardens, but to reproduce the elements that make them places to be in their own right. Once the garden space is defined, its outer perimeters delineated, the subdivision into sections or smaller "rooms" will come naturally, reflecting the way we use and move through the garden. As we shape our flower beds we can take advantage of the many microclimates created by hedges and walls, finding spots where tender things may now thrive.

Perhaps the most important contextual point is that we must adapt what we love and admire from great gardens to our own without trying to imitate them directly. Our gardens, too, must be intimate environments that suit our needs.

COHERENCE: MAKING OUR GARDENS OUR OWN

What we can best extrapolate from the great gardens are principles of composition. Most of the gardens vary a good deal within themselves; with relative formality nearest the house and wilder, more natural plantings on the outskirts of the properties. Although the nature of the planting changes, the character does not because all great gardens are children of a powerful, personal vision, and all have an interior consistency that carries through every part. Great gardeners develop planting styles as distinctive as most people's wardrobes, for gardens reveal truths of taste in exactly the same way as one's outfits and coordinated accessories do. In looking at Hidcote and Tintinhull, it is easy to see that they are related, yet each is stamped with the character and taste of its maker. What Johnston worked out on a large scale Mrs. Reiss reinterpreted in miniature; in our own gardens we can do exactly the same thing, each time with different and utterly personal results.

The lessons of Hidcote and the other great gardens are useful, indeed almost indispensable tools for the garden maker, yet none should be twisted into inflexible rules. Gardens made by the rules usually show it, and once we have gone through our training course we probably do better to trust our own eyes than rely on an arbitrary yardstick. Flower

North of Montreal, wild woods merge with carefully managed woodland plantings and wildflowers in Frank Cabot's garden. The transition from natural wilderness to the groomed lawns and formally shaped borders near the house is gradual and incremental rather than overt.

gardens need definition, but whether we choose to outline them with angular, sheared hedges or loose, flowering ones will depend entirely on our personal predilections, coupled with our intelligent observations. If you find yourself completely at a loss, find a professional who makes gardens you feel at home in and invest in some expertise. Don't feel you must implement all of the suggestions, or even any of them, right away, but study the plan until you understand it, then adapt it to your own ends, letting your own taste be your final guide. The result may not be textbook perfect, but if it suits you, delights you, and makes you long to be in it, that garden can only be called a success.

Once you have seen a good number of gardens it becomes second nature to analyze, however informally, their strengths and weaknesses. It is important to remember while you do this that most of the gardens open to the public are mature, whereas our own are apt to be young. What we instinctively feel is right for our garden probably is, and quite often both plans and plants that are impetuously dis-carded as failures are simply immature. Patience will be the anxious garden maker's best friend, patience and what Abraham Lincoln called the key to happiness—the ability to overlook. Gardens can be as awkward as adolescents while they grow. The wise, gardener and parent alike, take pleasure in the present whenever possible and trust in the wonderful properties of time. Along the way they overlook a good deal, realizing that it takes time to develop character and distinction, whether in a human or in a garden.

Garden making takes and deserves time. If the garden refuses to come together, take time to understand and refine your own inner vision. Look at the garden long, hard, and often. Act upon the evidence of your educated eyes, and you almost cannot help making the right garden for yourself. If you prefer sinuous curves, yet find yourself straightening out a certain border over time, your garden is probably teaching you that highly complicated plantings are best admired in an uncomplicated frame, or that a dash of formality is required to echo the long lines of the house.

Luxuriant masses of roses and flowering perennials are balanced by shrubs with interesting leaves and attractive foliage plants to extend the season of interest at Tintinhull House.

Once an alteration of this sort has been made, the transitional areas at either side may well need attention if they are to work with the old sections yet correspond to the new. Perhaps a pair of small evergreens could mark the ends of this more formal area, dividing it from more casual plantings; there are many possible solutions, but what ultimately matters most is twofold, the unity of the garden as a whole and your own satisfaction with it.

COLOR: ART IN THE GARDEN

The phrase "gardener's palette" refers as often to the range of plants used as to the actual colors favored in a given garden. The concerted flow of color through the garden, the color contrasts and color harmonies that obsess modern gardeners, are comparatively recent preoccupations that have gained force over the last hundred and fifty years. Before that, most flower gardens held a "riot of color" at the height of their season, and nobody worried much about the relationship of tonal values and color echoes.

The first recorded herbaceous (perennial) borders were made during the middle of the nineteenth century, and the growing interest in orchestrated color effects can be said to have developed in tandem with that in perennials. The outspoken garden writer William Robinson and many others encouraged the trend, but Gertrude Jekyll, the planter of Hestercombe and a sensitive, creative colorist, proved the most influential, laying out the definitive ground rules in her many books, particularly *Colour in the Flower Garden*, first published in 1908.

Like Monet, Jekyll was a trained artist with an eye for both form and color. She did not scorn any color, but prescribed the ways in which "difficult" colors, such as yellow, orange, and magenta, should be grouped and handled. She tempered bright hues with soft ones, and mellowed hot, heavy tones with gray, gentle blues, and chalky yellows rather than flat whites, which made too harsh a contrast. Jekyll's transitions were smooth, graded, and always harmonious, and she liked to re-

fresh the eye with restful, cool combinations between color climaxes. Using choice plants selected as much for their form and foliage as for flower color, she pioneered the highly sophisticated color schemes that continue to shape the twentieth-century English garden.

Jekyll taught several generations of gardeners the value of foliage as the firmest anchor for flowers, and to assist the flow of color through the seasons with their own tints. She mothered the concept of single color gardens, such as the white gardens at Hidcote and Sissinghurst, as well as color theme gardens in which two or three related colors would dominate. Though she had a somewhat didactic voice, she was the first to say that a slavish adherence to artificial rules could ruin a garden, pointing out that if a finishing touch of peach would improve a blue-and-white scheme, it was far better to bend a rule for the sake of the garden than to stick to the letter of the law.

At Giverny Monet knew no rules. He did precisely what looked right, not worrying a bit about theories or harmony, but relying entirely on his eye. His garden had little influence on the English, but did establish the tradition of the painterly garden in which plants are used to create massed effects, the key plants and combinations often as charac-

teristic as brushwork. Often sophisticated in terms of color, they are generally less so in plantmanship; most are by no means collector's gardens, though of full and assured beauty. My mother, who paints enormous, spare landscapes as well as sumptuous garden pictures, has an exceptional painterly garden—cheerful, crowded, and always full of flowers, with everything beautifully grouped and massed according to her instinct and eye. She, like Monet, is an advocate of the "no bad plants" school, which teaches that any plant of any color can look great, given the proper setting and companions. Her garden, which is in chilly Spokane, Washington, combines elements from both English and American garden traditions in its design. Besides wide gravel walks and rough-hewn wooden steps, fieldstone walls, and hedges of lilac, her garden holds enough evergreens to remain evocative and welcoming even in winter.

ABUNDANCE: PLANTING WITH A GENEROUS HAND

In all of the great flower gardens the same lesson is clear: Plant with a generous hand. Nowhere will we see bare earth or skimpy plantings, nor will we see straight rows of

In my mother's garden, a painterly sea of blossoms calls the visitor out of the house to wander along wide gravel paths, where every few steps reveal new vistas and every season brings fresh charms.

tightly trussed plants. What we see are controlled, naturalistic plantings that look completely comfortable, overlapping without overwhelming each other. Plants are mingled, often closely grown, yet the strong are not allowed to trample the meek. Shrubs are thinned to emphasize their natural shape, but suckers are rigorously removed. Self-sown seedlings are encouraged, yet never given their heads entirely; judicious thinning keeps the population down and ensures attractive placement. Perennials are set out in large clumps with smaller divisions tucked in nearby, threaded into and through neighboring plants to give the impression of a naturally spreading colony. Where quick colonizers run too freely their wandering children are kept firmly at bay. Through many such interventions, the balance of plants in a tightly planted border is maintained.

Though simple, planting with generosity is a hard rule to carry out until you are very familiar with your plants. Unless you are pretty sure what your plants will do, it is fatally easy to miscalculate; the only way to learn how to combine plants well is through experimentation. There will certainly be a few failures along the way, yet they are temporary and easily put right. Though most garden writers advise ample spacing, I personally prefer to overplant my borders, packing in far too many plants. This gives a lovely abundant look right away, but means that nearly everything needs moving or dividing within a few years. Since I am always refining and changing my garden, this prospect does not daunt me one bit.

In the newest beds, the spaces between young shrubs and perennials are filled with armloads of annuals—sweet peas, mignonette and fragrant nicotianas, dusky purple salvias and clary sages in pink or white, blue love-in-a-mist, and green bells of Ireland. This, too, gives a full and colorful look to the beds, most satisfying to the impatient who do not want to wait the five or ten years it takes for a properly planted border to mature.

MAKING A FLOWER GARDEN: TEN STEPS TO SUCCESS

1. *Define your space.*
This step is like putting up the walls of a room; it gives you observable boundaries within which to work.

2. *Determine the aim of your garden.*
With a clear goal, it becomes easier to plan and make choices. Is it to be a summer, year-round, or spring/fall garden? If you vacation all summer, have your garden perform when you are home to enjoy it.

3. *Know your plants.*
Before you can use plants well, you must be aware of the possibilities. You can learn from seeing plants in gardens, books, and nurseries, but the best experience comes from growing plants yourself. A nursery bed can hold unfamilar newcomers until you are able to place them where their natural tendencies are assets.

4. *Make each plant earn its place.*
Where space is at a premium every plant should contribute actively to the garden's beauty for as long as possible. Duds should be evicted ruthlessly.

5. *Choose a color theme.*
Broad or narrow, a seasonal color plan simplifies choices and placement and contributes a good deal toward keeping the garden coherent.

6. *Plant in size order.*
Begin planting the beds with the largest plants, work in the midsized shrubs and large perennials, then add the small plants last. It's just like getting dressed—foundation first.

7. *Give each bed a focal point.*
All the great gardens have at least one stunning plant group that photographs well. It is usually a strong, simple combination—one major architectural plant surrounded by large groups of one or two smaller plants. A single big picture can focus an entire small garden, but larger gardens will need one for each section.

8. *Stay in control.*
Relaxed planting requires vigilant grooming and frequent but subtle intervention. Flower gardens should look natural, yet nature must never control the garden.

9. *Make low maintenance the key to more, not less.*
The whole point of tricks and gadgets is not to get you out of the garden but to allow you to create more interesting plantings within it.

10. *Have fun.*
Above all, flower gardens are for pleasure. Whenever the garden stops being a positive pleasure it's time to reevaluate both goals and methods.

Above: *A profusion of well-grown delphiniums seen against the firm background of a dusky hedge makes a brief yet unforgettable display in Cabot's Canadian garden.*
Left: *Here, in one of Frank Cabot's borders, flowers are arranged in artful, pleasing clusters, appearing much as they might in a vase.*

CHAPTER SIX

TROPICAL GARDENS

Everything about the tropics is new and exciting to visitors from more temperate climates. The landscape often contains coconut palms bending over pristine white beaches, clipped tea plantations, high mountain coffee farms, flooded paddy fields, or jungle timber mills. Animals working in the countryside may include lanky mules, wallowing water buffaloes, and lumbering elephants.

The tropical garden is set with tall columnar palms, stately mahoganies, and spreading saman trees that create a vast canopy of shade from the intense, directly overhead sun. Frothy tree ferns, broad-leaved heliconias, and graceful gingers create a second level of shade for the wildly shaped and sometimes intensely colored tropical flowers. The architecture of the low, open tropical house—with its inviting verandas and private courtyards—allows the foliage and flowers of the garden to drift and mingle with indoor spaces.

The flowing sari, the pleated sarong, or the crisply starched guabera is often the garment of choice for the tropical gardener. Evidence of other fauna flourishing within the confines of the tropical garden may include the chattering of monkeys, the bagpipelike drone of the cicada, chirping frogs plopping into water, the swish of bats, a flash of bright bird wings, or the flicker of green lizards.

DEMYSTIFYING THE TROPICAL GARDEN

To the uninitiated, the *idea* of a tropical garden may be overwhelming: at first thought, rather casually carved from the jungle—incredibly, almost suffocatingly lush; weirdly, garishly floriferous, and perhaps just "too natural" to be a "real garden."

Tropical gardens are rarely mentioned in

general garden history books, relatively few books devoted to tropical gardens are available on bookstore shelves, and gardening and shelter magazines of broad distribution seldom cover gardens of the tropics. But like gardens in other latitudes, the tropical garden is an artifice of man—a living, artistic creation rendered in manipulated materials. Like gardens everywhere, it is a place of refuge, comfort, and beauty. As with any garden, from Versailles to the most humble cottage garden, once the tropical garden is understood in terms of design and content, it becomes an integral and enjoyable part of the overall appreciation of gardening.

The paradox of the tropical garden is aptly described by Dr. Alfred Byrd Graf, horticulturist, botanist, and plant explorer specializing in the earth's tropical regions, and author of the definitive work on tropical flora—the huge, two-volume *Exotica*. He writes: "The Tropics, because of the romance surrounding them, are frequently not truly understood. We imagine them as overflowing with color and exotic treasures, coddled by comfortable warmth, humidity, and sunshine. This is only true in part. The equatorial rainforest is not colorful. Typically it is a luxuriating scene of varied foliage in shades of green—an occasional bright spot the exception. Nor is the climate so ideal."

Although gardeners in temperate climates may scoff that the tropics are just one big garden anyway, the notion of "tropical paradise" is misleading. In his book on the exploration of the Pacific, *Lost Paradise*, Ian Cameron describes Polynesia in words that are true of any tropical region: ". . . the beauty of the . . . [cultivated] countryside bears little more relation to Nature than the beauty of the English countryside. The pre-Europeans . . . may indeed have lived in a Garden of Eden, but the garden was planted and tended by man."

WHAT IS INCLUDED AND WHAT WAS LEFT OUT

If ever to be published and read, any book is a finite project. In choosing what tropical gardens to include, it was decided that "tropical" would be strictly defined as those areas falling between the Tropic of Cancer (the parallel of latitude 23½ degrees north of the equator and the northernmost latitude reached by overhead

Previous page: *A thatched shepherd's hut perches above a tropical garden renovation in progress near Nykuning, Bali.*
Left: *In the Tavares garden in the Dominican Republic, mature specimens of* Vanda *orchids send sprays of flowers six feet (almost 2 meters) into the air, providing bright spots of color among the many shades of green foliage.*

Many tropical plants have become well known in temperate climates as houseplants or cosseted conservatory specimens. Wealthy Victorians had elaborate greenhouses and sponsored many plant-collecting trips to tropical areas. (Hothouse detail, Alessandro Saquirico, 1826, The Metropolitan Museum of Art, Harris Brisbane Dick Fund, 1939—39.54)

sun) and the Tropic of Capricorn (23½ degrees south of the equator and the southernmost latitude reached by overhead sun).

Within this 3,230-mile- (5,198-kilometer-) wide belt encircling the earth, there is a relatively mean temperature influenced by elevation, ocean currents, and rainfall. Although the flux of spring, summer, autumn, and winter does not occur here, there are two distinct tropical seasons. The wet season, occurring roughly between June and November with temperatures from 68° to 90° F (18° to 34° C), is marked by a high relative humidity. The dry season, falling between December and May, is cooler, with low humidity, and temperatures somewhere in the 66° to 88° F (17° to 32° C) range.

TROPICAL GARDEN DESIGN

Garden design is greatly influenced by climate and cultural influences. In the tropics there is no need for the grand parterre that looks so colorful even in winter from the upper stories of a cozy château. Warm weather the year round allows the tropical house and garden to be intimately related. In Venezuela, indoor and outdoor space merge on open, verandalike exterior corridors; an interior patio in the Dominican Republic is open to the sky; sunny or shaded courtyards create outdoor Sri Lankan garden rooms; and, in the case of the wall-less Balinese compound house, house and garden are separated by only a few steps.

Today most tropical gardens show the influence of colonial efforts as well as local habits. Foreign influence abounds in the tropics —just as it does everywhere else. Gardening is a cosmopolitan art, and garden history shows that almost every garden in the world is somehow influenced by other cultures. The manner in which distant customs and ideas of beauty are interpreted locally is a complex but fascinating part of the study of gardens.

Personal taste and skill in tropical design are what make the gardens individual. Water and shade elements, walls, paths, and garden structures are all a part of design—these and others form the embellishments added to any personal landscape.

TROPICAL GARDEN PLANTS

Some tropical areas claim more than a hundred thousand native plant species. In contrast, Hawaii technically has no native plants. (The islands were originally bare lava cones gradually softened by plants that had traversed two thousand miles of salt water.) When considering that tropical plants may require varying degrees of sunlight, ranging from full sun daily, to partial sun, all the way to no sun at all, it's obvious that the gardener in the tropics chooses his or her trees, shrubs, and flowers just like gardeners elsewhere. Some garden plants are native, many are imported, some have religious significance, some are grown as rarities, but most amateur gardeners anywhere grow plants because of their individual aesthetic appeal.

The flora of the tropical garden may seem a little strange at first glance, but upon closer inspection, anyone who has ever visited a florist or grown a houseplant will find that many of the plants are familiar. Some are even old favorites. Palms, impatiens, begonias, ferns,

orchids, dieffenbachias, arums, jasmine, gardenias, bamboos, shrimp plants, four-o'clocks, poinsettias, hibiscus, and many other plants that are found in pots in temperate zones just grow bigger (and better) in the tropical garden.

THE GARDENS: WHY AND WHERE

Because the tropical zone girds the entire planet, there is an amazing diversity among the gardens presented here. After attempts to group the gardens according to size, whether private or public, whether classic or modern, or by any other method, it became clear that the gardens naturally fell into order only when examined country by country. This is the way they were explored, and because of cultural influences, this is the way they make sense.

Included here are some seaside gardens and some located at higher elevations. A few are the works of garden designers specializing in tropical gardens, but most are the personal expressions of amateur gardeners. Most of the

The graceful lotus is a religious symbol in the East. All parts of the plant are edible. This water garden in Ubud, Bali, open to the public, stands between the Lotus Café and an ancient temple.

Bevis Bawa's garden, named Brief, is located near Bentota on the southwest coast of Sri Lanka. In this courtyard brightly colored bougainvillea enlivens a peaceful black reflecting pool.

gardens included are privately owned, a few are public botanic gardens and parks, and one is that intriguing combination of public and private, the hotel garden. Of the fourteen gardens included, each visited and photographed during early 1990, only a few have been published before. The six locations—Sri Lanka, Singapore, Bali, Hawaii, Venezuela, and the Dominican Republic—allowed exploration of many, but definitely not all, of the most interesting and beautiful tropical gardens existing today.

SRI LANKA: ANCIENT TRADITIONS AND MODERN REALITIES

The island of Sri Lanka, formerly known as Ceylon, has high interior mountains that gradually fall toward the wide white beaches of the Indian Ocean. In proportion to its size, Sri Lanka's botanical wealth, at least four thousand species, is equal to that of any other tropical country.

Although a cosmopolitan island, Sri Lanka has always been affected by its proximity to India. Its gardens exhibit touches of ancient Indian culture, as well as the garden traditions of the Mogul Empire. In the nineteenth century, the English introduced a plantation economy that drastically changed the natural landscape, but helped this island gradually move toward its place in the modern world as an international trader and tea supplier.

The ancient Indian landscape was marked by that country's lack of water. Tanks filled with flat, still water dotted the countryside. The ancient Hindus decorated their dry gardens with stone friezes, carved guardstones, and intricate moonstones inscribed with Buddhas and processional elephants. Later, Moguls from hilly, stream-fed regions conquered the country and began building their own gardens. They created reminders of their homeland by constructing long flat waterfalls and wide terraces featuring distant views.

Although none of the ancient classical gardens remain intact today, Sri Lanka's eminent garden designer, Bevis Bawa, has used many

these elements in the design of his stunning private garden, Brief. *The Oxford Companion to Gardens*, edited by Geoffrey Jellicoe et al., mentions the work of Bevis Bawa and his architect brother, Geoffrey, stating that "The finest modern gardens on the island are the ones they created for themselves," and although Brief is modern in age (begun in 1929), it has a distinctly classic atmosphere. It is located on the southwest coast, and the views along the road from Colombo to Brief are exactly the same as those described by plant explorer Dr. David Fairchild in 1938: "As the setting sun shimmered on myriad palm fronds, the fishermen were beaching their catamarans. Surely no tree exceeds the coconut palm in grace of form, and no place is more romantic than a coconut grove when the breezes rustle through the big green plumes and breakers roll up on the beach."

The driveway to the house and garden is marked with two large guardstones and flanked by a long tunnel of foliage. The house is large and low, with outdoor corridors and courtyards that merge indoor and outdoor

space in tropical style. Although Bawa is now an octogenarian and somewhat infirm, with his six-and-a-half-foot (2-meter) frame elegantly draped in a sarong, his hospitable greeting from the vine-draped veranda declares that the artist is still very much in residence.

There are three distinct areas in Bawa's five-acre creation. The first to be seen is just below the veranda. A long series of flat waterfalls mirrors sky and foliage in the Mogul style. Pillars of dwarf bamboo gracefully wave along a hundred and twenty feet (36½ meters) of reflecting planes of water. The gentle cascade ends in a summer pavilion topped with a carved pineapple.

To the left of the manmade waterfall is a set of broad, classic steps leading down to an elegant circular water tank. The small clearing surrounding the tank is planted with giant bamboo and a leafy ground cover Bawa jokingly calls *bimpol* for its resemblance to the dwarf coconut palm.

The third main garden area is yet another terrace of steps leading to a square lawn. At the foot, beautifully carved elephants parade

Above: *Bawa designed this long staircase to emphasize his classic circular pool. Sri Lankan gardens often show the influence of this island country's proximity to India, where flat, still bodies of water were a feature in ancient landscapes.*
Opposite page: *Sheila Sathananthan's garden outside Colombo, Sri Lanka, has broad green lawns that end at a canal of quiet water. Visible beyond the pot of green leaves is a double-flowered pink bougainvillea and a single-flowered red species, both trained as standards.*

around a moonstone, a configuration inspired by ancient Hindu art. From this terrace, tunnels of leaves mark pathways through the "forest" surrounding the garden. Also, from the highest stairs, broad views of surrounding paddy fields and coffee tree farms offer a panorama of the world beyond this tropical retreat.

Various bamboos and palms form a high, shady canopy decorated with colorful flamboyants *(Delonix regia)* and large specimens of *Dracaena*. A variegated variety, native to Sri Lanka and nicknamed Pride of India, is a dramatic evergreen with yellow- or cream-striped leathery leaves, and is very popular throughout the tropics as a showy garden shrub. Other golden tones shine from long strands of allamanda vine *(Allamanda cathartica)* from South America, showering sunny, velvety flowers from sky to earth.

Underneath the canopy are over fifty varieties of ferns, interspersed with many plants that are familiar to anyone who grows houseplants—dieffenbachia, aluminum plant *(Pilea cadierei)*, and Madagascar periwinkle

(Catharanthus). Among the more unusual flowers is the weird but compelling maroon-black blossom of the bat flower *(Tacca integrifolia)*. Tucked away in a dark corner of a secluded courtyard, this flower is almost too aptly named for comfort.

Whereas Bawa's garden is the classically inspired Sri Lankan country retreat, the modern suburban garden of Sheila Sathananthan honors certain traditions within a clipped modern vernacular. As one turns from a busy street on the outskirts of Colombo, a long wall with tiny green-leaved vines and standing pots of bougainvillea provides privacy for the peaceful entryway. Near the front door, the gray twisted trunk of a beautiful temple tree, or frangipani *(Plumeria)*, rises above variegated ground cover. Large Chinese jars, originally used for collecting latex, nestle at the base of the trunk and give homage to one of Sri Lanka's biggest industries. Rabbit's foot and maidenhair ferns create a soft green background to the boldly marked "face" of *Alocasia* × *amazonica*.

From the dramatic plantings of red- and

yellow-flowered heliconias at the rear of the house, broad lawns sweep toward a still canal of water. Beautiful specimen plants fill hundreds of pots throughout the garden. Ornamental trees, such as *Tabebuia rosea*, sealing-wax palms *(Cyrostachys)*, and araucarias provide vertical interest to the flat garden, and trees grown for their edible fruits—mango, cashew, breadfruit, rambutan, and jackfruit —add further shady areas.

Sathananthan is an accomplished amateur gardener. Wearing a flowing silk sari as she clips a wayward branch from a standard bougainvillea with double blossoms, she points to a nearby five-foot- (1½-meter-) long reptile that is sunning himself on the banks of the canal. The animal looks like an ugly gray alligator, with a huge wide mouth curled in an ominous grin. She explains that the damage created among the plants by the lizards' strong, swishing tails is supposedly a bad omen for the household, but her laugh gives notice that she holds little fear of this superstition. Although reverent and cognizant of traditional ways, Sathananthan has created her garden to suit a modern Sri Lankan lifestyle.

Sri Lanka has two upland botanic gardens open to the public, and although they are now somewhat past their prime in certain areas, both remain beautiful and certainly horticulturally interesting.

Peradeniya Botanic Garden is located near

Kandy, a city that David Fairchild described fifty years ago as "the greatest tourist center of the tropics." Huge elephants, still used as work animals, lumber along roadways buzzing with speeding, honking cars, but, truthfully, the glory that was once Kandy is now somewhat faded.

Because the British plantation economy depended upon botanical research, this 147-acre botanic garden (elevation 1,550 feet, or 472½ meters) was established in 1821 in a bend of the Mahaweli-Ganga River. Peradeniya has more than ten thousand trees, and although most of them are labeled (and sometimes mislabeled), the names are often so outdated that further research by the amateur may be stymied. Magnificent specimens of trees, many endangered in the wild, are now at the peak of their maturity here.

A *Ficus religiosa*, or bo tree, sacred in India to Hindus and Buddhists, stands near a stately avenue of *Araucaria heterophylla*, the Norfolk Island pine, and *A. columnaris*, the New Caledonian pine. In another area, the large "flying buttresses" of the Java almond (labeled *Cannarium commune*) provide support for these enormously tall trees in shallow sandy soil.

The garden also contains three graceful palm avenues. The oldest is called the palmyra *(Borassus flabellifer)* avenue and was planted in 1887 with native African palms popular throughout the tropics as an ingredient in the making of strong toddy. In 1905 a second curved avenue, labeled cabbage palms, but probably *Roystonea oleracea*, was planted. The third avenue was planted in 1950 with the royal palm *(R. regia)* from Cuba.

A large cannonball tree *(Couroupita guianensis)* is hung with enough eponymous fruit to seemingly feed vast ranks of old-fashioned artillery. Nearby, a grove of leafless trees is full of thousands of fruit bats. Large as chickens, the bats' upside-down posture and loud whistling noises add an oddly comic-fright touch to the brightly sunlit gardens.

Traveling from Peradeniya to Nuwara Eliya, home of Hakgala Botanic Gardens, requires a long trip along tiny roads winding up into the tea plantation highlands. Here the entire landscape takes on the appearance of a manically tended shrub garden. Low green tea bushes form perfect mounds across red hillsides planted here and there with silk oak *(Grevillea robusta)*, dadop *(Erythrina subumbrans)*, and eucalyptus. Although the tea industry helped establish a modern economy,

deforestation of the mountains to make way for the plantations led to the extinction of the native Sri Lankan elephant's habitat.

Located at an elevation of 6,200 feet (1,890 meters), Hakgala Botanic Gardens was founded in 1861 as an experimental cinchona plantation. (The bark of this tree is a source for quinine. This area of Sri Lanka was selected for its cultivation because of its similarity to the highlands of Peru where cinchona grows naturally.) Fifty-five acres in extent, the gardens contain the romantic remains of a once fine collection of flower gardens set among beautiful trees and sweeping hillside lawns. The wild garden features giant tree ferns *(Cyathea)*, including the woolly tree fern that has flourished on earth for over 250 million years. As wild wanderoo monkeys swing and chatter through the trees, regret over the gradual loss of the gardens is offset by the wonderful realization that the primeval atmosphere at Hakgala has been deliciously preserved.

SINGAPORE: PALMS AND ORCHIDS

In contrast to the genteel decline of Sri Lanka's botanic gardens is the modern hustle and bustle of the Singapore Botanic Gardens. Singapore is located in the Malay archipelago in the South China Sea, and this island

Left: *Hakgala Botanic Gardens, founded in 1861, is located near Nuwara Eliya at an elevation of 6,200 feet (1,890 meters). Tree ferns and wild monkeys create an exotic atmosphere in the fernery.*
Right: *The palm symbolizes and sustains life in the tropics. Singapore Botanic Gardens' Palm Valley contains many of the world's finest palm specimens.*

nation is the most developed equatorial country in the world. Towering skyscrapers, a thriving economy, and general prosperity place it very much in the center of a bustling new Asian world.

The climate in Singapore is one of the wettest on earth, and upon entering the 116-acre botanic gardens in early morning, one finds that the moist, springlike atmosphere makes a pleasant contrast to the hot asphalt outside the gates. Large, well-tended lawns sparkle with dew, and beautiful specimens of wrightia (an Old World tropical tree) and scented plumeria vie for attention next to the magnificent coral inflorescence of *Amherstia nobilis* (considered by many to be the world's most beautiful tree). When laid out in 1822, the gardens were menaced by tigers, but today's animal life is less threatening, with the common birdwing butterfly *(Troides helena)* and bright blue white-breasted kingfishers *(Halcyon smyrnensis)* flying above small herds of fluorescent-clad joggers.

The botanic gardens were the dream of Sir Thomas Stamford Raffles. In a lifetime filled with interesting pursuits, he found time to make significant contributions to natural history and, for his efforts, was knighted. Also, a plant bearing the world's largest flower, *Rafflesia arnoldi*, was named in his honor. Raffles planted the first botanic garden in Singapore with a hundred and twenty-five trees and a thousand seedlings of *Myristica fragrans*, the conical tree that grows in the understory of the tropical forest and provides the spices nutmeg and mace.

After various stops and starts, the present location of the gardens was acquired in 1859. In 1888 Henry Nichols "Rubber" Ridley became director, and led the tireless research that resulted in the efficient growing, tapping, and production of rubber. At the height of the "rubber rush" at the beginning of this century, the botanic gardens had distributed over seven million seeds of the para rubber tree *(Hevea brasiliensis)* and economic botany became very important to the prosperity of the entire country.

Jack Kramer, author of *World Wildlife Fund Book of Orchids*, writes: "Invariably the plants most people associate with the tropics are palms and orchids." The Singapore Botanic Gardens have beautiful displays and collections of both large families.

The palm is the root of all tropical life, providing essentials such as food, shelter, fuel, and fibers for weaving. Palms also contribute to the "extras in life," yielding spices, oils, gums, poisons, medicines, and intoxicating beverages. A former botanist of the garden,

C. X. Furtado, once pointed out that, using the trunk of a coconut palm, one could make a boat, and from other tree parts, outfit the vessel with "ropes, sails, cloth, flour, oil, sugar, wine, vinegar, spoons, brushes, drinking vessels, and more."

Among the intriguing trunks and green fronds of the botanic garden's Palm Valley, there are the rattan palm *(Calamus)*, the toddy palm or palmyra *(Borassus flabellifer)*, and the rare double coconut palm *(Lodoicea maldivica)* that produces the world's largest and heaviest seeds, about one foot (30½ centimeters) long and weighing between twenty-six and thirty-six pounds (12 and 16 kilograms). Elsewhere there is an avenue of sealing-wax palms *(Cyrostachys lakka)* with their bright scarlet leaf stalks that look like huge displays of open lipsticks. The graceful appearance of a huge clump of nibung palms *(Oncosperma tigillarium)* belies the fact that these trees possess the extremely durable wood necessary to construct the big fish traps of Southeast Asia called *kelongs*. Far from an unaesthetic collection of trees, the botanic gardens' Palm Valley and other palm groupings offer some of the coolest and most inviting spaces in Singapore.

Amazed by their fragile beauty or dazzled by their showy flowers, many forget that the delicate-appearing orchid is also a plant of significant economic value. The botanic gardens have been actively involved in the hybridization of this family of plants since 1925, helping to make Singapore one of the leading orchid suppliers in the world.

The orchid family is huge, with over thirty-five thousand species distributed (unevenly) over the world. The ancient Greeks associated the shape of its tubers with the human male sexual organs and concoctions made from them were used to treat various love-related maladies. The Aztecs used the vanilla bean from the orchid *Vanilla planifolia* to flavor chocolate long before Columbus came to America.

Orchids captured the imagination of Europeans when the first imported specimen flowered in England in 1733. For many decades after, subsequent orchid flowerings were often reported in newspapers. After the infamous mutiny on the *Bounty*, Captain Bligh was sent to the South Pacific to collect orchids and, between 1840 and 1850, England experienced a short-lived floral frenzy called orchidomania. Just as Holland's tulipmania had more to do with monetary speculation than

Singapore Botanic Gardens' collection of orchids contains more than twelve thousand plants. The gardens specialize in orchid hybridization, helping Singapore to be a world leader in the orchid trade.

horticultural appreciation, the orchid remained a relatively difficult plant for the ordinary grower.

In 1925 Singapore Botanic Gardens began a program of hybridization with particular emphasis on orchids. By the 1930s director Eric Holttum became the father of Singapore's orchid trade and a very important contributor to the development of the commercial cultivation of orchids throughout Southeast Asia.

In the past, Singaporeans complained that their botanic garden was "green, green, and more green," and ever responsive to public demand, the botanic gardens added a huge display area for orchids. Here there are masses of color provided by more than twelve thousand thriving plants. Four hundred endangered species are preserved, as well as more than five hundred named hybrids. The standards of the Singapore cut flower trade—*Dendrobium, Vanda,* and *Aranda*—are displayed alongside spidery *Arachnis*, butterfly-shaped *Oncidium*, mothlike *Phalaenopsis*, and corsage-sized *Cattleya*. The effect is stunning and probably unequaled in glory in the rest of the world.

Dr. Tan Wee Kiat is the current director of the gardens and a world-respected orchidologist. As he walks through the orchid shade house where much of his work takes place, he points out that the economic future of orchid breeding is very much on his mind. He plans to have the gardens develop further hybrids for commercial use and for landscaping public areas, but also wants to serve his local community by breeding orchids suitable for growing in the high-rise apartments that most Singaporeans inhabit.

Apart from the wonderful opportunity to learn about palms and orchids, the gardens offer other enjoyable areas. The herbarium is a leading center for taxonomic research and is open to interested members of the public. It contains over 600,000 specimens in dried, preserved, or spirit collections, and unlike many herbariums, is in a good state of repair. There is also a library containing more than twenty thousand botanical and horticultural books, most of them written in English. A rare book collection specializes in botanical works from the 1700s through the last century.

An especially poignant note in the gardens is almost ten acres of preserved rain forest. As one of the last stands on the island, its monkeys having only recently departed, its future usefulness is ensured. With much of the world's rain forest disappearing, Singapore is keeping this area as a reminder of the days when tigers roamed the island.

BALI: FRANGIPANI AND LOTUS

Bali is one of the 13,677 Indonesian islands. Between Bali and the Lesser Sundas is the Lombok Strait marking the Wallace Line—an imaginary line delineating the boundary between the habitats of Asiatic and Austronesia flowers and animals. Bali is, without doubt, one of the most beautiful places on earth.

Although Marco Polo visited the area in 1292, the first Europeans to set foot in Bali were Dutch sailors who landed in 1597. The entranced visitors were befriended by the king, who was described as "a fat, jovial man who surrounded himself with dozens of wives, owned fifty dwarfs as retainers, and drove a chariot drawn by white water buffaloes."

It is immediately obvious that summer and winter monsoons give Bali ample water. The countryside is full of deep, rushing brown rivers and bright green rice growing from curving, terraced paddies. Domesticated ducks and water buffaloes splash together in the flooded fields.

Fantastically carved temples and shrines appear nearly every hundred yards (91 meters), and outdoor studios for carvers, painters, and musicians are as frequently placed as

urban bus stops. Within the traditional Balinese domestic compound, older women still frequently follow the bare-breasted manner of dress.

The gardens of Bali are marked by the three pervasive qualities of Balinese culture: the daily observance of religious duties, deep respect for the creative artist, and adherence to traditional lifestyles.

In relatively undeveloped countries, where funding for such amenities as public parks and gardens is very limited, the hotel garden provides a unique opportunity for designing large, extravagantly planted, and well-maintained gardens that are (somewhat) available to the public. The Bali Hyatt at Sanur is a wonderfully executed example of tropical hotel garden style.

Australian Made Wijaya and his associate were hired in 1981 to elaborate upon thirty acres of garden originally laid out in a former coconut plantation. Entry to the garden is through the expansive open-air lobby constructed of coconut beams and thatched with ribbons of elephant grass. There is little to mark what is indoors and what is outdoors. As one walks through the lobby into the garden, pleasant gamelan music (played on an instrument that resembles a xylophone) gradually gives way to the swish of palm fronds and the sounds of water.

Wijaya describes this creation as "a splendidly ordered jungle," and within its confines are hundreds of tropical plants, neatly and correctly labeled. Waterways and lotus ponds sparkle between tall trees dripping with lush, large-leaved vines. Magenta bougainvillea grows rampant among white frangipani.

Open areas relieve any feelings of "horticultural oppression" and provide space for performances of the highly stylized Balinese dancing. Throughout the garden are primitive statues and several shrines protected by lacy, tasseled umbrellas. Here, as everywhere else in Bali, daily offerings of frangipani and fruit are placed on woven palm fronds.

Wijaya's own house and garden, located inland at Sayan, is another example of splendidly ordered jungle, but here on a much more intimate scale. This tropical "country" garden winds along paths past the various small wooden buildings that compose Wijaya's compound. Along a slate path are two rectangular pools filled with lotus, umbrella-shaped papyrus, and other water-loving plants.

Throughout the garden Wijaya has used

many beautiful crotons, the brightly colored trees and shrubs popular in the tropics. (Actually *Codiaeum*, they are unrelated to the true *Croton* genus that has no ornamental value at all, but everyone calls these showy plants crotons anyway.) The leaves of these plants are shiny and incredibly colored, looking as if a classroom of children had been set free in the garden with their crayons. Many shades of green, yellow, red, pink, orange, and even deep blue-black appear on thick, leathery leaves that resist wind tear more readily than more delicate foliage. Here they are set among red heliconias, purple bougainvillea, and blue-green and white aloes.

All this excitement of color ends abruptly at a small terrace that overlooks a deep river gorge terraced with paddy fields. In this borrowed landscape, the noise and turbulence of the rapids make a fantastic contrast to the still, quiet water of the rice fields. As the sunset spreads across the horizon toward high blue mountains in the distance, the sky lights up with all the colors of Wijaya's domesticated jungle.

At Puri Kaleran in Ubud, a young Australian-American couple has created an enclosed garden among the courtyards of a minor palace. (*Puri* means palace.) Gates, walls, and house are ornamented with elaborate Balinese carvings. The Balinese owners, from one branch of a former royal family, rent their traditionally styled compound to Lyn and Cody Shwaiko with the understanding that the old "queen-mother" will return periodically to make offerings at the family's ancestral shrine.

When Lyn first moved to the *puri* the prospects of a garden looked slim. Some Balinese practice a custom found in many hot regions (including southern areas of the United States) wherein the earth around the house is swept daily. This practice compacts the soil, keeping it clean and bare, and although trees and a few bushes may grow, there are no grass or flower beds to tend.

But the Shwaikos wanted a garden in their tropical home and, by continually building up and hand-sifting the soil, eventually they were able to introduce an abundance of flowers, ferns, and trees into the small courtyard areas that cuddle up within the compound. Lyn laughs about the long process saying, "This isn't the sort of place where one can just order a truckload of topsoil, but once it was all done I found out just how quickly a tropical garden will grow. Tiny little plants reach gargantuan sizes quickly, and baby ferns will sprout up everywhere, even on window ledges and the sides of other pots.

"The most difficult aspect of tropical gardening is to keep it all under control. Everything just grows and grows. Once a twelve-foot- [3½-meter-] tall frangipani blew down in a storm. As it lay on the ground and gradually lost all its leaves, I became attracted to the beautiful shape of its bare trunk. Eventually four people helped me shift the huge old skeleton and we decided to stick the trunk—which had snapped off flat at the ground and was about ten inches [25 centimeters] in diameter—upright into the ground like a piece of sculpture. Imagine our surprise when within a month, the entire tree had leafed out again. Today it flourishes and makes hundreds of flowers for the owners' temple decorations!"

Because frangipani—called temple tree in Old World parts of the tropics and *jepun* in Bali—is highly prized for offerings, it is easy to assume that this ubiquitous and highly scented tree is an Eastern Hemisphere native. Actually, it is a rather modern introduction, and the three species most common in Southeast Asia are native to tropical America. (Its genus name, *Plumeria,* derives from the name of Charles Plumier (1646–1706), a French botanist who traveled widely in those New World regions.)

Used medicinally in the seventeenth century as a diuretic and treatment for venereal diseases, frangipani was brought by the Spanish to the Philippines. It gradually spread to other Eastern countries and acquired entirely more appealing uses. Balinese carvers prize the wood highly and both men and women wear frangipani in their hair. Because its pretty blossoms fall from the tree while still fresh in appearance and keep a crisp, sweet composure and scent for days after, it is the perfect flower for the countless offerings made daily in temples.

Other plants in the Shwaiko garden include magnificent ferns. Two epiphytes (plants that do not root in the earth, but rather grow, in many cases, on the bark of another plant) that were once collected high in the mountains and now thrive at the *puri* are huge, spiky bird's-nest ferns and long, cascading staghorn ferns.

The staghorn *(Platycerium coronarium),* called *semun bidaduri* in Southeast Asia, creates its own hanging basket. Specialized downward-hanging leaves gradually die off and curl inward, holding and compressing accumulated debris against the plant's roots. Other long, drooping, branched leaves tumble off the root ball and give the plant its common name.

The bird's-nest fern has a more upright posture and, as its broad, pointed leaf looks like a human spleen, the Latin name *Asplenium nidus* was assigned. Asians call it *paku langsuyar* and it is well liked for its carefree habits.

Right: This lush garden was, until recently, the bare, swept-earth courtyard of a Balinese palace and temple. Lyn and Cody Shwaiko created their garden by hand-sifting the soil and planting native and exotic plants. Left: A frangipani blossom, here fallen from the tree onto the leaves of another plant, stays fresh and sweet-smelling when plucked. Although native to the Western Hemisphere, the trees are now ubiquitous in the East where the flowers are essential for making temple offerings.

The leaves serve as funnels to direct water and organic litter into the spongy mass at the center of the fern. From this the plant derives its nutrients and may grow as big as a medium-sized shrub.

The Shwaiko garden is filled with many "houseplant" flowers and shrubs, including a large variety of begonias and a few African violets exactly like those grown by Lyn's mother inside her Australian home. Large-leaved caladiums look as if they have been sprinkled with dots of red and white confetti, and tiny species orchids create a special sensation when they flower. Lyn says, "Although the flowers are not as showy as the hybrids, I know the day that they bloom as soon as I wake up—the entire compound fills with their fragrance." It is an entirely old-fashioned scent

for a newly created but old-fashioned garden.

A few houses away from Puri Kaleran in Ubud are the new house and modern garden belonging to photographer Rio Helmi. A well-traveled Indonesian, he rides a huge black motorcycle and often relaxes in a sarong. In the process of publishing a book on Balinese style, Helmi designed and built his compound adapting old traditions into a strikingly modern setting.

At the entrance to the garden, large stepping-stones curve and disappear behind a small slate wall that blocks views of the interior of the compound. This wall is called an *aling aling* and is traditionally used as a guard against evil spirits. The devilish little troublemakers cannot turn corners in the dark so the wall protects the compound against their entry during their nighttime witching hours.

Past the *aling aling* is a courtyard filled with flat, dark pebbles. Delicate trunks of bamboo sprout between the stones. This area is especially peaceful in the rain, when its only colors are shiny green and shiny black. Concrete stepping-stones, cast in bamboo frames to give bamboo impressions, lead to the other small buildings of the compound. These individually serve as a children's room, studio, master bedroom, guest quarters, and bathroom. Around a corner, the raised open platform that serves as the living room is completely open to a small but spectacular lotus pond and the bright green lawn beyond.

During the wet season curtains of rain dripping off the edges of the fringed thatched roof make the only wall between garden and house. Mercurylike drops of water are caught in the slightly cupped lotus leaves that stand about a yard above the surface of the water. The large clear pink flowers grow even taller than the leaves, rising at least a foot above the lofty foliage. In a heavy rain the flower cup slowly fills with water, and as it does, its long, slender stalk begins to sway back and forth with the extra weight. Eventually the flower rocks just enough to spill its contents back into the pond, and, released of its burden, slowly dances back to its original upright position. Then the process begins again, and with a pond full of lotus, the swaying and spilling of pink flowers is like an elaborately choreographed dance.

The lotus *(Nelumbo nucifera)* is an important religious symbol in the East. This fragrant flower has strong, earthy connections to male and female sexuality, and it is believed that Brahma was born from the lotus issuing from Vishnu's navel. Its connection with life-giving also probably arises from the fact that all parts of the plant are edible. The seed head, a flat-topped cup pierced with deep holes, protects its seeds. The stalk can be boiled or steamed like asparagus, and the rhizomes produce an easily digestible starch used in Oriental cooking.

Much of the symbolism and physical

Right: *Wijaya's own garden near Sayan features a terrace with a magnificent borrowed landscape of rice paddies and distant mountains.* Bottom left: *Like most tropical gardens, the Shwaiko garden in Ubud, Bali, contains many plants grown for their decorative leaves, such as these stunning caladiums.*

Left: *This garden on Kauai, Hawaii, was created fifty years ago by the Allerton family of Chicago. Formal elements, unusual in most tropical gardens, include a copy of Canova's* Diana *standing at one end of a pool edged in lava rock.*

Bottom left: *A gazebo standing in what the Allerton family called "the outdoor living room" is decorated with bronze castings purchased in Italy. The heads, copied from originals salvaged from the ashes of Mount Vesuvius, refer to Hawaii's volcanic origins.*

The waterway in the mermaid garden at Allerton Gardens was copied from the Villa Caprarola in Italy. Two mermaids, originally lighting fixtures on a steamship, face each other across a pool surrounded by palms and bamboos.

beauty of the lotus arises from its unusual growth habit. Unlike water lilies that float upon the surface of pools and streams, the pristine lotus flower pushes up from the mud and water where its roots are hidden. Whether one looks upon the lotus for physical or spiritual sustenance, it remains a tropical flower of special beauty and grace.

HAWAII: PRIVATE PARADISE AND THE NATIONAL TROPICAL BOTANICAL GARDEN

Tropical gardens of the Western Hemisphere have a distinctly different feel from those of the Eastern Hemisphere. Although the plants are basically the same, the design of New World tropical gardens is often closely linked to European garden traditions, Italian and Spanish sensibilities often prevailing.

In *Hawaii Is a Garden*, author Jeri Bostwick points out: "The Hawaiian Islands came boiling out of the earth's core . . . barren gray-brown mountains of lava towering 30,000 feet [9,144 meters] from the ocean bottom. Flowers and trees, so much a part of the islands today, arrived slowly. Some came on the wings of trade winds . . . some floated

on the crest of the ocean, some were carried by birds on their feathers, or rode with man on canoes, frigates, steamships, and planes. Each had crossed nearly 2,000 miles [3,220 kilometers] of ocean to produce the lush mountains and valleys where a practiced eye can count forty-three shades of green on a sunny day."

The Hawaiian Islands are equally distant from Asia and North America, and collectively form the only state in North America that falls between the Tropics of Cancer and Capricorn. Kauai, the northernmost island, receives the most rain and was long ago nicknamed "the garden island." It is here that Queen Emma built her summer house and garden in 1870.

Queen Emma, widow of King Kamehameha, built a tiny house on the cliffs of the Lawai valley on the south coast of Kauai. A keen gardener, she was responsible for many introductions to the islands, including bougainvillea species, mangoes, and tamarinds.

After she died the next owner respectfully moved her house from clifftop to valley floor, planting the hillside behind it with scarlet *Bougainvillea spectabilis*. In 1937, when Chicago philanthropist Robert Allerton and his architect son, John, visited the Lawai valley, the hills behind Queen Emma's house were bril-

liant red and her former garden was a sugarcane plantation. The Allertons decided immediately to buy the property. They built a house next to Queen Emma's and started a horticultural odyssey that today forms the Allerton Gardens and the National Tropical Botanical Garden. Both gardens are now open to the public.

Cecil Beaton visited Allerton Gardens in their prime and described them as "a masterpiece of tropical romanticism." Located on one hundred acres at the lowest end of the valley, a long series of garden rooms—decorated with European sculptures and exotic plants—winds along terraces in which taro was once cultivated. The Allertons took advantage of the terracing (and existing walls and water) in laying out their rooms, and as son John later explained, "Each garden is a surprise. One isn't anxious to reach an objective. . . . One is gradually led to see what is ahead." After meandering through the many rooms, the eventual destination is the wide beach and rolling breakers located beyond the house at the end of the valley.

The sound of water plays throughout the garden. A carved narrow waterway is modeled after the one at Villa Caprarola in Italy and is embellished with two bronze mermaids. The mermaids were originally lighting fixtures on the steamship *Columbus* and Allerton first saw them at the Italian exhibit at the 1939 New York World's Fair. He had them cast and now they frolic among bananas, bamboos, and palms.

Other European elements adapted to the exotic locale are a beautiful white pavilion overlooking a calm pool edged in lava paving. A copy of Canova's eighteenth-century *Diana* stands opposite the pedimented and latticed garden structure. Two oblique references to Hawaii's fiery origins are to be found in the Phoenix pavilion and in the cupids and busts cast from those originally found in the ashes from Vesuvius.

The Allertons had originally gardened at The Farms, their large estate in Monticello, Illinois, but obviously had no trouble learning the ways of tropical plants. The "walls" of their outdoor living room are planted with *Polyscias guilfoylei*, also known as panax or wild coffee, and the ceilings are the spreading branches of massive, but delicately leaved saman trees.

Bright tropical colors shine from the ti plant, or Hawaiian good luck plant *(Cordyline terminalis)*, and the matte turquoise florets of the jade vine *(Strongylodon macrobotrys)*. The light wine-colored flowers of the Queen Emma lily *(Crinum augustum)*, sprout on red stems from massive evergreen plants that can reach eight feet (2½ meters) in height and diameter. This huge plant, native to Mauritius and the Seychelles, has long swordlike leaves draped with silky burgundy-colored floss. It is a majestic tribute to the woman who introduced it to the island and cultivated it in her gardens.

Apart from the gardens he created for his family, Robert Allerton was determined to help establish a tropical botanical garden in Hawaii. Just before his death he contributed a million dollars to this cause and, in 1969, 186 acres of land were purchased. Adjoining the Allerton Gardens and rolling further up the Lawai Valley, the National Tropical Botanical Garden was established with the following goals: to study tropical plants of nutritional value, to conserve rare and endangered species, to develop tropical fruits, and to examine plants of unexplored potential.

The botanical garden has a variety of growing areas, including marshland, dry cliffs, shady woods, and open grasslands. The upper reaches are six hundred feet (183 meters) above sea level and receive significantly more rain (seventy inches [178 centimeters] yearly average) than regions closer to sea level (thirty inches [76 centimeters] annually). There are sweeping views of the steep valley cliffs covered in Australian pines *(Casuarina equisetifolia)* and Java plums *(Syzygium cumini)*, and the sounds of running water and birdsong echo throughout.

The National Tropical Botanical Garden has the world's foremost collection of *Erythrina* trees. Also called coral trees, they are beloved in hot climates for their showy flowers and their use in medicinal preparations, and here are undergoing carefully controlled hybridization. There is also an important collection of five hundred palm species, all started from seed as there now is a ban on importing live plant material to the islands for reasons of disease and pest control.

Throughout the gardens are many cultivars of brightly colored hibiscus, as well as four hibiscus species, including *Hibiscus waimae*, one of the rare scented hibiscus. Other perfumed rarities are found in a pond where the six-foot- (almost 2-meter-) wide leaves of the royal water lily *(Victoria amazonica)* float

There is no wall between the front of Helmi's living room and the garden. A small lotus pool is edged with concrete slabs cast in bamboo forms.

among large fragrant red-and-white flowers. Everywhere the secret scent of ilang-ilang *(Cananga odorata)* is released from wispy green flowers invisible in the tree's lofty canopy.

In a state where visitors are traditionally greeted with a beautiful lei of flowers, it is appropriate that the garden grows many of the plants used to make these floral necklaces. These include the crown plant *(Calotropis gigantea)*, pikake *(Jasminum sambac,* also used to flavor tea), and several deliciously sweet frangipanis.

The botanic garden has various satellite gardens throughout the islands, and maintains The Kampong in Florida, the former house and garden of Dr. David Fairchild, the horticulturist and plant explorer who described the coconut palm beaches of Sri Lanka earlier in this chapter.

VENEZUELA: FROM THE COLONIAL PERIOD TO ROBERTO BURLE MARX

The northern countries of South America, especially Colombia and Venezuela, serve as a linking habitat between the flora of Central America and that of the Amazon region. This area is noted for its partially dry, partially wet climate. Venezuela has a broad Caribbean coastline and high, cool forests where the temperature sometimes drops to 46° F (9° C). Here many epiphytes flourish and a single *Cattleya mossiae,* the Easter orchid, may produce as many as twenty-two flowers at one time.

Caracas, the capital of this former Spanish colony, is located three thousand feet (914 meters) above sea level. Although May through November is the rainy season and the remaining months are generally very dry and warm, temperatures remain fairly springlike throughout the year.

The city was founded in 1567 and shortly after, in 1590, the house and original garden at the Hacienda La Vega was established on a large land grant outside the town. Today this private estate remains in the hands of the original family, but where it was once surrounded by tropical forest and cane fields, it is now a refuge in the heart of an urban industrial area.

Although the garden has changed during its four hundred–year existence, the links to its Spanish heritage—and the Moorish and Italian influences that strongly affected garden styles in that European country—remain evident. Spanish-Moorish garden style is very important in the New World tropics and is also seen in semitropical parts of mainland North America, especially in California and

Hacienda La Vega was established in 1590 on a large land grant now completely surrounded by urban Caracas, Venezuela. Two grand corridors mix indoor and outdoor space in tropical style. Other interior-exterior spaces include several peaceful indoor patios influenced by Moorish traditions.

Florida. It differs from the Mogul style, discussed earlier, in that Moorish gardens do not have large pools of water or stylized waterfalls and are usually smallish, with an urban character. The traditional Moorish garden often had no grass and was enclosed by stuccoed walls. Tiles, paving, benches, and pots were meticulously arranged to establish a sense of order, coolness, and privacy.

At Hacienda La Vega the Spanish-Moorish influence is best preserved in indoor-outdoor spaces called corridors and patios. The magnificent corridors—one over ninety yards (82 meters) long, the other sixty (55 meters), and both at least eight yards (7 meters) wide—are marked with beautiful white columns and form two sides of the large, elegant tropical house. The shorter corridor is filled with dark furniture of the colonial period and faces the side garden. The longer corridor has many separate groupings of lacy white wickerwork furniture and opens onto the main garden. Potted ferns and orchids are arranged on tables and upon the beautifully tiled floors.

The interior patios create a sense of peaceful outdoors within the house. In one patio, tiled floors give way to a wide band of stone paving, and then onto grass. Here the plantings are restrained, with shrubs planted in the corners and large baskets of hanging ferns. A small, simple Moorish fountain in the center is accented with potted plants. Another patio is even more sedate, with pots of azaleas arranged on a tiled floor, their delicate flowers glowing like votive candles against the whitewashed walls.

The walled garden that surrounds the house and its exterior corridors was redesigned in 1640 to reflect a later trend in Spanish garden style. When Emperor Charles V (1516–56) built himself a new palace in the Italian style, he began a sixteenth-century Spanish craze for houses and gardens built in the same manner. This trend slowly drifted toward the Spanish colonies, and by the seventeenth century the gardens at Hacienda La Vega were remade in the Italian fashion. Four fountains and paths winding like ribbons decorate a lushly planted garden. About two hundred years later Victorian statues were added to further "modernize" the garden's look.

Today, from the fern- and orchid-festooned long corridor, there is a beautiful view into the main garden of a pair of delicately branched, pale orange frangipanis planted against massive, dark green cypresses. A brick-paved walk, scattered with the pale orange blossoms, leads to a central fountain. Swept-earth ribbon paths curl away from the main axis, and disappear around curves of tropical shrubs and trees.

Flowering trees in the garden include mauve-flowered jacarandas and showy ornamental acacias. Mango trees (*Mangifera indica*, cultivated for more than four thousand years), along with the cypresses, add evergreen elements to the garden. The lofty plumes of royal palms *(Roystonea)* are native to this part of South America, and at one end of the long corridor stands a large traveler's palm *(Ravenala madagascariensis)*. This beautifully formed tree is a favorite in dry countries because its flower bracts and leaf sheaths collect and store rain that can be used for emergency drinking water.

A small but lovely example of a colonial Spanish-Moorish garden (open to the public) is found at the Quinta de Anauco, the Museum of Colonial Art in Caracas. Originally the residence of General Francisco Rodriguez del Toro, the house was finished in the early 1800s, just about the time that Venezuela began to break its ties with Spain.

A garden adjoins the exterior corridor and features a small fountain and good paving work. The beds are filled with various plants of the colonial period, including the now ubiquitous bright yellow marigold *(Tagetes)* originally from this part of the world. They acquired the misnomers French and African marigolds after early Spanish explorers distributed the seeds throughout other countries where, subsequently, the flowers were "rediscovered" and renamed after their foster homes.

In the main interior patio there is a beautiful Moorish fountain surrounded by a star of pebble paving. Here the beds are crowded with plants that would have been grown during the colonial period for food, medicine, or for their attractive aromas. Against white adobe walls grow pomegranates, hot peppers, limes, coffee, cacao, violets, gardenias, jasmine, and rose mallow petunias.

During the heyday of the Quinta de Anauco, the study of botany became very important in Venezuela. In contrast to the rigid formality of Caracas's classically designed urban squares, nineteenth-century garden owners began using lush natural vegetation extensively. By the second half of that century, botanists and scientists were warning that clearing and cutting the forests above Caracas could lead to disaster, and, with harrowing foresight, Julio Churion published *The Causes of Drought and the Necessity of Afforestation* in 1877.

This movement toward the horticultural use of native vegetation and the need for plant conservation later gained a successful advocate in the person of Brazilian landscape architect Roberto Burle Marx. But it was not until after the Venezuelan oil boom of the early 1950s that Burle Marx, in association with architects Stoddard and Tabora, came to Caracas to help establish a new exciting standard for contemporary tropical landscape design.

Burle Marx has been designing gardens, mainly in the tropics, for almost sixty years. He is a lively, productive octogenarian with a boyish mop of white curls who, at the end of a particularly enjoyable meal, may burst into joyous song in any of the six languages he speaks. Besides the prodigious amounts of landscape architecture he has produced, Burle Marx is also a proficient painter, sculptor, printmaker, and designer of fabrics, tapestries, and murals.

In an interview published in 1989, Burle Marx explained how his love for tropical plants began: "In 1928 I went to Europe for the first time and lived in Berlin for a year and a half. It was in Berlin that I first saw many Brazilian plants that were not part of Brazilian gardens in those days. My need to collect them increased—their beauty was extraordinary. It was in these amazing European greenhouses that I started to love the Brazilian flora."

Four years after his visit to Europe, Burle Marx designed his first garden for the Schwartz residence in Rio de Janeiro. A garden by Burle Marx is characterized by his modern designs for tiled walls, outdoor murals, and pavings; by his highly developed, yet naturally inspired plant groupings; and by his enhancement of natural landscapes that often include lakes, mountains, and other natural vista-makers.

After Burle Marx's Brazilian work brought him international renown, he began undertaking major projects abroad. Between 1956 and 1961 he designed various public spaces in Venezuela, including clubs, hospitals, and a cemetery, as well as over a dozen private gardens. His first major project in Caracas was the Parque Del Este, a 175-acre public park begun in 1956. The best way to see the park is from the cable car that rises

high up the mountain behind Parque Del Este. From this vantage point the design of the entire park is visible, a clear example of what Sir Geoffrey Jellicoe meant when he wrote "The translation of abstract art into landscape originated . . . through Roberto Burle Marx." Wide winding paths meander lazily around hillocks and knot crazily in other areas; a boating pond is decorated with tree specimens. Although there were once grand plans for a planetarium, athletic fields, restaurants, a zoo, and an open-air theater, in recent years the park has suffered from a lack of public funds.

But Burle Marx is far from an artist in an ivory tower, and in an interview in 1989 he spoke about his role in the highly political issue of tropical rain forest destruction: "We are currently witnessing a great destruction of flora and the disappearance of many . . . species that have never been utilized in gardens. . . . Current devastation needs to be reversed at two different levels, that of the natural and that of urban environments.

Right: *Brazilian Roberto Burle Marx is the foremost designer of tropical gardens and an advocate of tropical forest and plant conservation. He designed this garden for Odette Monteiro at the foot of the Serra dos Órgãos in Brazil in 1948.* Below: *In the seventeenth century the grounds at Hacienda La Vega were redesigned to reflect a colonial Spanish trend for gardens in the Italian fashion. Here two huge frangipanis bloom against dark green cypresses.*

"Not only do we need to protect regions of floral importance . . . but also *all* cities, towns, and municipalities should have parks and green areas to perpetuate the little native flora they have left. . . . A landscape architect can actually show and perpetuate the botanic structure of a region. . . . The importance of the landscape architect in environmental conservation is unquestionable."

THE DOMINICAN REPUBLIC: THE TROPICS TAMED

The subject of tropical gardens of the world —their plant material and design elements— is so vast that it is comforting to end this chapter with a garden that is close to home. Christopher Columbus's journey to the Far East took him instead to the West Indies. On his second voyage there, in 1493, natives gave him pineapples—although a South American plant, already a cultivated crop in this part of

the world. He took one home as a present for Queen Isabella, and the delicious fruit at once captured her fancy, and five hundred years later remains a symbol of hospitality.

The Caribbean islands and West Indies are among mainland North America's closest truly tropical neighbors. Cuba, Puerto Rico, and the Dominican Republic—all islands traversed by mountain chains—receive ample rains and are characterized by their deep red loam and abundant vegetation. Huge mahogany trees, giant samans, and the Caribbean royal palm are native to the rich forests, and trees are usually loaded with epiphytic ferns and orchids. Tree ferns and heliconias form a lower canopy and delicate begonias grow scattered on the jungle floor.

Some of the islands have botanic gardens that originally began as private collections, the oldest of these started in 1765 on St. Vincent. Andromeda Gardens, laid out in 1954, is another important West Indian garden, but, as is often the case, the best gardens remain pri-

vately owned and are tended and developed by successive generations of the same family. The beautifully designed and masterfully planted garden at the Tavares family's Villa Pancha in the Dominican Republic is an exceptional example of the tropical garden in all its sophisticated glorious beauty.

The garden at Villa Pancha was begun more than sixty years ago by a young wife who had had a childhood fascination with tropical plants. She had spent extended periods with a family friend in New Jersey who maintained a rare plants greenhouse, and it was there that the unusual plants of the tropics became her favorites. After she married and moved to her lifelong tropical home, these exotics became the familiar beautiful outdoor plants that formed her family's large tropical garden.

Doña Maria Grieser de Tavares instilled a love of plants and gardening in her three children, and after a generation of collecting plants throughout the world's tropical belt by the entire family, Villa Pancha's undulating flower beds burst with many plants that were the first of their kind to be grown in the Dominican Republic. Exotic and native plants are carefully blended and appear as if flourishing in their natural habitats. Huge mature trees spill orchids and ferns from their branches and, at the same time, shade more tender terrestrial plants growing underneath. Every corner of the garden glows with dozens of variations on a green theme and shimmers with carefully orchestrated, bright moments of color.

The design of the house is in the tropical Spanish tradition, with a carefully arranged, simply planted sunny interior patio that serves as the heart and hub of household activity. A central raised star of ceramic tiles holds a potted tree with pinkish red blossoms to complement the color of the slanting tiled roof.

From the wide open terrace (similar in idea to an exterior corridor, but more roomlike in appearance) the modern informal design of the garden is apparent. A large saman tree *(Samanea saman)* hosts sprays of pink Central American orchids high in its branches and enormous balls of staghorn ferns hang from heavy chains. A low ground cover of pale pink begonias and tiny ferns (originally brought by Doña Maria from New Jersey) carpets the bed underneath the branches. Small ornamental palms and darker pink begonias grow over six feet (almost 2 meters) tall.

The mature trees of the garden provide the ample shade that makes this tropical garden a comfortable refuge from the hot sun. The mahoganies *(Swietenia mahagoni* and *S. macrophylla)* are the most important export timber trees in the region, and these evergreens can attain seventy-five feet (23 meters) in height. Another important native is the saman. Its fernlike leaves grow high in delicately twisting lateral branches that form an umbrella-shaped tree structure. The shaggy bark of the tree makes it a perfect host for other small plants to grow upon, and for two months this gentle giant of a tree flowers with small pale pink-and-white powder-puff blossoms.

Other specimen trees planted throughout the garden include a wide variety of palms, araucarias, cecropias, and a *Ceiba pentandra*, or kapok tree. This enormous tree annually scatters fluff balls of white cottony fibers—traditionally used for stuffing pillows and mattresses—across the lawn. The Mexican Mayas believed that the first man was born from the sacred ceiba tree, and it is pleasant to think that the Adam of the Mayas had nice soft cushions to rest upon.

Under all these shady trees, large gracefully shaped beds are set amid green grass. Curving walls of rustling heliconias, bananas, torch gingers *(Nicolaia)*, and crotons conceal one garden area from the next. A pink ornamental shell ginger *(Alpinia zerumbet,* native to India and Burma) was collected many years ago in Hawaii by a family member and made its debut in the Dominican Republic at Villa Pancha.

Further foliage variations are provided by the yellow-and-green spiky-leaved Pride of India, Australian tree ferns, caladiums, and a variety of other plants known to the family only by their own personal common names, such as "microphone ginger," "music sheet plant," and "woodpeckers' tongues." Shaded by a large tree is a naturalistic grouping of thick-leaved bromeliads, ornamental cousins of the pineapple given to Columbus centuries ago. Nestled among the evergreen leaves of *Medinilla magnifica* are grapelike clusters of pinkish purple beadlike flowers, and the once-ominous black bat flower *(Tacca integrifolia)* appears to fly gracefully above its shiny green leaves.

The most exciting color moments in the garden are provided by the enormous orchid collection that has flourished for more than half a century at Villa Pancha. Red renantheras explode like fireworks. Fine coteries of cattleyas seem to gossip in little out-of-the-way corners. Masses of oncidiums sparkle like little stars, and sheets of tiny native orchids fall like curtains from tree branches. Amazing arandas and arachnis from Singapore join vandas and ascocendas from Thailand to create a United Nations of orchid colors.

Another area features broad terraced steps and a long cascade of water that descend into a garden of extraordinary beauty and calm. This is *el jardin blanco*, a sophisticated tropical twist upon Vita Sackville-West's white garden at Sissinghurst. Here pristine arches of bridal veil, jasmine, coral vine, and petrea take turns blooming. Pale balloons of agapanthas, clouds of scented gardenias, and stands of white-faced caladiums adjoin cool green lawns. Tiny white oxalis petals shine against flagstone steps, and euphorbias with small creamy flowers held amidst spines grow in pots. White orchids in all shapes and sizes flutter and spill. Huge snowdrifts of woody jasmine and pure white impatiens create a cool tropical setting.

Under a shaded pergola dripping with stalactites of white thunbergia vine, Gustavo Tavares, son of Doña Maria, sits and talks about plans that he and his sisters have for the garden at Villa Pancha. Close by, shiny green lizards rest immobile on rocks, and the water song of the nearby cascade is accented with birds singing, chirping, and whistling like flirtatious construction workers.

Palm and banana leaves swish in the wind like old-fashioned fans as Tavares, appropriately dressed in a delicately tucked and crisply starched white guabera, enjoys the universal favorite pastime of gardeners—looking at and talking about gardens. Chatting pleasantly and exchanging "plant gossip," he gradually pauses to glance at the white tropical wonder billowing, rolling, and drifting before him. With a sudden sense of amazement he says, "I don't know how it would have ever been done in color!"

The fact that man gardens at all is a sign of respect to the indomitability of nature. The tropics may seem like a wonderful natural paradise, but one should not forget that the tropical garden is a work of art composed by man. In the words of Roberto Burle Marx: "A garden is nature organized *by* man *for* man."

Left: *The trunks of tree ferns provide support for many mature specimens of orchids in the Tavares garden, their gray wirelike aerial roots zigzagging through their neat, daggerlike foliage.*
Opposite page: *Shiny white pebbles define undulating beds of orchids. The original garden layout at Villa Pancha was determined by using garden hoses to define graceful curves.*

El jardin blanco *at the Tavares garden is a sophisticated play on Vita Sackville-West's white garden. Agapanthas, jasmine, gardenias, and other white tropical flowers festoon pergolas, arches, and pools.*

CHAPTER SEVEN

COUNTRY GARDENS

The image we carry of a garden in the country—a soft, gentle, romantic place heady with smells—is one that has developed over the centuries, each nationality having its own version, the differences based upon climate, landscape, and social structure. The three are inseparable; the permutations innumerable.

The place of a garden in the country has much to do with the landscape in which it sits, and how that landscape was and still is worked. The cottage garden in Britain, for example, was originally owned by a worker of the land—a farmer, forester, or manual laborer. Each of their homes was different, although built from the same stone or brick perhaps, if locally available, giving a sense of regional identity, and each had its place socially in the community.

The nuances of social position were expressed in the form of the house and reinforced by the size of the garden that accompanied it, so that not only different scales of country house emerge, but different styles of country garden, both tempered by the landscape in which they sit. Those who owned the land on which the traditional country cottage and garden stood (and who almost owned the workers on it, too) lived in grander houses whose style was more elegant and that warranted a garden not of its region—rather, to emphasize their superiority it was often purposely at odds with it—in a fashionable national style of the period. Thus the landed of Renaissance Europe carved their gardens out of their landscapes and imposed a rigidity upon their rural forms, clipped and alléed to express their control of all that they surveyed from their pampered loggia.

Even in eighteenth-century England the gentleman's park, a picturesque idyll of country, was only an idealized version of a classic landscape, with very little to do with real coun-

Preceding page: *The look of arum lilies bordering a pastoral stream at Ninfa, just two hours south of Rome, illustrates perfectly the romantic ideal of a country landscape.*

Left: *The old walls and architectural remnants of this once medieval village provide startling focal points throughout the lush gardens of Ninfa.*

tryside. So although the grander houses of Europe and their surrounds might be located in the country, their form very often had little to do with the essence of the country itself.

This distancing of house and its immediate surround from what was seen as the vulgarities of raw nature was always paralleled by a romantic streak that saw the lifestyle of those "without the pale" as being one of bliss, controlled by the rising and setting sun, and by the elements of nature. An even greater distancing of the aristocracy from their roots took place in the nineteenth century when, to shelter and husband newly introduced plant material, walls were built and hedges were grown, significantly separating the garden from the countryside.

UTILITY AND THE COUNTRY GARDEN

The earliest country garden was never a fashionable concept of decorative horticulture; rather, it was a utilitarian space surrounding the home of ordinary country folk, providing fruit, herbs, vegetables, and cut flowers for daily use. Originally the garden was regarded as a retreat from the harshness of nature—its overpowering scale and its lurking dangers. It was a nightly enclosure for beast, and it protected all who lived within.

Slowly, though, the need for enclosure diminished and the early gardens became a microcosm of the surrounding worked land. In Tuscany, for example, vines would grow, and between the vines, vegetables—artichokes, beans, onions—and herbs. Where space was at a premium the vines might be strung between olive trees in the warmer parts of the countryside or, on the tops of Tuscan hills where it was colder, between nut or pear trees. Around the house a few flowers might be planted, probably not for use inside the house, but for the glory of God at church, or for placement on the local shrine.

In essence this was the framework of all early working gardens, although geographic location would have altered the range of produce grown. The garden might also have had a building for storage, a place for the pig, and would, of course, have had a privy—the last providing organic content to husband the crops and increase their yield. Such a garden might also include a well or perhaps a dovecote.

BAYLEAF—A FOURTEENTH-CENTURY GARDEN

Medieval farming was accomplished by strip cultivation. Each village was surrounded by two or three large open and unhedged fields that were divided into any number of strips, all individually owned but farmed in common. Within this system were common pasture, arable land, and land held fallow. The arable land was divided into furlongs and a rotational cropping program was employed.

All these subdivisions must have given farmed landscapes the look of a checkerboard. It's a pattern you can see from the air in northern France and the Low Countries, although it is the result of different agricultural practices.

It is this checkerboard system that has been brought within the hurdle-enclosed pale at Bayleaf. Beds are set out for a rotation of crops, with adjacent areas for herbs. Sprinkled among the vegetables are what appear to us to be cottage garden flowers; they were, in fact, an early form of companion planting, certain flowers held to possess the power to either stimulate the growth of particular vegetables or to ward off insects. There are also fruit trees that were by no means meant to be decorative. This garden provided the farmer's wife with all she needed for her table.

The prosperous farmer, with a larger family and staff to feed, would have increased the size of his garden and, to manage the space, watering, and general maintenance of it more efficiently, would have introduced pathways into the layout. Having no concept of asymmetry, he would have had a formal layout, and would have followed the basic grid or pattern of all early gardens, such a pattern having been derived from those of irrigation systems and the Middle Eastern quartered prototype. He would have seen this patterning at his landlord's house, further ornamented there with the beds being edged, perhaps in box (though box was not used as an edging till the seventeenth century). This type of lay-

out is seen in the paintings of the medieval masters, and still exists within the cloistered layouts of monasteries and schools of learning. It paralleled the changing fashions of the decorative garden and might well have accompanied it—though it remained walled, both for reasons of shelter in colder northern climates and to be hidden, for not until the nineteenth century did the working garden become a thing of decoration in itself within larger garden layouts.

ROMANCE AND THE RURAL LIFE

This form of early garden was the prototype

The landed gentry of the late seventeenth and early eighteenth centuries saw an "improved" natural landscape as the ideal; this version at Rousham in Oxfordshire was designed by William Kent.

for country gardens around the world as new territories became colonized. Different plants in different locations give a different look, but early layouts are remarkably similar and must have been for generations. Our image of the cottage garden starts to change in the nineteenth century when, with an emergent industrial society and its accompanying urban housing, a creeping nostalgia for a simpler lifestyle redirected new middle-class images back toward the country. A mood of romanticism fostered by the Arts and Crafts Movement of William Morris (and by the romantic writings of William and Dorothy Wordsworth) and the earthy arabesques of Art Nouveau brought a love of organic forms and

nature into fashion. For their inspiration they sought the rural ways of the quieter Middle Ages, the cottage and its herby garden with good old-fashioned flowers, the surrounding primrose woods, and the gentle pastoral of country life. (As a concept this was pure unfettered nostalgia, for most cottagers had been only too happy to leave an impoverished, harsh, underpaid, and underfed lifestyle for more urban areas or to even take a ship to other parts of the world to escape.)

The mood infused the grander garden layout too, and simple flowers and gentle colors became *de rigueur*, the artificiality of the Victorian garden being replaced by an Edwardian pastoral. The farm and cottage garden them-

THE TUDOR GARDEN

This is a garden of the sixteenth century—not a grand garden by any means, but one owned by someone of substance. The garden is still enclosed and inward looking, but the early strip patterns employed in gardens like Bayleaf have now become slightly more decorative. Although their proportions are similar, the strips now surround a central knot of clipped and interlaced herbs, resulting in an embroidered effect.

The contents of the beds would probably have been very similar to those of the farm-house garden, full of vegetables and herbs for culinary and medicinal use. Surrounding the practical elements of the garden are more decorative ones—an arbor of ash or hazel poles to support a vine or honeysuckle and a fountain that in its day would have been filled up constantly by the gardener, carrying the water from the well in a leather bucket. This garden also contained a small enclosed bee garden, with the bee skeps worked into the surrounding wall to keep them dry.

The Orchard *by Pierre Bonnard (1899). Painters and writers of the late nineteenth century sought to direct their audience toward the romance of the countryside again. (National Gallery of Art, Washington, D.C., Rosenwald Collection)*

selves did not change—British agriculture was at a low, but the pull of the countryside and the garden within it was constant, in literature and in painting, and with better transport the facility to enjoy it was increased as well.

Another manifestation of the desire to bring some of the green back into industrialized urban areas was, and still is in many countries, the city dweller who plants and grows his vegetables and flowers within an allotment of land at some distance from his house. In Europe the allotment concept has been the norm for some time, an escape from the apartment on weekends. An extension of this is the summer dacha living of well-to-do Russian families; their literature reflects its influence, overflowing with the yearning for the flowering of lilacs, the cherry orchard, the trembling poplar, and the silver birch.

In nineteenth-century England Queen Victoria and Prince Albert set a precedent for

the wealthy having alternative country homes to which they moved at different times of the year. This was different from returning to family estates, and soon fostered in the lower classes as well an appreciation for rural life. Part of smart country living was, of course, the growing of vegetables and fruit for the household. These nineteenth- and early-twentieth-century vegetable gardens, still walled, are legend, for their productivity was phenomenal, husbanded by country gardeners whose families had perhaps performed the same function for generations previous.

After World War II labor was at a premium, and many of these vegetable gardens were neglected; the fashionable herbaceous border became the mixed border filled with lower maintenance bulbs and shrubs along with the perennials, a general awareness of maintenance tempering the look of grander country gardens. Labor shortages in the house

made it fashionable to move to smaller homes and slowly, very slowly, the smaller garden surrounding the smaller country house became the norm.

A great turn-of-the-century influence on the way in which we now think of the countryside was Gertrude Jekyll, who worked with the architect Sir Edwin Lutyens, who died in 1945 and is said to have been the last great architect of the country house. Jekyll was a plantswoman who, being forced to give up painting in midlife because of poor eyesight, turned her artistic eye to the sympathetic arrangement of plants, mainly perennials, in the border. In two of her books, *Home and Gardens* (1900) and *Wood and Garden* (1899), she draws a romantic picture of the vanishing Surrey countryside and its inhabitants, along with its cottage gardens. This was the inspiration for her style of planting, which paralleled the way country folk gardened in their own small plots. Jekyll's deep-felt attachment to the coun-

try lifestyle and its seasonal nuances resulted in natural plant groupings that had a truly earthy feel for location and that set her landscape philosophy way ahead of its time.

It was perhaps Jekyll's misfortune that only the more obvious bits of her philosophy were imbibed—the clematis twining through the apple tree and a general rustification of the prim Victorian garden look. I believe large sections of her writing were misinterpreted and resulted in a country garden style characterized by a mishmash of soft, romantic plantings that overlaid a classic garden plan. Such a garden was cottagey by feel, harking back to the idyll of thatch and the simple, uncluttered country life, but it missed the point that the true cottage style was a holistic approach to living and gardening out of sheer necessity, any excesses pared away to subsistence level.

The new twentieth-century British gardener was extremely well informed horticul-

Above: *Hestercombe in Somerset is a restored garden designed by Sir Edwin Lutyens but planted by Gertrude Jekyll. Although we remember her for her use of perennials, she was an early-twentieth-century advocate of country ways, the cottage garden, and the interaction between the two.*

Opposite page: *The true cottager's garden was a subsistence garden, for it fed the family. Such a garden must have been planted at Hidcote Bartram for generations.*

turally, having learned the craft of the garden from practical experience. Just such a gardener was Lawrence Johnston at Hidcote Manor.

HIDCOTE VILLAGE

The real country garden is a distillation of the country around it—as we saw in the early Tuscan enclosure—rather than a refinement. The cottages at Hidcote Bartram, outside the walls of the garden of Hidcote Manor, look into surrounding fields; there is a meandering stream with ducks and geese strolling beneath pollarded willows on its bank, sheep with lambs, and strutting fowl. The stream runs into the village pond, and not too far off is the abandoned well. In the common land verge at the roadside are wildflowers beneath thorn (*Crataegus*), heavy with May blossom. In and out of this are the cottage frontages onto the road—their muddled and weedy plantings of irises, violets, bluebells, tulips, and forget-me-nots only once removed from those growing naturally in the verge opposite. Behind the cottages, though, and often cited as the *raison d'être* of their gardens, are the vegetable patches. Traditionally, it was upon his own garden produce that the country person had to survive, supplemented with dairy produce from the farm and, no doubt, with poached game from the master's land. The average person was tied to his cottage and the land he worked around it; out of it he sought his livelihood, food, his total existence. The relationship of the countryman to the earth of his garden and its surround was as close as that of the native Indian of North America to his plain.

This feeling for land, earth, and the produce raised from it was expressed in the dedication applied to the vegetable garden, which included some fruit as well. Herbs were traditionally part of this symbiosis too, for not until the eighteenth century did Britons breed up the turnip needed to overwinter cattle. Previously most were killed and their meat salted and herbs used to disguise the salty taste of the meat, should the cottager be lucky enough to get any. Herbs were also used for medicinal reasons and to strew upon the earth floor to provide insulation and to give off the fragrance of their essential oils.

Within the walls of the grander country garden, vegetables give way to decorative flowers in a more gracious layout, that of Lawrence Johnston at Hidcote Manor. The cottage becomes a decorative element beyond the walled enclosure.

UPTON HOUSE

Tucked under the garden wall, before the level drops away, is a mixed country border. While the overall grandeur of the Upton House gardens may seem unattainable to the average person today, each section within the garden illustrates simple gardening principles and styles appropriate for smaller scale applications.

Another garden of this period, and perhaps a unique one, is that of Upton House in War-wickshire. The long, low house is approached down a drive dead center of the front door. Though seventeenth century in origin, the house was enlarged and improved in 1927 to become the country home of the second Vis-count Bearsted, housing one of the finest art collections of the twentieth century.

You should approach the garden through the house, passing paintings by the eighteenth-century English landscape painters John Con-stable and George Stubbs. At the threshold,

across a magnificent lawn framed by yew and cedars, you see such a landscape actualized, a pastoral scene across the valley, flecked with sheep and lambs, rolling away into the War-wickshire landscape. This, you feel, is truly a country house in a country garden setting. Though built in its present state only in this century, the terraced garden below the lawn must have been worked for generations, for beneath terraces of garden walks is an im-maculate vegetable garden, facing due south.

The towering cedars of Lebanon, planted about 1740, command the whole garden. As you progress down a flight of steps, across the terraces and through the vegetable garden to-

ward the bottom pond, you become aware of a flowering cherry garden as well, all pink and white foam and froth among dark yew, and, around the corner, a boggy garden, too. But it is the panoramic countryside beyond this garden which is so spectacular and which gives it stability in scale with the cedars and the lawn and house above it, striking in their simplicity. Of horticultural expertise there is plenty apparent, but it is subservient and somehow transitory to the total layout of this beautiful spot.

The Upton House garden is perhaps unusual for a twentieth-century garden, for although it holds its surrounding country view at a distance—framing it, not dissimilar to the Stubbs you pass on approaching it—it is part of it also. And like the Stubbs, this garden captures a moment when master and steed seem at one with *their* countryside.

THE COUNTRY GARDEN TODAY

In Europe from the beginning of the twentieth century a new enlightenment known as the modernist movement swept through the arts —in music, painting, sculpture, architecture, philosophy, and lifestyle. In the visual arts it was a concern for line and form, much influenced from Japan and interpreted by the Bauhaus as industrial form following utilitarian

This old medieval stew pond (in which fish were bred for the table) at the foot of the path both separates and connects the garden and the agricultural landscape on the other side of the valley.

Concealed below the decorative garden of Upton House in Warwickshire, vegetables are still grown for the household as they have been since the seventeenth century.

function. This movement influenced a succession of landscape designers as well, including Thomas Church working in the Bay Area of San Francisco. Slowly their work, originally for a private clientele, was recognized and the new landscape movement infused public areas—the corporate building, the factory, the campus, and public housing. As they became larger so did their landscapes. These new landscapes were no longer gardens, but rather reinterpretations of the eighteenth-century English parkland—a new pastoral of contoured ground forms, grouped trees, and landscaped water.

The brave new world of the modernist, however, somehow turned sour in the middle of the century, as the scale of new development and vast public landscapes seemed overwhelming. There was however, an emergent concern for green and garden on a smaller scale. The feel for country, perhaps lurking there in all of us, called out for intimate garden spaces in urban areas.

The word "holistic" entered our vocabulary and organically grown food became a general concern. Suddenly the vegetable and herb garden was back in vogue, gardened along country lines, for its randomness was its appeal. Apartment dwellers again sought the suburban allotment, which, after a period of dereliction, was at a premium. The gardening wheel had turned again.

Since the 1960s and 70s we have sought to control the spraying of chemicals on our food and to preserve our flora as well as fauna. Both sides of the Atlantic are now looking at their landscapes and countryside, and are seeing their unique qualities. People are questioning the usual approach to garden design —the modernist plan with contrived, alien plantings—and are seeking to reinterpret the essence of their location within both their private gardens and their public landscaped areas.

It is time for a new look at the garden in its country setting. That the turn-of-the-century country house garden in Britain is still regarded as the norm is unrealistic. Many surround large properties that have been bequeathed to the National Trust, since the owner could no longer support them. These were and are managed by an informed staff, and a place like Sissinghurst, long held as the epitome of an English family garden, now entertains in excess of a hundred thousand people a year. It is now a public showplace—a horticultural theme park—very different from its origins.

The British garden has been caught in a historical time warp, which all too sadly many gardeners around the world have tried to emulate in their native countries, constantly chiding themselves that they cannot create in Toronto or Albuquerque what they have been told is a typical English perennial border. Additionally, climatic changes, whether due to ice cap movement, a break in the ozone layer, or nuclear fallout, have produced extremes in temperature which have been accompanied by an increasing lack of water worldwide as we humans greedily tap into natural underground aquifers.

This further compounds the problems of horticulturists/gardeners seeking to create an alien look, and slowly, very slowly, as the increasing roar of environmental pressure groups is heard, the gardener is beginning to realize that perhaps more native forms of garden, furnished with indigenous plants, might make for not only a more labor-saving garden, able to stand the local climate—its heat and cold, its water excesses and droughts—but one that looks at peace with its surround as well. Hedges can be reduced to look at the view beyond, since there is an increasing affinity

Above: Here runner beans are grown up a tepee of cane at Tintinhull House; traditionally, brushwood was used for this function and can still be employed to support perennials as well. The background plant—a great favorite— is Euphorbia wulfenii, *the gold form.*
Right: *At Tintinhull House, Penelope Hobhouse has used catmint, or catnip* (Nepeta), *on either side of a gravel path, which plays host to bees all summer.*

between in and out, and wildflowers and rougher grasses can be allowed within the garden's scheme. In fact, by managing what happens naturally, with the occasional intercession, your country garden will look, not like something from Gloucestershire or Giverny, but of its own location, alive with its own flora and abundant with local fauna as well.

The new country garden is still composed of many elements of the cottager's plot and the overriding mood is still one of relaxation. And where maintenance was once manual, mechanical devices have altered the feel of the garden to a degree as well. Riding mowers prefer curves to right angles, for instance, though edging tools can give a clean look far removed from the cottager's burgeoning vegetation. Perhaps unique to Britain is a curious breed of yeomen and -women gardeners who spend much of their lives in their gardens, seeking to create these moods of the country, which are equally viable as an objective in town.

The meadow or prairie garden, pioneered in the United States, is an extension of the full cottage look, and if it can be combined with an old orchard so much the better. In Britain the wildflower garden is very much a late-spring, early-summer occurrence; it follows the bulbs, when, according to soil, Queen Anne's lace and dog daisies appear, along with buttercups, poppies, cornflowers, and so on. To the ecologist the dog daisy is a flower of the hayfield, the buttercup is a flower of the damp meadow or neglected cornfield, and the field poppy is common over disturbed ground and mixed in among cereal crops, but all, being indigenous, are accommodating, if not downright invasive. This is country gardening with a bias toward conservation. Relevant to the horticulturist, it calls for an observation of the local countryside—its soil and natural plant arrangements, the trees and shrubs, as well as the wildflowers. These native plants cope best with that particular climate, hot or cold, its water excesses and droughts, and all the nuances of the individual microclimates of a private garden.

The word that keeps coming to mind to conjure up the country look is romantic, for really what one is seeking is a sort of pastoral

Opposite page: *A Pissarro landscape of flowing trees in a kitchen garden against a village landscape.* (Potager et arbres en fleurs, *Giraudon/Art Resource, New York*)
Above: *The same Pissarro feeling translated into the reality of an orchard in bloom at Glenwood Farm in spring.*

idyll, an antidote to urban living, a fragrant June abundance of flower and foliage—its carefree lifestyle (to the uninitiated) devoid of stress and strain. I think of the orchard at Sissinghurst as pure country gardening, along with the meadow beneath the house at Great Dixter with its front lawn full of wildflowers. Their borders, whether mixed or perennial, are much too sophisticated to be real country.

Perhaps perversely, the moment a garden is good enough to be public it has lost the charm and essence of unsophisticated country. For many the essence of country gardening is still the vegetable patch, with its herb garden and nearby orchard. And it is the home harvest of fruit and vegetables which sustained the original cottage dwellers.

The cottage garden idiom described at Hidcote Bartram pervades the country garden mood today for, with our growing concern for landscape and the environment in general, the new country garden coexists with its environment in a happy symbiosis, practical in its maintenance and at home in its surround.

A COUNTRY GARDEN CONCLUSION

Much of my work has to do with rationalizing the layout of older gardens that were once worked by a staff, but now have only part-time help, if any at all.

By reducing labor-intensive garden areas, softening the layout and often opening it up to the view beyond, one creates what is ultimately called a cottagey look. Actually, it's only rationalizing the garden to the different lifestyle of the current owners, what they can look after and the machinery they have with which to do it.

The accompanying garden plans illustrate the point. The house is a modest late-nine-

teenth-century country house, with a small walled garden. It is now owned by a working couple. When they bought the property, the layout was very labor-intensive (see the plan below), with a rose arbor and rose garden, a collapsing garden pavilion, a weedy sunken area, rockery, and so on. The garden was enclosed by shrubbery studded with overgrown conifers. There was really nowhere to relax, even if there was time to do so, since the whole layout was too much to cope with.

I addressed this problem (see the plan to the right) by removing many of the decaying nineteenth-century features, backfilling the

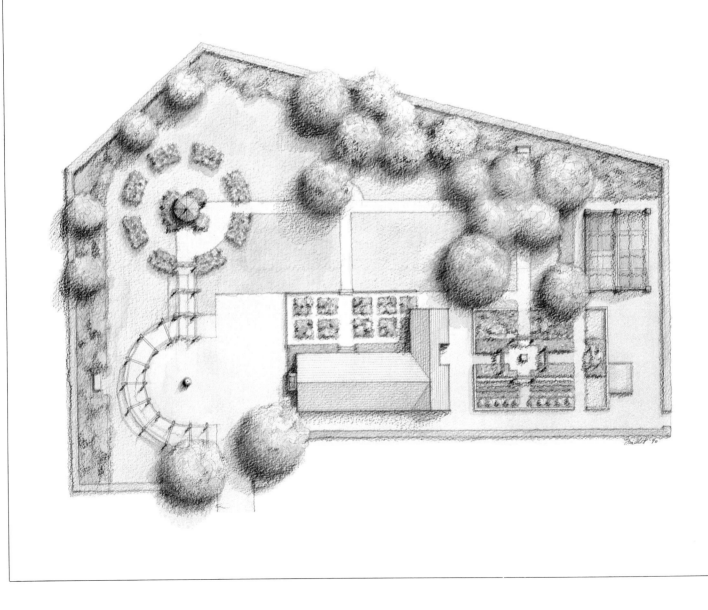

sunken area with rubble from the house alterations, and laying a terrace over it to provide a sheltered sitting area. The gravel drive was extended around it, the whole providing a planting area with tubs of annuals for seasonal interest.

The hedge and shrubbery were grubbed out to open the garden to a view of the fields beyond and provide a flowing patterned path through the old orchard, which has been supplemented with new fruit trees. The older plum trees have clematis and the odd rose growing up through them. All right angles have been eliminated to allow the easy passage

of the riding mower, which the client enjoys using on weekends to cut the grass.

The fruit cage (the enclosure for protecting berries that appears at the top right-hand corner of each plan) remains, as does the vegetable garden, with an herb bed at the center.

This sort of rationalization of a country garden is increasingly the norm in Britain—it's the new cottage garden look, with relaxed borders of mixed shrubs, herbs, and perennial material. It's manageable and allows for plant interest—not just color—throughout the year.

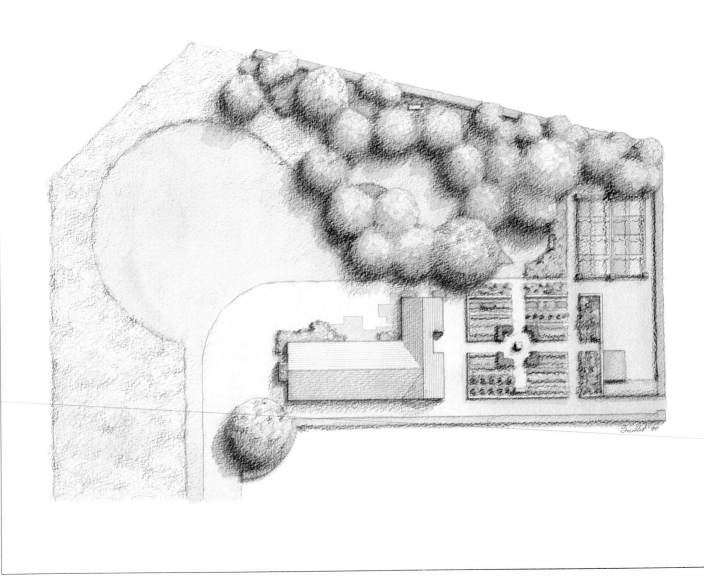

Above: *Vegetables are grown at Barnsley House in a decorative manner, crop interplanted with crop, known as companion planting.*
Right: *Grasses are used to soften the edge of a reflecting pool in one of the several distinct gardens within Rosemary Verey's garden at Barnsley House.*

Opposite page: *Rock roses*
(Helianthemum) *are
planted among paving
between an avenue of Irish
yew* (Taxus baccata
'Fastigiata') *in this famous
central garden walk at
Barnsley House.*
Above: *A country garden
in Maine with the ocean
beyond, which makes a
serene backdrop to the
tapestry of flowers
contained within. The style
of fencing used here is
sympathetic to the setting of
the garden.*

Left: *A wildflower meadow at the Villa Reale, Ninfa. The contrast of formal hedging with the sheet of buttercups is stunning.*

Following pages: *The quintessential "country road," here leading to the gardens at Ninfa, Italy. Innately pleasing and inviting, it seems almost of a bygone era. How will our reinvigorated concern with the landscape and countryside affect the look of the garden?*

CHAPTER EIGHT

PUBLIC GARDENS

There seems no greater magic for the urban dweller than the sudden glimpse of greenery set within the rigid confines of the city. That brief verdant sight can often provoke a sentimental stirring for the natural world, transforming even a single moment to one of optimism and assurance which gives hope to life. That momentary view of nature, even in its most abstract form, reconfirms our simple existence and unique relationship with the world. Throughout the centuries of civilization, we have molded our surroundings, reflecting our most current philosophies of an idealized paradise. When these civilizations eventually advanced, with towns and settlements expanding to become cities and major metropolises, the public park as we know it today was first conceived. Created as a safeguard for communities against rapid growth,

the park became the link, for some the only link, between the urban environment and the distant natural world.

THE FIRST PUBLIC SPACES

When the ancient Greeks set small groves of sacred olives or plane trees in marketplaces, gymnasia, or open squares, it was to provide the democratic society a place in which to spend a solitary moment or congregate with others in a peaceful and pleasant environment. Plato's Academy and Aristotle's Lyceum flourished within such grove backdrops, with the philosophers teaching as they strolled amid the shaded pathways, or *peripatos*—thereby the name Peripatetic school of philosophy. The creation of these ancient Greek, and later Roman, communal sites was motivated by the desire to provide a refuge of natural beauty that would function as a counterpoint to the uncertain world beyond. The public space was an arena of cooperation and exchange, representing, as public parks do today, a shared garden to benefit the community as a whole, a peaceful common ground.

After the fall of Rome the concept of gardens with public access was not to resurface in the Western world again until the advent of the Italian Renaissance. After centuries of focus on the domestic enclosure and monastic isolation of the Middle Ages, change was signaled in movement outward beyond the fortified garden. The sixteenth-century French essayist Montaigne wrote after visiting the early Renaissance gardens in Italy: "And these are beauties that are open to anyone who likes them, who may sleep in them, and even take his friends, if the masters are not actually there." The spiritual foundation of this change was the rediscovery of the philosophies of the "ancients." One such garden complex was the Villa Borghese in Rome. Laid out in 1605 for Cardinal Scipione Borghese, the park, three miles in circumference, was one of the earliest villa-garden complexes in Rome. Large groves of trees were planted with intersecting walks punctuated with statues, fountains, and grottoes. Walled enclosures contained wild animals, such as lions and gazelles, and secret gardens were composed of fragrant shrubs and flowers. A casino, or ornamental pavilion, was built for receptions, around which were arranged formal parterres, orange trees in tubs, and fanciful aviaries. An inscription mounted at the villa's entrance, dating to 1620, and similar to the one made by Brezoni for the villa at San Vigilio, read, "Whoever thou art, now be a free man, and fear not the fetters of the law. Go where thou wilt, pluck what thou wilt. Here all is for the stranger more than for the one who owns."

THE ENGLISH LANDSCAPE INFLUENCE

In terms of both stylistic composition and historical context, the public park proper germinated from ideals and principles advanced, for the greatest part, in late-eighteenth-century English garden design theories. Lancelot "Capability" Brown, that century's most eloquent garden practitioner,

labored for over five decades, until his death in 1783, transforming existing formal grounds and creating a new Elysian vision that came to be known as English landscape.

Brown's doctrines were based on the earlier precedents of the English architect and garden designer William Kent (1684–1748). During a six-year sojourn in Rome to study painting, Kent traveled throughout Italy, inspecting, as did so many of his future clients, the ancient Roman ruins, Renaissance villas, and their garden compositions. By 1719 Kent had returned to England, where new philosophies concerning man's relationship with nature were evolving. Inspired by the literary works of Addison and the new gardens of Pope and Bridgeman, Kent began to chart a changing course of garden design in England. He proposed treating the garden in a painterly manner, softening the contour and line by opening up the garden's previous stiff formality. Banished from the English manorial horizons were the geometric groupings of topiaried yews, the intricately florid parterres, and the squadronlike formations of pleached limes and hornbeam that were integral to formal designs.

The term "parklike" described these modern landscapes that imitated nature. The compartmentalized gardens bounded by surrounds of stone, trellis, or hedge annexed to the mansion houses were pulled down and wide, sweeping vistas were extended from doorstep to distant reaches. Serpentine promenades and irregular-shaped lakes replaced bisecting axial walks and symmetrical stone-rimmed pools of water. Whether rivers were rechanneled, mounds built up, or shady woods planted, the key underlying philosophy was to compose a natural scene, one more natural and more pleasing than the original.

The individual tree played a major role in these newly conceived compositions. No longer treated as geometric abstractions as they were in formal designs, their habits were allowed natural expression. Although this period witnessed the increased introduction of plants and trees collected from foreign voyages, the exotic specimens were rarely planted by Brown in his designs. He also relegated all flowers to unseen enclosures as he believed them distracting. Axial perspectives receding to infinity, an important feature in formal gardens which tends to increase visual depth, were replaced with gentler views. "Clumps" of native oak and beech dotted the lawns and contoured meadows, and

Previous page: *Set amid the dappled shadows of the Luxembourg Gardens in Paris is the Medici Fountain, which offers a cool, pleasant retreat for garden strollers. Originally part of an early-seventeenth-century grotto construction, the fountain was moved to its present site within the park grounds in 1862 and a wide water canal was added. The rusticated facade contains in the central niche a sculptural group by Ottin of Polyphemus discovering the young lovers Acis and Galatea.*

After decades of neglect, the crab-apple row in Central Park's Conservatory Garden has grown to create a variegated tunnel of light and shade. The green canopy is enhanced by the trees' vividly graphic branches, providing a peaceful sanctuary for the urban dwellers who use the intimate garden.

Brown often foreshortened his new vistas with the use of the "belt," a ring of woods planted to enclose a site's far-off reaches.

By 1775 many of the major French gardens contained an English park feature. Adjacent to the Petit Trianon in the park at Versailles, an elaborate landscape garden was created for Marie Antoinette with winding rivers, hillocks, grottoes, bridges, and temples. Framed by the outlying countryside, the garden was the artificially conceived representation of a pastoral scene, a conceit that was to reach its zenith of expression ten years later with the building of the mock peasant village Le Hameau, which was frequented by the queen and her intimate circle, all dressed as shepherdesses and farmers.

By the second half of the eighteenth century, the converging influences of English garden theory and the taste for romantic abandonment produced a new style in European gardens that was reflected in the literary works of Voltaire and later Rousseau. Artists such as Fragonard and Hubert Robert, based at the Villa Medici in Rome, the site of the French Academy, produced works that captured the spirit of the by now romantically overgrown Italian Renaissance gardens, such as the Medici gardens themselves and those of Villa d'Este (both were laid out in the last quarter of the sixteenth century), and the ruins of Hadrian's classical villa at Tivoli, which dates to the first century A.D. These paintings, expressing a picturesque dereliction, caught the imagination of the French court. Already enraptured by a craze for the exotic, the French called their attempts at this "landscape" style *anglo-chinois*, in the belief that the English landscape movement was originally inspired by the naturalistic garden style of China.

The French landscape garden was to remain the site of a wide array of *fabriques*, or constructions, from Turkish tents and minarets to Egyptian pyramids, Chinese pagodas, and imitation antique ruins until the revolution in 1789. This new garden style was to exercise an influential role in design as the French interpretation of the English landscape style spread throughout Europe and as far as Russia under Catherine the Great.

It was odd that the century that produced the clean sweeps of Capability Brown also promoted the cult of exaggerated imitation broadly inspired by the cultures of China, Egypt, and antiquity. By the end of the eighteenth century, these crosscurrents of garden design philosophy were embattled. In the midst of the tumult appeared Humphrey Repton.

A self-proclaimed "landscape gardener," the first use of the title, Repton fused these two garden factions to form a stylistic movement that was to take garden design into the nineteenth century and lead the way to the public park proper. "I have adopted the term 'landscape gardener' as most proper," wrote Repton, "because the art can only be advanced and perfected by the united powers of the landscape painter and the practical gardener." Unlike his English predecessors, Repton was prolific in his writing, producing three major publications along with his famous trademark "Red Books." Across Europe and America his synthesis of quarreling ideals and concepts influenced future generations of landscape designers. Although thoroughly entrenched in the Brownian ideals of improving the natural setting, he drew from the picturesque the concepts of creating striking variations in tone and atmosphere through color, form, and, at times, theatrical devices.

By the beginning of the nineteenth century, the vast range of exotic trees, shrubs, and flowers that had been introduced to Eu-

Bottom left: *Seen from the interior of the rocky grotto at Stourhead in Wiltshire, England, this vista extends out across the great lake. Conceived over a thirty-year period, Stourhead is a prime example of the artificially contrived private park setting known as the landscape garden that caught the imagination and delight of eighteenth-century men and women in England and the Continent.*

Right: *At various points around the lake at Stourhead, buildings and monuments or "follies" appear and disappear amid the luxuriant vegetation, such as this five-arched stone bridge or the Temple of Flora rising on the lake's distant reaches.*

rope from the sixteenth century onward had become a flood, and nurseries quickly made them available to clients willing to experiment. During the 1620s and 30s the two Tradescants, father and son, introduced many trees, including fruit bushes and other plants, both from Europe and Virginia. Among those exported from America were Virginia creeper *(Parthenocissus quinquefolia)*, staghorn sumac *(Rhus typhina)*, Virginia spiderwort *(Tradescantia virginiana)*, tulip tree *(Liriodendron tulipifera)*, and swamp cypress *(Taxodium distichum)*. The black locust *(Robinia pseudacacia)*, today almost a ubiquitous hedgerow "weed," arrived in Europe in the first years of the seventeenth century. Later in that century, Henry Compton, Bishop of London, cultivated over a thousand exotic species in his garden at Fulham Palace, most of them introduced from North America through the agency of John Bannister. Among these were swamp bay *(Magnolia virginiana)*, balsam fir

(*Abies balsamea*), honey locust *(Gleditsia tricanthos)*, sweet gum *(Liquidambar styraciflua)*, and scarlet oak *(Quercus coccinea)*. Flowering shrubs included oak-leaved hydrangeas and kalmias.

By Repton's time these plants were in great demand and his "American gardens" (some of which still survive at Bicton in Devon and at Fonthill Abbey in Wiltshire) set a new fashion. In these gardens, usually a section of a larger landscape, North American specimens (and exotics from other parts of the world requiring similar conditions) were given moist acid loam in which they could thrive.

Repton also reintroduced the flower garden. His designs for circular mounds of flowers were forerunners of the century's later passion for carpet-bedding, and his "flower basket," a bedded-out plot raked to a central point and encircled by low metal or wooden hoops, was used well into the twentieth century. Architectural features, such as trellis, terraces, gravel walks, and stone and iron balustrades, returned to use, often overplanted with flowering climbers that softened their linear qualities. Advocating an enlivened landscape that contained motion, Repton inhabited the meadow vistas with cows or sheep to break what he termed "the still life quality." In one instance he instructed the building of a rusticated hut set in a verdant view so that a fire could be lit at the hearth and the smoke allowed

This view down the long central axis in the Luxembourg Gardens is accentuated by the pleached chestnut trees flanking the wide grass lawn. The Luxembourg Palace facade, built in the early years of the seventeenth century for Queen Marie de Medici, is framed within the tree rows, an important concept in French formal gardens.

to animate the valley scene. It was a ritual that was repeated every day at Endsleigh in Devon until 1940.

Although Repton cannot be credited with the inception of a new genre of landscape treatment, his important contribution was the union of various ideals that were to have their greatest moment of expression in the creation of the large-scale public parks. Repton's career, like that of Kent and Brown, was focused on the private exclusive world that he strove to enhance through balance and harmony. But those self-contained domains, at times open to the public, remained far removed from the changing social environment. The public parks of the future were to be designed for the recreation and enjoyment of the new urban populations and, for generations of landscape designers to follow, were to become the zenith of one's career, overshadowing the importance of private commissions.

THE RISE OF THE CITIES

The early nineteenth century marked the rise of the industrial city as European and American urban centers swelled with growing populations from rural, agriculturally based communities. The psychological distance between the city and country increased. By 1819, when the Factory Act was made law in England to protect women and children in the workplace, social awareness and reform were dominant issues. The burgeoning cityscape formed the grim backdrop for the socially conscious novels of Dickens and Zola which championed the need for great change. Escape from the city existed for the landed gentry and the new industrial rich to their country seats for retirement, and for the rising middle classes to suburban villas, but for the working classes, the largest majority of urban inhabitants, there was little relief.

Although most European cities provided garden spaces in which the public was allowed entrance at times, many remained royal domains attached to city palaces which could be closed off at a whim. In France it took the French Revolution to transfer ownership of Versailles and other similiar vast estates to the people. During Georgian times a great number of small planted squares were created in London, but their access was reserved for the surrounding residents who also maintained them. Crown properties such as Hyde Park, Green Park, St. James Park, and Regent's Park were open to the public, but for the most part situated in the fashionable quarters of London and not readily accessible to the working class neighborhoods that could have most benefited from them.

Two men, through their work and writing, were influential in inspiring the development of public parks: the Scotsman John Claudius Loudon in Britain and the American Andrew Jackson Downing. Loudon was perhaps most important for his prolific writings, over sixty million words devoted to garden theory and its related subjects, in which he advocated the necessity for public gardens. Loudon's two park designs, the Terrace Gardens (which was never implemented) and the Derby Arboretum of 1839, were the first attempts to create spaces intended for both recreational and educational purposes with public access. Apart from his conceptual designs for "ring parks" that would surround city centers with bands of greenery, Loudon's greatest strength lay in his power to awaken his large readership through his books and numerous articles.

Andrew Jackson Downing had a massive impact on his American readers, being the first author in the United States to write about the principles of garden design, in *Landscape Gardening*, published in 1841. Explicating the Reptonian tradition of design, Downing proposed design schemes, for the modest American house to the impressive suburban villa, which were often accompanied by lessons on "good gardening taste." Downing was a great agitator for the creation of public gardens and was widely responsible for the decision to lay out a large-scale public park in New York City. After Downing's unexpected death by drowning in 1852, his assistant, the English architect Calvert Vaux, working with Frederick Law Olmsted, designed Central Park in 1857.

The first park truly conceived of as "public" in England and financed with public funds was Birkenhead Park in Liverpool, built in 1843. Pivotal primarily because of its creation rather than its design, it made an impression on Frederick Olmsted, who visited the site in 1850. Birkenhead was laid out in the landscape tradition of Brown and Repton by Joseph Paxton, the former head gardener at Chatsworth, also a keen botanist and architect of the Crystal Palace. The 125-acre site was made accessible to the public by a double road system—a wide carriage drive for heavier traffic that encircled the park grounds and a secondary pathway for pedestrians. Groups of trees were planted along the routes, leaving large open lawns in between. Two narrow irregular-shaped lakes completed the design, both dotted with miniature islands reachable by bridges built in an array of architectural styles. The park's success lay in the definition of access systems that was to be fully developed in other public parks, most effectively in Central Park nine years later.

THE GREENING OF PARIS

Whereas Birkenhead was created from barren, undeveloped land, most European public park models, unlike their American counterparts, were assembled from existing sites within the urban structure.

There was no larger nor more ambitious development of this kind than the verdant metamorphosis of Paris. From 1852 to 1871 the city radically changed character, resulting in a city panorama that remains basically as it was when the work was completed. This first modern venture into what contemporary vocabulary terms "urban renewal" was due in great part to the personal initiatives of the newly proclaimed French emperor, Napoleon III.

Returning from exile in London, Napoleon III found Paris in dire need of revitalization. Overcrowding and poor sanitary conditions produced desolate, unhealthy environments; in 1848–49 nineteen thousand Parisians died of cholera. Four gardens, none of them municipal, served over one and a half million inhabitants. The emperor's many years abroad had instilled in him a great admiration for the English landscape style and their ventures into creating public open space. One of his first acts of power was the transfer of a 1,100-acre wooded site, known as the Bois de Boulogne, from state property to the city of Paris for the construction of a public park.

After Napoleon's nomination of Georges Eugène Haussmann as prefect of Paris in 1853, the transformation of the city began. Haussmann's responsibilities included the creation of the new public parks and squares, tree plantings, and general architectural adornment, yet, apart from selecting the team of designers, engineers, and plantsmen that made the verdant change possible, his input was slight. Headed by Jean-

Claude Alphand, a civil engineer by training, and assisted by Edouard André and the newly appointed chief city gardener, Jean-Pierre Barillet-Deschamps, the team was to work in every quarter of the city.

Alphand's first task was the Bois de Boulogne, which he completed in three short years. The surrounding wall was pulled down and, as a result of land transfers, the park was increased in size to extend down to the Seine. All but two of the original axial drives were replaced with sixty miles (95 kilometers) of winding lanes, bridle paths, and carriage roads laid out within the replanted woods. Massive regrading gave topographical relief to the flat site, as did large stones and boulders transported from Fontainebleau. Alphand's engineering skills were required in the construction of two lakes, one with a small island, that were connected by a twenty-foot- (6-meter-) high waterfall. With the advances of the period in hydrodynamics, a second waterfall, forty-two feet high by thirty feet wide (13 meters by 9 meters), was also built. This engineering feat was set into a grottolike scene that was to become a common feature in future park designs. From this dramatic focal point a sinuous stream snaked along the wooded trails, planted with aquatic plants and ferns. Promenade walks were laid out around the perimeters of the few open meadows that had been cleared from the forest setting.

Barillet-Deschamps was responsible for replanting the woods, and he did this predominantly with oaks and elms, along with large numbers of ornamental groupings; in all, over 200,000 trees were planted. Set within the promenade clearings and around the public areas, such as the lakes, restaurants, cascades, and entrances, were evergreen trees and shrubs. Year-round interest was the principal reason for planting large masses of pines, especially Austrian black pine *(Pinus nigra)*, Lawson's false cypress *(Chamaecyparis lawsoniana)*—a North American native—and Canadian hemlock *(Tsuga canadensis)*.

The ornamental plantings were divided into three design categories that were to remain standards in French landscape terminology well into the twentieth century. The first, the *groupe*, was the practice of planting two or more of the same variety of tree close together and was generally utilized at pathway intersections or as punctuation on lawns or in clearings. Low underplantings were not used with

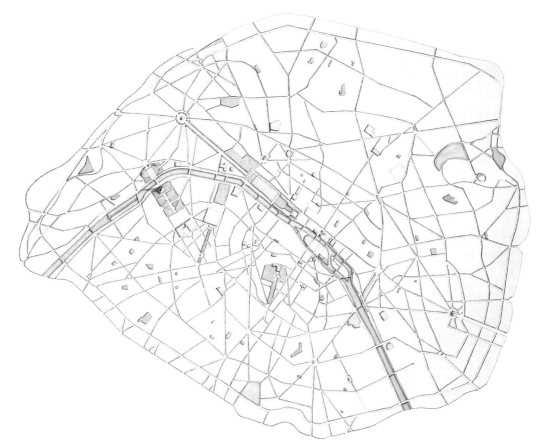

the arrangement, as the trees were to provide contrasting interest without blocking out entire views. The second schematic, called the *massif*, was just the opposite and was used to screen unwanted features or in isolated situations where its silhouette would read as a dark, impenetrable mass. The understory of these densely planted tree groups mainly consisted of European shrubs—viburnums, dogwoods, and buckthorns. The third planting, which was employed most often in the creation of wooded expanses, was the *futaie*, which consisted of intermixing tree varieties without the use of underplantings and arranging them in symmetrical rows or in irregular formations, depending on the site.

Other features of the park that have changed little since 1865 include the small children's zoo, numerous restaurants, Swiss chalet–style cafes and pavilions, and the famous Bagatelle garden, which was originally laid out as an English park by the Scotsman Thomas Blaikie in the late 1770s. The park is still as popular with Parisians as it was during the Second Empire, when it became the fashionable spot for afternoon drives and outdoor dining for the wealthier classes.

While landscaping the park Haussmann also laid out the grand Avenue de l'Emperatrice, now know as the Avenue Foch. Treated as the formal approach to the Bois, the avenue is nearly twice as wide as other city thoroughfares and is further distinguished by flanking gardens more than a hundred feet (30½ meters) across. Here, beneath the canopies of Oriental planes, Barillet-Deschamps planted a luxurious collection of flowering shrubs and, in irregular-shaped plots, an eclectic selection of much-admired bedding-out annuals. The avenue's design was just one example of how the landscape was extended from the limited confines of the park into the city beyond.

In conjunction with the prefect's reorganization of the city's major street system, over seventy small parks or planted squares were created. Loosely patterned after the privately maintained garden squares the emperor had admired in London, the French square was to be open to the public and located in the city's most densely populated quarters. Most of the miniature parks followed a general scheme of evergreen shrub borders enclosing central grassed areas planted with a few specimen trees. Along with such commonly employed shrubs as box and yew, the borders also contained such imported exotics as *Aucuba japonica*, recently in-

Above: *The gently
undulating lawns in the
Bagatalle landscape garden
are punctuated by groups of
trees, many consisting of
foreign species employed for
their contrasting color and
form, such as the blue
Atlas cedar.*
Left: *Hidden within the
landscape garden at
Bagatelle in the Bois de
Boulogne is one mid-
nineteenth-century garden
feature, the towering water
cascade.*

troduced from Japan, California allspice *(Calycanthus occidentalis)*, and Oregon grape *(Mahonia aquifolium)*. Imported trees were used in the squares to provide each with a special atmosphere. Planted among the plane and linden trees were Japanese pagoda tree *(Sophora japonica)*, paulownia, tulip tree *(Liriodendron)*, southern magnolia *(Magnolia grandiflora)*, and Lawson's false cypress *(Chamaecyparis lawsoniana)*. The squares remain small verdant islands today and, with their benches and characteristic metal chairs, places for moments of quiet within the urban scramble. Their tradition continues, the number of little pocket parks having doubled since their original creation.

Alphand and his team of designers were equally responsible for the public transformation of many former royal parks and gardens, the Parc Monceau and the Luxembourg Palace gardens being two such examples.

The Parc Monceau on the Right Bank was in its original layout one of France's earliest *anglo-chinois* gardens, built as the Duc de Chartres's Parisian pleasure grounds. The plan by Carmontell, worked on by Thomas Blaikie, had rolling vistas, serpentine lakes and streams, and its most notable feature, innumerable *fabriques* that ran the gamut from Dutch windmills to Egyptian pyramids and Italian vineyards. Confiscated during the revolution and briefly opened as a public park, the land was returned to the family with the restoration of the monarchy in 1814. In 1860 just under half of the original site was transferred to the city of Paris. Alphand simplified many of the path systems while redesigning the overgrown meadows and lawns, and restored as many of the original *fabriques* as possible. Barillet-Deschamps planted large numbers of trees and shrubs along with flower beds that included a vast carpet of roses composed of 'General Jacqueminot', 'La Reine', and 'Souvenir de la Malmaison'. Alphand built a lake with a winding stream and, because they proved so popular at the Bois de Boulogne, a grotto and waterfall. The park exists today almost as it did over a hundred and thirty years ago and still holds a great fascination for the crowds of neighborhood children, as hidden moss-covered pyramids and ruined colonnades rise above shady mounds of aucuba and dark yews.

The Luxembourg Palace and adjoining

gardens were built in 1612 for Marie de Medici in the manner of the period, with embroidered parterres set within a sunken central area on axis with the palace's garden facade. In the late seventeenth century the parterres were redesigned in a cross formation with rounded ends that remains today, forming bays from which steps rise to the wooded areas of the park. By the mid-nineteenth century the embroidered parterres had been replaced by large grass lawns framed by wide flower borders. Perhaps no other Parisian park today rivals the Luxembourg for the Second Empire's great love of bedding out.

From spring through late fall the garden is overwhelmed by a riot of color and plant combinations, from the beds that border the grass parterres and the numerous vases and urns, to the hidden "basket" beds planted within the confines of the "English park." Barillet-Deschamps's original plant combinations included lilacs and honeysuckle standards set within vivid beds of cannas, hollyhocks, dahlias, and bright pelargoniums. The original tree plantings were replaced in the 1860s with sugar maples for their colorful autumnal foliage and white- and red-flowering varieties of horse chestnut for their late-spring blossoms. Summer brings out orange and palm trees set in painted boxes and tubs, just as is done at Versailles, which animate the central sunken area. In a corner at the far reaches of the park are the vegetables and espaliered fruit trees. In the great French kitchen garden tradition, once each individual apple or pear has developed enough, it is wrapped in its own paper bag and tied with a string, protected from insects and birds until the fruit is ready to be picked. Beehives and beekeeping classes are held in a shady confine of the park and courses on plant identification in one of the small pavilions. Throughout the park are fixed benches and movable armchairs, adding to its intimate atmosphere. Of all the Parisian parks, the Luxembourg Gardens is the most successful in its attempt to bring the pleasures of both park and garden together on a human scale.

What linked these varied expressions of "urban renewal" in Paris was the grand-scale use of trees. As the city expanded at an alarm-

Left: The Place de Furstenberg is quietly nestled in the densely crowded Sixth Arrondissement on Paris's Left Bank. The small square is transformed by the inclusion of four trees which humanizes the intimate site.
Right: Framed within a tunnel of chestnut trees, two Caisse de Versailles, or planter boxes, contain towering palms. Following the French tradition of cultivating exotic tree specimens, the Luxembourg Gardens are dotted with palms and orange trees during the warm months. As at Versailles, the tender specimens are overwintered in greenhouses, or orangeries.

ing rate and the nearby countryside ceased to be within view, it was the introduction of the tree-lined street and planted square in Haussmann's time that humanized a cityscape that had come to overwhelm the pedestrian scale. In seventeenth-century France, Louis XIV's powerful controller general of finance, Jean-Baptiste Colbert, ordered the planting of plane and elm trees to line the major thoroughfares leading into Paris. These leafy drives of evenly spaced rows of trees provided shaded and protected routes for the city's visitors while si-

multaneously heightening the sense of arrival and the expectation of grandeur. The practice soon became commonplace throughout the French countryside as principal roadways were aligned with ribbons of greenery. By lining the newly created mid-nineteenth-century boulevards and avenues with trees, Haussmann provided the urban framework with a verdant lushness that provoked memories of the distant countryside in a most abstract and conceptual form.

Above: *A sculptural fountain terminates the long southern perspective at Luxembourg Gardens. The avenue of chestnut trees is pruned annually to enhance the axis and direct the view of the extended vista.*
Right: *Common in so many French formal gardens is the play of light and shadow, the positive and negative. Here in Luxembourg Gardens the tunnel of tree rows provides a cool promenade as it flanks the wide, open grass lawn.*

CONSERVATORY GARDEN

In the far northeastern reaches of Central Park lies a small enclosed site that acts as the park's only gesture toward the formal garden. The juxtaposition of the garden's intimate scale with Olmsted's sweeping designs increases its secret, jewellike quality. The Conservatory Garden's precarious position further enhances its unique atmosphere, as it borders both the urban environment and the encircling verdant landscape of the park.

Conceived as a WPA program to replace the site of the park's former greenhouses in 1935, the garden was rescued from years of neglect in 1982 and restored to a place of special beauty. From the great flight of steps that descends into the garden at Fifth Avenue (shown at right center of the plan), the immediate sensation is one of entering an extraordinarily distinctive and reserved world. Sheared yew hedges and flanking billowing crab-apple trees frame a broad grass lawn that, in context, is very different from the park's acres of green turf. A planted terraced slope rises at the far end, atop which one can view the small complex below. A trellised pergola crowns the summit with a gnarled wisteria that provides cool summer shade. The stepped incline is planted with clipped spirea and yew, with bold rows of vibrant bluebells outlining each terraced edge during the midspring weeks. The North Garden, to the right of the entrance, projects a vivid display of color twice a year. Surrounded by waist-high hedges of Japanese quince, spirea, and metal hoops of climbing roses, concentric beds contain masses of tulips in spring—over twenty thousand—and chrysanthemums in the fall. The central fountain is ringed by a second series of beds with a florid parterre scroll design planted with santolina and supplemented with additional seasonal annuals for color. It is a garden of bold, bright color and form which seems to energize by its striking show.

Its counterpart on the opposite side of the great lawn, the South, or Secret, Garden, demands a slower pace, as its subtleties are finer. Redesigning from the original layout by Betty Sprout, the Conservatory Garden's director, Lynden Miller, has transformed the U-shaped beds into English-style perennial borders. Here visitors spend summer afternoons marveling at the contrasting colors and palettelike effects of foliage and flower forms, while others are noting down combinations for future attempts back home.

CENTRAL PARK AND WASHINGTON, D.C.

Though built concurrently with the public gardens of Paris, Central Park provoked an altogether different approach. Whereas the Parisian parks reflected the Second Empire's passion for parade and spectacle, fused with the dramatic, their American counterparts mirrored the spirit of that nation's relationship with the wild and the natural. Although both philosophies strove to integrate nature with the changing city for public benefit, it was the 1857 Olmsted and Vaux design of the eight-hundred-acre site for Central Park that most completely realized this concept.

Deeply rooted in Brown and Repton's principles, the Olmsted and Vaux design was also influenced by the writings of Loudon and Downing. Their plan resulted in a modern ideal where the functions of both city and nature were able to coexist without encroaching upon each other. The design transported the visitor away from the surrounding world to one of pastoral scenery. From the sunken cross-park roads that eliminate the intrusion of urban traffic to the variety of landscape experiences, the park provides an entirely self-contained naturalistic environment. A range of architectural features supports the countrylike atmosphere—rusticated balustrades, benches, boathouses, shady vine-clad walks. Pavilions and park service structures were treated in a pastoral vocabulary that recalls farm constructions and fanciful visions of an idyllic countryside. Olmsted and Vaux created their own influential interpretation of the elysian vision in the United States.

The second half of the nineteenth century witnessed the adoption by major American cities of the Central Park concept while simultaneously large tracts of virgin lands were set aside for public use and ownership in undeveloped regions of the country. The National Park system was created by congressional legislation and then signed by President Grant in 1872 to preserve, protect, and maintain what came to be called Yellowstone Park in Idaho, Montana, and Wyoming. Sites of scenic beauty later added to the roster included Yosemite Park in California and Mount Rainier in Washington. With this increased awareness of the natural untouched landscape developed regional landscape and architectural movements in the United States, such as Frank

A promenade avenue amid New York's Central Park contrasts with its Parisian park counterparts. Here fixed benches line the wide pedestrian concourse and the trees flanking the walk are allowed to grow in their natural shape and form, creating a naturalistic setting.

*The entrance to the South,
or Secret, Garden in New
York's Central Park
Conservatory Garden. In
spring, billowing lilacs
encircle the U-shaped
garden, reflecting the vivid
hues of the bulb plantings.
By midsummer the beds
have taken on a riot of
color as the perennial
borders reflect an English-
style planting scheme.*

Lloyd Wright's Prairie School from which rose an expanded consciousness and employment of indigenous plant materials. Jens Jensen, a Danish-born American landscape architect, practiced in Chicago at the turn of the century both in public works, as the director of the city's park system, and for private commissions. His designs emphasized the horizontal line—the prevailing theme in the Prairie School—by use of native trees and shrubs, including hawthorns, flowering dogwoods, and crab apples, often set bordering broad meadow treatments of ornamental grasses and wildflowers.

At the turn of the century the United States produced one of the most classical expressions of formal design in a public forum: the revival of Pierre L'Enfant's original layout for Washington, D.C. Created by Congress in 1790, the site for the nation's future federal seat was the decision of George Washington, as was the choice of L'Enfant, a French military engineer, as the city's architect. Working closely with the president, L'Enfant produced a grand layout in the traditional French formal style. Long axial sight lines radiating from Capitol Hill and the White House—both of which he sited—converge perpendicularly to each other, while diagonal drives connect the two, a design similiar in relationship to that existing between the château and the Grand Trianon at Versailles. Bisecting boulevards with squares and planted spaces with vistas to the new capital were emphasized. Required by Jefferson and Congress to incorporate a grid street structure, L'Enfant proposed a variety of open urban spaces to relieve the boredom of the pattern.

The majestic vista down the Potomac River from the porch at Mount Vernon. The tree plantings along the banks were an important design feature that George Washington incorporated into the general scheme of the grounds. Termed "clever trees" by Washington, for their sudden bursts of blossoms, the groupings include dogwoods, sassafras, and shad which enlivened the river views during the early spring months when outdoor promenades were limited to the covered porch.

One of George Washington's first undertakings upon acquiring Mount Vernon was the laying out of the kitchen garden. Here, within the geometric beds linked with grass paths, the cultivation of vegetables and herbs, along with such fruits as apples, pears, and peaches, enabled the large plantation complex to be self-sufficient.

Congress approved the final layout and work commenced. Soon after, L'Enfant was relieved of his position as relations between the designer and the government commission set up to oversee the work had deteriorated. By 1800 the federal government was transferred officially to Washington from Philadelphia, yet large tracts of swampy land still remained undeveloped. In the century that followed, the plan was little consulted as the city expanded. Perhaps the greatest intrusion on the original conception was the construction of a train station in the central Mall, destroying the grand perspective set up from Capitol Hill down to the Potomac River.

In 1900 a congressional commission was formed to study the city's urban planning problem. Named for Senator McMillian, who advocated immediate action, the four-

man body was composed of professionals in several fields. Frederick Olmsted, Jr., son of the creator of Central Park, was joined by Charles McKim, the noted architect; Augustus Saint-Gaudens, the sculptor; and Charles Moore, who dealt with administrative responsibilities. The McMillian Commission toured Europe for two and a half months inspecting endless sites, including the Bois de Boulogne, the Tuileries, and the Luxembourg Gardens in Paris, Villa d'Este and Hadrian's villa at Tivoli, and Hyde Park in London, along with others in Venice, Rome, Vienna, and Budapest. Their final decision was to readopt L'Enfant's plan, with the inclusion of wide tree borders flanking the Mall to hide the nineteenth-century intrusions into the space, along with a formal treatment at the intersection of the sight lines from the White

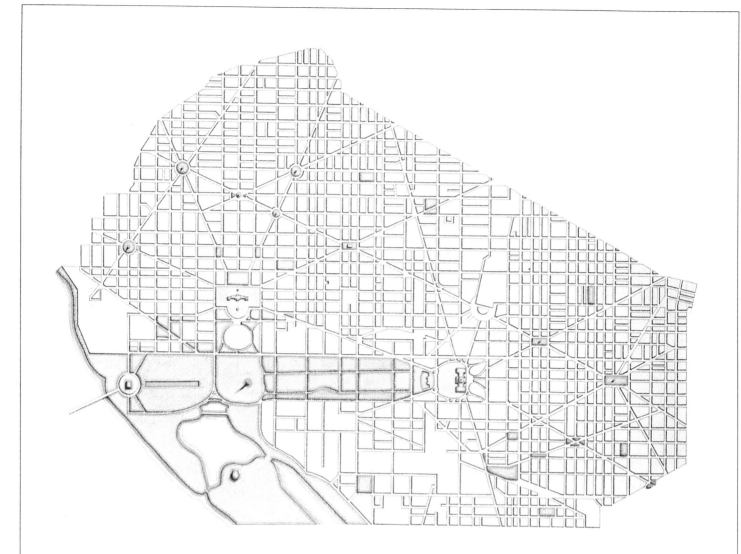

WASHINGTON, D.C.

The plan of Washington, D.C., as it exists today. Radiating from both the White House and Capitol Hill are two important axial perspectives from which radiate wide avenues and vistas. Conceived by the Frenchman Pierre L'Enfant in 1791, the city's original layout reflected late-eighteenth-century ideals and theories regarding the logical organization of space and their interconnecting relationships in creating a large-scale sense of majesty. By the mid-nineteenth century, L'Enfant's plan had long been abandoned as the city expanded. That changed in 1901 when the McMillian Commission was formed with the task of replanning the city. The commission's recommendations and subtle modifications restored the formality of L'Enfant's design, providing the city with a unique sense of force and grandeur.

FEDERAL RESERVE GARDEN

Wolfgang Oehme and James van Sweden's influential work over the past decade includes this redesign of the Federal Reserve gardens in Washington, D.C. Replacing traditional plantings commonly found in such institutional sites, the team employed their signature plant materials, which include ornamental grasses and herbaceous perennials. Credited with the formation of a new American style of garden, Oehme and van Sweden plant with broad, dramatic strokes, massing single species and varieties, such as *Bergenia*, *Epimedium*, *Miscanthus sinensis*, and *Sedum* 'Autumn Joy' and 'Ruby Glow'.

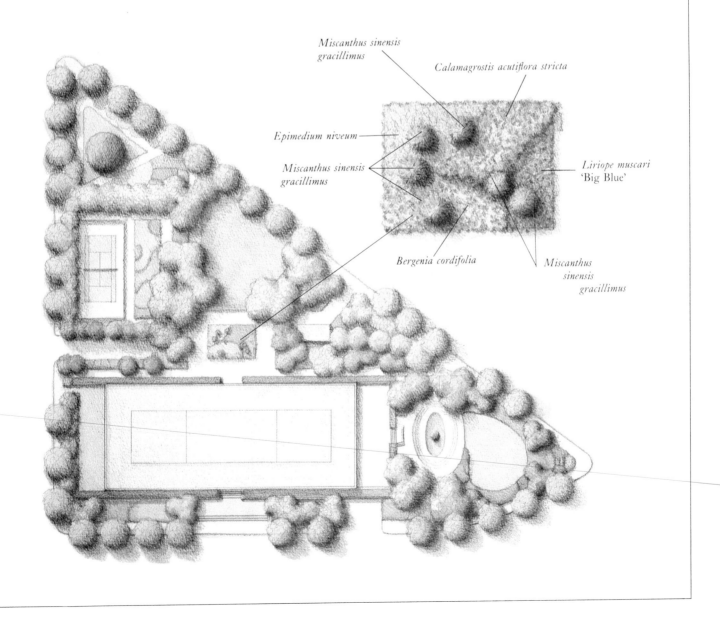

Miscanthus sinensis gracillimus

Calamagrostis acutiflora stricta

Epimedium niveum

Miscanthus sinensis gracillimus

Liriope muscari 'Big Blue'

Bergenia cordifolia

Miscanthus sinensis gracillimus

Left: *Spring sets forth a sweep of pastel pinks and whites at the Lincoln Memorial Park on the outskirts of Springfield, Illinois, designed in the early twentieth century by the influential Danish-born American landscape architect Jens Jensen, who was credited with the formation of the Prairie School of landscape, with his employment of indigenous plant materials within a naturalistic setting. Here Jensen used informal groupings of native redbud trees and dogwoods to create a naturalistic effect that relied more on trees and shrubs for seasonal color and interest.*

Bottom left: *A view from the enclosed perennial garden at Wave Hill down across to the Hudson River. Located north of Manhattan on the steep banks of the Hudson, Wave Hill is just one of the many parks in the United States that were once private estates.*

Opposite page: *Situated on the banks of Lake Ontario, the Royal Botanical Gardens at Hamilton, Ontario, are world famous for their large collection of flowering shrubs, most notably lilacs. Increasingly popular with the garden-loving public, the botanical gardens provide both educational and recreational facilities for many urban dwellers.*

House and Capitol Hill. Their proposal also included the siting of such future monuments as the Lincoln Memorial. Washington, D.C., as we experience it today, with its grand avenues and verdant expanses of lawn and trees, is the direct result of the 1901 McMillian plan, which restored its late-eighteenth-century formal layout.

Washington continues to be at the forefront of contemporary landscape treatment, incorporating innovative designs within formal compositions, most notably the widely acclaimed work of the landscape office of Wolfgang Oehme and James van Sweden. This Washington-based firm has been responsible for revolutionizing planting concepts in the last decade and credited with the creation of the "new American garden" through their characteristic use of herbaceous plants and ornamental grasses. They transformed the planting scheme of the Federal Reserve Bank building from its traditional treatment of lawn, boxwood, and azaleas to one of continuous change and vivid color. Large blocks of single flower plantings are laid out in such bold schemes as masses of black-eyed Susans followed by 'Autumn Joy' sedums all set against contrasting ornamental grasses and evergreen hollies. Oehme and van Sweden's innovative designs are also conscious of the contemporary problems facing gardens and large-scale planting—water and maintenance. Their plantings tend to need little of either.

SUBURBIA AND THE FUTURE OF PUBLIC PARKS

The great expansion and economic growth experienced in the United States during the early decades of the twentieth century meant the increased affluence of the middle class, which in turn manifested itself in the establishment of the suburban township or "green village." This development would later have far-reaching implications for urban parks and public spaces. The first attempts at planned suburban communities included the construction of Forest Hills Gardens in Queens, New York, in 1909 by Olmsted Brothers, and Hare and Hare's 1913 design for Kansas City's Garden Club district. These first "bedroom communities" were verdant housing developments intended for the increasing numbers of commuting urban workers.

With the post–World War II economic boom came an even greater flux of middle-class inhabitants from the densely populated urban centers to what were to represent the final achievement of the great American dream: suburbia and the individual house and garden. Numerous American cities saw their financial bases weakened as a result of this mass exodus, which produced great financial strains on city municipalities struggling both to maintain existing park systems and plan future facilities. Few private urban ventures provided public areas before the late 1960s, one such exception being New York City's Rockefeller Center, constructed in the 1930s. The complex of commercial office buildings also includes public spaces such as restaurants, shops, and theaters, along with fountains, flower and shrubbery beds, and tree plantings, all of which continue to delight native New Yorkers and visitors alike. Rockefeller Center's conceptual arrangement of public space set within a commercial context was to become mandatory five decades later for large-scale building in midtown Manhattan, resulting in such recent examples as the IBM Bamboo Garden.

Throughout the 1970s and 80s civic governments, realizing the increased needs of their inhabitants for green space, began to rely more heavily on both corporate and private sponsors, along with public support groups, to supplement public funds in helping maintain and, in some instances, restore areas of neglect in city parks. Private concerns and commercial ventures have also transformed and renovated historic and former industrial sites, such as Ghirardelli Square in San Francisco or Faneuil Hall in Boston, into popular spaces that rely on landscaped features. Urban renewal became the key word as faded "downtown" districts were rejuvenated with the additions of public squares and plazas, many conceptually influenced by Italian Renaissance models, which drew both people and businesses back to once-forgotten areas.

Although gardens and parks have become increasingly vital for the city dweller as a counterbalance to the rigid urban framework, it is essential to exploit further alternatives to provide additional greenery. One such means has been the transformation of former private estate gardens to public access and use. Successful transitions have resulted in gardens or parks, some of which are botanical in nature, such as Wave Hill in the Bronx borough of New York City or the Huntington Gardens in San Marino, California. Others, like Swan House in Atlanta, Filoli in San Francisco's peninsula area, or Washington, D.C.'s Dumbarton Oaks, have become favorite public gardens as they retain their former highly personal atmosphere, resulting in unique and intimate spaces for the general public and interesting alternatives to the nineteenth-century elysian park compositions.

As the twentieth century draws to a close, major city centers arduously maintain their existing spaces while designs for future parks are continually being proposed and realized. This passionate battle has resulted in urban landscapes greener today than they were even a generation ago. Enterprising and ambitious grand park propositions continue to dominate urban issues as alternatives to the late-nineteenth-century parks are presented in both Europe and the United States. One such garden complex, the Moody Historical Garden currently under construction in Galveston, Texas, continues the spirit for innovative design and will provide the city inhabitants with green spaces in an altogether original and exciting manner. Financed privately by the Moody Foundation, the intricately envisioned garden complex was created by the English designer and landscape historian Sir Geoffrey Jellicoe. The twenty-year program, begun in 1985, signals an entirely individual and novel approach toward public park design. Conceived to be experienced either from a sinuous boat ride that takes the visitor on an aquatic promenade, or by foot, the garden is composed of

Ragdale, one of the few vestiges of unspoiled natural prairie land still existing in North America, lies thirty miles (48 kilometers) from Chicago in the exclusive township of Lake Forest, Illinois. Created at the turn of the century by the Chicago-based architect Howard Van Doren Shaw as a country retreat, the fifty-acre estate included wildflower plantings, serpentine drives, and groves of cottonwoods, swamp willows, ash, and oaks. Today the property is managed by the Ragdale Foundation, formed in 1976 and jointly owned by the Nature Conservancy and the Lake Forest Open Lands Association. The prairie lands are ablaze with color from spring until late October with violets, both blue and white varieties, sunflowers, coneflowers, prairie docks, and bluestem turkeyfoot grass. The foundation maintains residences on the property for artists, providing studios for writers and painters set within the richly diverse prairie landscape.

small, intimate, roomlike gardens that depict fifteen different interpretations of garden cultures in an almost surreal manner. From Adam and Eve's garden of paradise, past ancient Egypt, Rome, eastern Mogul India, China, and Japan, the visitor experiences the general atmospheres that compose garden styles up to the nineteenth century's landscape movement. Most of the Western cultures are set within a grid formation, which also makes reference to an influential twentieth-century garden feature, the exterior room, or garden compartment, as perfected at Sissinghurst and Hidcote. The intimate atmosphere of the various garden rooms reflects the utilization of a domestic schematic applied on a public scale. Diverging from the classical nineteenth-century concepts for public park design, the new directional design schematics have also been incorporated in the proposed layouts of two other large-scale parks—South Garden in

New York City's Battery Park City complex and the vast Jardin Javel-Citroën, currently under construction in Paris. All three designs will provide a multitude of garden experiences for the increasingly garden-conscious general public through the use of "garden room" configurations.

As the world's natural environments have come under direct threat of destruction and concerns for the earth's safety become more complex, we must continue, to an even greater degree, to maintain and protect both the natural world and the one we have created, as the two are vital to our existence. The public park as a concept has expanded far beyond its original creators' definition to now encompass all our surroundings. Although we seem far from that lost idealized paradise that a garden can abstractly represent, it can reappear very quickly with even the slightest verdant image, but only if we wish it.

By the mid-nineteenth century, the public park became the center for daily social activity for many well-to-do Parisians. Here in his masterpiece Music at the Tuileries, *painted in 1862, Manet captured the gay spirit and atmosphere so characteristic of the newly created public parks of the Second Empire. The ambience of an outdoor* salon *still exists in many Parisian parks today; though many are set within a formal design, a informality prevails and visitors can draw up chairs to create an intimate tête-à-tête or enjoy a large gathering. (Bridgeman/Art Resource, New York)*

Early morning at Luxembourg Gardens in Paris. The characteristic metal chairs await visitors who, by the end of the day, move them around completely.

ABOUT THE CONTRIBUTORS

The volunteer director of special projects at the Brooklyn Botanic Garden, ELVIN MCDONALD has written over forty books on gardening, most recently *Northeast Gardening* and *House Beautiful's Outdoor Living*. He was the garden editor of *House Beautiful* for twelve years, was a founding editor of *Flower and Garden* magazine, is on the advisory board of *Garden Design* magazine, and is the secretary of the American Horticultural Society.

A gardener and gardening consultant of world renown, PENOLOPE HOBHOUSE has written numerous books on the topic, including *Color in Your Garden*, *The Country Garden*, and *Garden Style*. A regular contributor to gardening magazines and journals on both sides of the Atlantic, she also lectures widely in Britain, Europe, and the United States. She is at present in charge of the National Trust garden at Tintinhull House in Somerset, England.

ALLEN PATERSON trained in horticulture at the University Botanic Garden, Cambridge, and the Royal Botanic Gardens, Kew. In 1973 he became curator of the historic Chelsea Physic Garden in London, where he remained until 1981, when he was appointed director of the Royal Botanical Gardens at Hamilton, Ontario. He travels and lectures widely and has led plant-study tours to Ecuador and the Galápagos, the Himalayas, and the Mediterranean. He is the author of several books on horticultural topics, most recently *Plants for Shade and Woodland*, and is a Distinguished Advisor to the Board of the Brooklyn Botanic Garden.

The director of the Japanese Association for the Conservation of Architectural Monuments and a professor of architecture at Kogakuin University in Tokyo, TEIJI ITOH is an authority on Japanese garden and architectural design. His books on garden design include *The Gardens of Japan*, *The Imperial Gardens of Japan*, and *Space and Illusion in the Japanese Garden*.

A contributing editor to *Horticulture* magazine and a regular columnist for *Seattle Weekly*, ANN LOVEJOY writes regularly for *Harrowsmith*, *House & Garden*, and many other gardening and plant society publications. Her most recent books include

The Year in Bloom and *The Border in Bloom*. She is also the editor of the anthology *New Voices in American Garden Writing*. She gardens on an old farm on an island in Puget Sound, outside Seattle, Washington.

KATHERINE WHITESIDE has traveled around the world to write on gardening subjects for such magazines as *House & Garden, Connoisseur, Garden Design*, and *Landscape Architecture*. She is the author of *Antique Flowers*, a collaboration with her husband, photographer Mick Hales, and their monthly garden column appeared in newspapers across the country. She lives in Cold Spring, New York.

A garden designer of world reputation, JOHN BROOKES is the author of thirteen books on gardening, including *The Garden Book, The New Small Garden Book*, and *The Country Garden*. He is the founder of the Clock House School of Garden Design in West Sussex, England, and gives garden design workshops around the world, in addition to maintaining his private practice.

The author of *Private Gardens of Paris*, MADISON COX lived in Paris for ten years. His landscape commissions include many private gardens as well as the Franco-American Museum in France. He runs a private design practice in New York City and is a contributing editor of *Elle Decor*. His articles have appeared in numerous European and American magazines.

MICK HALES is an internationally known photographer who specializes in gardens and architectural design. He photographed the best-selling calendar *Gardens* and the book *Antique Flowers*. His work appears in *House & Garden, House Beautiful, Town & Country*, and numerous other magazines.

A photographer specializing in fashion and gardens, ERICA LENNARD has had her work exhibited in galleries around the world. She has collaborated on numerous books and her photography has appeared in magazines worldwide, including *Garden Design, European Travel and Life, House & Garden*, and *Metropolitan Home*. She lives in New York City.

PHOTO CREDITS AND COPYRIGHTS

GLOSSARY

allée—French, usually denoting a passage lined with clipped or pleached trees.

bassin—French formal pool usually lined with stone.

belvedere—an Italian garden building and viewpoint.

berceau—French term for an arbor enclosed by shade-giving plants.

bosco—a grove of trees, in Italy usually evergreen oaks, pines, and cypresses.

bosquet—French for a formal decorative grove of trees; at Versailles containing a series of garden themes.

charmille—from the French for *hornbeam*. A tree-lined walk where the walls of "green" are cut to an even height.

corona—the cup or trumpet of a daffodil or narcissus.

cotyledon—the vestigial leaf or leaves present within a seed that frequently emerge above soil level at the time of germination.

dicotyledon—one of the two primary divisions of flowering plants, having two (more rarely) seed leaves *(cotyledons)*. Most woody plants belong to the dicots, as they are abbreviated; they have leaves with netted or branched veins and their floral parts are in fours or fives.

giardino inglese—a private retiring garden, not literally a secret garden.

giochi d'acqua—an Italian water joke.

ha-ha—a dry ditch with an invisible raised retaining wall that conceals the boundaries of the garden so that they merge with the landscape.

jardin anglais—French term for a garden laid out in the English landscape style.

jardin anglo-chinois—a French interpretation of the English landscape style with Oriental overtones perpetuated throughout Europe.

knot—a geometric formal pattern where dwarf hedges interweave that was popular in the Italian and French Renaissance. Interpreted in Tudor England as patterns from strapwork plaster ceilings and embroidered "up and over" stitches.

labyrinth—also known as a *maze*, this was a confusing pattern symbolic in the Christian church of man's journey through life and his search for eternity.

monocotyledon—one of the two primary divisions of flowering plants, having only one seed leaf *(cotyledon)*. Grasses, palms, orchids, and most bulbous plants are monocots, as they are abbreviated. Their leaf veins are mainly parallel and their floral parts occur in threes.

tunic—the outer coat of a bulb or corm.

BIBLIOGRAPHY AND FURTHER RECOMMENDED READING

CHAPTER 1

Beales, Peter. *Classic Roses*. New York: Henry Holt & Co., 1985.

Fisher, John. *The Companion to Roses*. Boston: Salem House Publishers, Ltd., 1987.

Gibson, Michael. *The Rose Gardens of England*. Chester, Conn.: The Globe Pequot Press, 1988.

LeRougetel, Hazel. *A Heritage of Roses*. Owings Mills, Md.: Stemmer House Publishers, Inc., 1988.

Thomas, Graham Stuart. The introduction to his revision of *Roses*, by Gertrude Jekyll and Edward Mawley. Salem, N.H.: Ayer Company Publishers, Ltd., 1983.

Wells, Robert W. *Papa Floribunda: A Biography of Eugene S. Boerner*. Milwaukee, Wis.: BBG Publishing Co., 1989.

CHAPTER 2

Bloomfield, Reginald. *The Formal Garden in England*. New York: Macmillan Publishing Co., 1901.

Dumbarton Oaks Publications, ed. Elizabeth MacDougall. Including *Ancient Roman Gardens* and *The Islamic Garden*. 1976.

Elliot, Brent. *Victorian Gardens*. London: B. T. Batsford, Ltd., 1986.

Gothein, Marie-Louise. *A History of Garden Art*. New York: Hacker Art Books, 1979.

Hervey, John. *Medieval Gardens*. London: B. T. Batsford, Ltd., 1981.

Jacques, David, and Arend Jan van der Horst. *The Gardens of William and Mary*. Portland, Oreg.: International Specialized Book Services, 1988.

Loudon, John Claudius. *Encyclopædia of Gardening*. London: Longman, Hurst, Rees, Orme, Brown & Green, 1825.

The Oxford Companion to Gardens, ed. Patrick Goode and Michael Lancaster. Oxford: Oxford University Press, 1986.

Thacker, Christopher. *The History of Gardens*. Berkeley: University of California Press, 1979.

Woodbridge, Kenneth. *Princely Gardens*. London: Thames & Hudson, 1986.

CHAPTER 3

Mathew, Brian. *The Larger Bulbs*. London: B. T. Batsford, Ltd., 1978.

———. *The Smaller Bulbs*. London: B. T. Batsford, Ltd., 1987.

Phillips, Roger, and Martyn Rix. *The Bulb Book*. London: Pan Books, Ltd., 1981.

Taylor's Guide to Bulbs. Boston: Houghton Mifflin Co., 1984.

Thomas, Graham S. *The Art of Planting*. Boston: David R. Godine, Inc., 1984.

Wilder, Louise Beebe. *Adventures with Hardy Bulbs*. New York: Collier Books, 1990.

CHAPTER 4

Hayakawa, Masao. *The Garden Art of Japan*. New York: John Weatherhill, Inc., 1973.

Itoh, Teiji. *The Gardens of Japan*. New York: Kodansha International USA, Ltd., 1984.

———. *The Imperial Gardens of Japan*. New York: John Weatherhill, Inc., 1970.

———. *Space and Illusion in the Japanese Garden*. New York: John Weatherhill, Inc., 1980.

Ohashi, Haruzo. *Japanese Courtyard Gardens*. Briarcliff Manor, N.Y.: Japan Publications (USA), Inc., 1988.

———. *The Japanese Garden: Islands of Serenity*. Briarcliff Manor, N.Y.: Japan Publications (USA), Inc., 1986.

———. *Japanese Gardens of the Modern Era*. Briarcliff Manor, N.Y.: Japan Publications (USA), Inc., 1987.

Shigemori, Kanto. *The Japanese Courtyard Garden: Landscapes for Small Places*. New York: John Weatherhill, Inc., 1981.

Slawson, David A. *Secret Teachings in the Art of Japanese Gardens: Design Principles, Aesthetic Values*. New York: Kodansha International USA, Ltd., 1987.

Treib, Marc, and Ron Herman. *A Guide to the Gardens of Kyoto*. Distributed by C. E. Tuttle, Inc., Rutland, Vt., 1980.

CHAPTER 5

Barton, Barbara. *Gardening by Mail*. Boston: Houghton Mifflin Co., 1990.

Brookes, John. *The Garden Book*. New York: Crown Publishers, Inc., 1984.

Ferguson, Nicola. *Right Plant, Right Place*. New York: Summit Books, 1984.

Fish, Margery. *A Flower for Every Day*. Winchester, Mass.: Faber & Faber, Inc., 1981.

Hobhouse, Penelope. *Color in Your Garden*. Boston: Little, Brown & Co., 1985.

Lloyd, Christopher. *The Adventurous Gardener*. New York: Random House, Inc., 1984.

———. *Foliage Plants*. New York: Random House, Inc., 1985.

Sackville-West, Vita. *Vita Sackville-West's Garden Book*. New York: Atheneum, 1983.

Thomas, Graham S. *Perennial Garden Plants*. London: J. M. Dent & Sons, Ltd., 1982.

CHAPTER 6

"Allerton Gardens." Kauai, Hawaii: National Tropical Botanical Garden.

Bostwick, Jeri. *Hawaii Is a Garden*. Honolulu: Mutual Publishing of Honolulu, 1988.

Cameron, Ian. *Lost Paradise: The Exploration of the Pacific*. Topsfield, Mass.: Salem House Publishers, Ltd., 1987.

Clay, Horace F., and James C. Hubbard. *Tropical Exotics*. Honolulu: University of Hawaii Press, 1987.

Dworsky, Susan. "Two in the Tropics." *Horticulture Magazine* (March 1986): 57.

Eiseman, Fred, and Margaret Eiseman. *The Flowers of Bali*. Singapore: Periplus Editions, 1988.

Ekanayake, D. T. *The Botanic Gardens of Sri Lanka*. Kandy: Rotary Club, 1985.

Fairchild, David. *The World Was My Garden*. New York: Charles Scribner's Sons, 1941.

"A Garden Called Brief." *Shenelle* 5 (Sri Lanka, 1989).

Graf, Alfred B. *Exotica: International Series Four*, Volumes 1 and 2. East Rutherford, N.J.: Roehrs Co., 1985.

———. *Exotic Plant Manual: Fourth Edition*. East Rutherford, N.J.: Roehrs Co., 1974.

Hargreaves, Dorothy, and Bob Hargreaves. *Tropical Blossoms*. Kailua, Hawaii: Ross Hargreaves Co., 1960.

———. *Tropical Trees*. Kailua, Hawaii: Ross Hargreaves Co., 1960.

Hodge, Peggy H. *Tropical Gardening*. Rutland, Vt.: Charles E. Tuttle Co. Inc., 1970.

Jellicoe, Sir Geoffrey, et al. *The Oxford Companion to Gardens*. New York: Oxford University Press, 1987.

"Kauai." *The Magazine of the Garden Island* (July 1987): 24.

King, Ronald. *The Quest for Paradise*. New York: W. H. Smith Publishers, Inc., 1979.

Kramer, Jack. *World Wildlife Fund Book of Orchids*. New York: Abbeville Press, Inc., 1989.

Lara-Resende, Magda de Moura. "The Landscape Architect as Conservationist: An Interview with Roberto Burle Marx." *Orion Magazine* (Autumn 1989): 42.

Motta, Flávio L. *Roberto Burle Marx: e a Nova Visão da Paisagem*. São Paulo, Brazil: Nobel, 1985.

Museo de Arte Colonial: Quinta de Anauco. Caracas: Venezuelan Association of Friends of Colonial Art, 1978.

"National Tropical Botanical Garden." Kauai, Hawaii: National Tropical Botanical Garden.

Otis, Denise. "Artist of the Garden: Roberto Burle Marx." *House & Garden* (September 1986): 166.

———. "Burle Marx at Eighty." *Orion Magazine* (Autumn 1989): 47.

Padilla, Victoria. *Bromeliads*. New York: Crown Publishers, Inc., 1986.

"The Peradeniya Botanic Garden." Colombo, Sri Lanka: Ceylon Tourist Board, 1990.

"Singapore Botanic Gardens." Singapore: Singapore Botanic Gardens, 1990.

Tay Eng Pin et al. *Pictorial Guide to Singapore Botanic Gardens*. Singapore: Singapore Botanic Gardens, 1989.

Tinsley, Bonnie. *Visions of Delight: The Singapore Botanic Gardens Through the Ages*. Singapore: Singapore Botanic Gardens, 1989.

"Tropical Discovery on Kauai." *Sunset Magazine* (February 1984).

Veevers-Carter, W. *A Garden of Eden: Plant Life in South-East Asia*. New York: Oxford University Press, 1989.

Wellingham-Jones, Patricia. "Olu Pua Botanical Garden." *Pacific Horticulture Magazine* (Spring 1988): 50.

Whiteside, Katherine. "The Tropical Garden of Villa Pancha." *House & Garden* (November 1983): 124.

CHAPTER 7

Brookes, John. *The Country Garden*. New York: Crown Publishers, Inc., 1987.

———. *A Place in the Country*. London: Thames & Hudson, 1984.

Fairbrother, Nan. *New Lives, New Landscapes*. London: Architectural Press, Ltd., 1970.

Griswold, Mac. *Pleasures of the Garden*. New York: Harry N. Abrams, Inc., 1987.

Hoskins, W. G. *The Making of the English Landscape*. London: Pelican Books, 1970.

Jekyll, Gertrude. *Home and Garden: Notes and Thoughts, Practical and Critical of a Worker in Both*. Ithaca, N.Y.: Antique Collector's Club, 1982.

Jensen, Jens. *Siftings—The Major Portion of the Clearing and Collected Writings*. Ralph Fletcher Seymour, 1939.

Ottesen, Carole. *The New American Garden*. New York: Macmillan Publishing Co., 1988.

Taylor, Christopher. *Fields in the English Landscape*. London: J. M. Dent & Sons, Ltd., 1975.

Thorpe, Patricia. *The American Weekend Garden*. New York: Random House, Inc., 1988.

CHAPTER 8

Coffin, David R. *The Villa in the Life of Renaissance Rome*. Princeton, N.J.: Princeton University Press, 1979.

Kinkead, Eugene. *Central Park 1857–1995: The Birth, Decline and Renewal of a National Treasure*. New York: W.W. Norton & Co., 1990.

Loudon, John Cladius. *The Suburban Garden and Villa Companion*. London: Longman, Orme, Brown, Green & Longmans, 1838.

Newton, Norton T. *Design of the Land: The Development of Landscape Architecture*. Cambridge, Mass.: The Belknap Press of Harvard University Press, 1971.

Pinkney, David H. *Napoleon III and the Rebuilding of Paris*. Princeton, N.J.: Princeton University Press, 1958.

Roberts, Martha McMillian. *Public Gardens and Arboretums of the United States*. New York: Holt, Rinehart & Winston, 1962.

Scott, Frank J. *The Art of Beautifying Suburban Home Grounds*. Watkins Glen, N.Y.: Library of Victorian Culture, American Life Foundation, 1982.

Turner, Roger. *Capability Brown and the Eighteenth Century English Landscape*. New York: Rizzoli International Publications, Inc., 1985.

INDEX